D0492804

THE GLOBAL AUCTION

PHILLIP BROWN, HUGH LAUDER, AND DAVID ASHTON

THE GLOBAL AUCTION

The Broken Promises of Education,
Jobs and Incomes

LRC Stoke Park
GUILDFORD COLLEGE

OXFORD

UNIVERSITY PRESS

2011

331.7
BRO
182918

OXFORD
UNIVERSITY PRESS

Oxford University Press, Inc., publishes works that further
Oxford University's objective of excellence
in research, scholarship, and education.

Oxford   New York
Auckland   Cape Town   Dar es Salaam   Hong Kong   Karachi
Kuala Lumpur   Madrid   Melbourne   Mexico City   Nairobi
New Delhi   Shanghai   Taipei   Toronto

With offices in
Argentina   Austria   Brazil   Chile   Czech Republic   France   Greece
Guatemala   Hungary   Italy   Japan   Poland   Portugal   Singapore
South Korea   Switzerland   Thailand   Turkey   Ukraine   Vietnam

Copyright © 2011 by Oxford University Press, Inc.

Published by Oxford University Press, Inc.
198 Madison Avenue, New York, New York 10016

www.oup.com

Oxford is a registered trademark of Oxford University Press

All rights reserved. No part of this publication may be reproduced,
stored in a retrieval system, or transmitted, in any form or by any means,
electronic, mechanical, photocopying, recording, or otherwise,
without the prior permission of Oxford University Press.

Library of Congress Cataloging-in-Publication Data
Brown, Phillip, 1957–
The global auction : the broken promises of education, jobs,
and incomes / Phillip Brown, Hugh Lauder, and David Ashton.
p.   cm.
Includes bibliographical references and index.
ISBN 978-0-19-973168-8
1. Social mobility—United States.   2. Educational attainment—United States.
3. Labor market—United States.   4. American Dream.
I. Lauder, Hugh.   II. Ashton, David.   III. Title.
HN90.S65B77 2010
331.70086'220973—dc22   2010009401

1 3 5 7 9 8 6 4 2

Printed in the United States of America
on acid-free paper

THIS BOOK IS DEDICATED TO A. H. (CHELLY) HALSEY
SCHOLAR, INSPIRATION, FRIEND

Acknowledgments

THIS BOOK IS the result of an enduring fascination with the global economy and its consequences for prosperity and social justice. We have enjoyed a great privilege, ringside seats that we've used to interview major players involved in the rise of the Asian Tiger economies in the 1990s through to the more recent rise of China and India. While many intellectuals and media commentators have debated the relative merits of global free trade, offshoring, and the impact of new technologies on the future global workforce, we have been keen to reserve judgment. It was only after talking to around 200 corporate executives and national policy makers in seven countries that we were led to an "inconvenient truth" that has provided the motivation for writing this book. We believe that everyone has a right to know that the opportunity bargain based on better education, better jobs, and better incomes can no longer deliver the American Dream. How individuals, companies, and nations respond to these changing circumstances, especially following the financial crash in 2008, will inevitably shape the fate of future generations in America and beyond.

What we describe in the following pages derives from the ideas and observations of many outstanding people involved in shaping their organization's or nation's policies aimed at delivering success in the global economy. Because we wanted people to "tell it as it is" rather than present us with "cheerleader" accounts, all our discussions were treated as confidential. Consequently, the names of individuals and companies are anonymous. Those who were involved in the research will know who they are, so a big "thanks" to all those we met in America, Britain, China, Germany, India, Singapore, and South Korea.

Without the Internet (a significant source of information about companies and government policies in different parts of the world), this project would have been very difficult. But without the help of key people in each country, this project would have been impossible. We owe a major debt of gratitude to In Sub Park, Liu Xin, Xu Jing, C. D. Wee, Gopinathan Saravanan, Yasho Verma, K. M.Shashidharna, Aslesha Khandeparkar, Kent Hughes, Joan Wills, Phyllis Eisen, Jane Houzer, Helen Bostock, Alister Jones, and Hilary Fleming.

Along with those who helped us organize interviews, numerous other people helped in other ways, including Susannah John, Ian Jamieson, Ian Jones, Dan Gordon, Ewart Keep, Rajani Naidoo, Jim Truesdale, John Squier, Alan Brown, Simon Head, Chelly Halsey, Stuart Maister, Helen Butler, and Sandra Bonney. A special thanks also goes to Gerbrand Tholen for his contribution to the statistical work that informs this book and to Ceri Brown, who helped us to master the qualitative software used to explore our interview data.

The reason there is so little hands-on research of this kind is largely because it is expensive both in time and money. We are therefore greatly indebted to the Economic and Social Research Council of Great Britain and the Centre for Skills, Knowledge and Organizational Performance (SKOPE) for funding a number of related studies over the past 15 years. While we have written many academic papers and policy reports that directly relate to issues in Britain, we felt it important to write a more wide-ranging book because the issues it raises are relevant not only to the United States but are truly global.

Finally, we'd like to acknowledge the outstanding contribution of James Cook, our editor at Oxford University Press in New York. He has not only shared our vision but has been instrumental in improving the quality of the product.

Contents

CHAPTER ONE

Introduction

Democratic nations, left to themselves, are slow to embark on great ventures;
they are only dragged into revolutions in spite of themselves.

—*Alexis de Tocqueville, 1835.*[1]

LEXIS DE TOCQUEVILLE arrived in America in early April 1831, and his initial impressions left him stunned by seeing so many things of interest, but most of all, he viewed America as a land of opportunity. In a letter to his good friend Ernest de Chabrol, he confessed, "There is here not one man without a reasonable hope of attaining the good things of life...granted a taste for work, his future is assured."

If de Tocqueville returned to America today, what would be his reaction? There is little doubt that he would again be stunned by the changes. In the 1830s, there were no radios, televisions, or computers. He would be amazed by the palaces of consumption in cities large and small and be impressed by his foresight in recognizing that prosperity had been extended to a majority of American families. He would also be surprised to find a black president, given that black Americans had been enslaved and excluded from white society, and by the advances made by women. But is it unlikely that he would miss the realities of a dark age in bright lights.

Although he believed that America was the first nation to win the cause for equality, he would no doubt be surprised by the fragility of the American Dream and amazed to find millions of Americans relying on food stamps. He would also discover that middle-class families were far from happy and fearful for the future of their offspring. He would also realize that these problems are deeply rooted. The road to recovery in the aftermath of the 2008 financial crash would not restore the American Dream as many had hoped.

If his return journey had taken him beyond the United States, he would also have noticed that the idea of an affluent and fair society had spread to many parts of the world. It is equally valid to talk about the Chinese Dream or Indian Dream, as all have expressed a commitment to economic growth as a way of extending opportunities and a better life for all. But he would also discover that the age of uncertainty was not an exclusively American or European phenomenon. The spectacular growth rates achieved in the world's most populace countries have done little to remove fears of rising inequality and social unrest even as unprecedented numbers of Chinese and Indian families join the ranks of the global middle classes.

Our purpose is not to repeat de Tocqueville's tour of America but to understand the future of the American Dream, a task that can no longer be restricted to studying what lies within national borders. The world has become more integrated and networked, especially in economic activities. The market value of American workers is no longer judged solely in comparison to their neighbors. It is judged in a global auction for jobs. To capture these changes and what they mean for American and European workers and families, we set out on a journey that included seven countries—America, Britain, China, Germany, India, Singapore, and South Korea. Drawing on more than a decade of research, which involved an intensive 3-year study leading up to the second Wall Street crash, we visited 18 cities, including the Asian economic powerhouses of Bangalore, Beijing, Guangzhou, Hong Kong, Mumbai, New Delhi, Seoul, Shanghai, and Singapore.

We wanted to test the official account of how middle-class prosperity could be delivered in the future. Is it true that a knowledge-driven economy accelerates the demand for employees with a college education? Will it be enough for individuals to invest in their talents and abilities as they had done in the past to secure a well-paid job via educational achievement? Could America succeed in attracting a large share of the global supply of high-skill, high-wage jobs?

To find some answers, we talked to more than 200 managers, executives, and policy makers of many different nationalities. We met people in corporate headquarters, regional offices, hi-tech factories, research facilities, and government departments, along with taxi drivers, hotel employees, and fellow airline passengers. We paid particular attention to leading transnational companies as they defined the rules of the economic game. But we did not limit ourselves to American corporations. We also interviewed leading companies from Britain, Germany, South Korea, China, and India that will make investment decisions in the coming decades profoundly affecting the opportunities and prosperity of American workers.

As social scientists, we wanted to ensure the impartial rigor of our investigations, yet realized that our findings needed to be shared with a wide audience rather than remain locked away in specialist journals. We were observing an economic power shift that threatens the foundations of prosperity and social justice that many of those in governments throughout the developed world would rather we did not publicize. We had discovered another inconvenient truth that everyone has a right to know.

Those we met offer the reader a window on the changing economic world that for us evoked a sense of admiration and foreboding in equal measure. The exploitation of women, men, and children is the dark side of Asia's economic revolution, but it is only part of the story unfolding today. The other story line is the breakneck speed at which China and India, along with other emerging economies across Asia, South America, and Eastern Europe, have geared up to compete for high-value goods and services. This is shattering the view that the economic world would remain divided between *head* nations, such as America, Britain, and Germany and *body* nations, including China, India, and Vietnam.[2] Such ideas fail to understand how the global economy allows emerging economies to leapfrog decades of industrial development to create a high-skill, low-wage workforce capable of competing successfully for hi-tech, high-value employment. These workforces challenge the economic livelihoods of those in stable, well-paid, middle-class jobs once assumed to be safely lodged in America and other affluent economies.

The availability of cheap brainpower will continue to threaten the prosperity of Western workers long after recovery from economic recession. It challenges the very opportunities Tocqueville identified as standing at the heart of the American Dream in 1831 and on which President Obama staked his political credibility on rebuilding.

The Opportunity Bargain

After World War II, countries on both sides of the Atlantic enjoyed unprecedented prosperity. This prosperity was built on a model of economic nationalism intended to spread the benefits of economic growth to the majority rather than to a privileged few. Individuals and families were linked to national economic growth by extending opportunities to education and well-paid jobs alongside welfare support for those who required it.

John Maynard Keynes's classic work on *The General Theory of Employment, Interest and Money*, published in 1936, shaped economic thinking at the time by rejecting the neoliberal view that capitalist economies were self-correcting and required little government intervention. Hence, economies which had fallen into recession would automatically bounce back to a period of boom and full employment.

Keynes rejected this idea and argued that governments could intervene effectively in market economies to solve the problem of recession, or what one of his contemporaries called the "gales of creative destruction."[3] Thus, when demand for goods slackened and workers were threatened with unemployment, governments could act to keep the wheels of industry turning. Keynes also endorsed the idea of a welfare state to protect people from the chronic insecurities that characterize the boom-and-bust nature of capitalist development.

By the 1980s, neoliberal ideas had regained popularity. Under Ronald Reagan in America and Margaret Thatcher in Britain, there was a return to preaching the virtues of free trade, self-interest, and the power of the market to deliver prosperity and justice. Keynes's ideas were renounced as a recipe for big government and a growing underclass living off state handouts.

Hence, the tenets of neoliberalism encouraged people to believe that welfare support introduced in the 1950s and 1960s was misguided because it rewarded failure and feckless behavior, whereas free markets offered a fair and efficient system where talent and hard work would be appropriately rewarded. As a result, the fate of individuals and families became heavily reliant on maintaining, if not increasing, the market value of their knowledge, skills, and credentials. Jobs and rewards would flow to individuals able to upgrade their skills to meet the competitive conditions of the knowledge economy, where opportunities were assumed to expand as the economy relied on new ideas, technologies, and innovations.

Since the 1980s, politicians and opinion leaders, whether Republican or Democrat, continued to present the future economy as a world of smart people doing smart things in smart ways. It is a world of new opportunities for creative talent and prosperity for American workers and families based on faith in the market to deliver the middle-class dream. This faith resulted in an *opportunity bargain* on both sides of the Atlantic where the state's role was limited to creating opportunities for people through education to become marketable in the global competition, in which economic fate rested on success in the job market.

Today, billions of dollars are spent on mobilizing American and European workers in a bid to outsmart rivals in the competition for the best jobs, technologies, and companies. A vast edifice of policies, programs, and initiatives has been introduced in virtually all affluent countries in anticipation of an innovative age of high-skill, high-wage work. Higher education has been massively expanded, and it encourages individuals to take on personal debt to pay for college and university credentials in the belief that they will be well rewarded once they enter the job market.

This book explains why much of this money, effort, and enterprise will be wasted, as the neoliberal opportunity bargain fails to deliver on the promise of education, jobs, and rewards. Schooled in the belief that "learning equals earning," many Americans have unrealistic expectations of a world that does not owe them a living.

It has left them ill-prepared to meet the challenges posed by the new era of knowledge capitalism because they are caught in a gale of creative destruction that makes it difficult to find individual solutions to changing economic realities. The demand for managerial and professional jobs in the United States is not only far less than commonly assumed, but the quality of working life and rewards associated with those jobs will not live up to expectations. The idea that learning equals earning fails to acknowledge that most of those with a university degree in America have not witnessed an increase in income since the early 1970s. The only winners among college graduates are a minority who succeed in the competition for the best jobs. This is squeezing and polarizing the American middle classes and posing fundamental challenges for policy makers.

This book shows how the fate of American workers is inextricably linked to a global auction for cut-priced brainpower that is weakening the trading position of many managers, professionals, and technicians previously associated with individual success and a comfortable standard of living. The promise of the good life for those with ability and the willingness to work hard has been broken. Behind the challenge to America's middle classes is a fundamental shift of power in the global economy that cannot be resolved through the job market no matter how much money is pumped into developing the skills of the American workforce. The neoliberal opportunity bargain, which offered families a path to individual and national prosperity through education, has been torn up.

If the American middle classes were created by industrial capitalism in the twentieth century, they are now being ripped apart by the global forces of knowledge capitalism. The problem confronting Western workers is that the rise in the value of knowledge, predicted by most commentators in the West, failed to materialize.

This is not to say that new ideas as a source of innovation have become any less important. Companies continue to need well-educated people with clever ideas, but some knowledge workers are believed to be much more valuable than others, leading to a significant decline in the value of various forms of knowledge work upon which the prosperity of Western middle classes depend.

We should not be surprised by this because, if knowledge is a key source of company profit, then the task of business is not to pay more for it but to pay less. This is why companies are seeking to distinguish between paying a premium for what is essential to the success of their businesses while reducing the cost of everything else. Yet, we have been led to believe that the value of a college education would continue to rise as the economy became more knowledge intensive. However, we lost sight of the age-old conflict between employees who want to increase the value of their labor and companies who want to maximize profits by reducing labor costs.

In the boom years, this conflict remained hidden, but the financial crash in America and Britain exposed a yawning gap between the interests of Wall Street and the middle class. It also hid the fact that the livelihoods of many Americans depend on selling an asset—brainpower—to companies that increasingly have other options. College-educated Americans were only sheltered from price competition as long as educated talent was in limited supply at home and only found in equally expensive countries like Japan, Germany, or Britain.

Reversing Fortunes

The competition for jobs has shifted from one largely restricted within clearly defined national boundaries to a global auction open to competition across borders. We are all familiar with art auctions held by Sotheby's and those on eBay. In these forward auctions, the highest bidder wins. For the majority of American, British, or German workers, a Sotheby-type progressive auction was assumed to reflect the increasing value of investments in what economists call human capital. The expertise for jobs involving research and design was believed to be in limited supply and located in the West. It was also taken for granted that when it comes to high-end activities, America and other affluent nations will always have the edge, given they possess more advanced technologies. Hence, the competition was not seen as a matter of cost but as the application of smart knowledge for which companies were willing to pay a premium.

But the global auction for jobs increasingly works in reverse to an auction where the highest bidder wins. In a reverse or Dutch auction, bids decline in value as the goal is to drive down prices. These auctions are becoming more popular on the Internet involving bidding competitions for business-to-business services. The German Web site *jobdumping.de* offered a stark example of a reverse auction. Cleaning, clerical, and catering jobs were offered by employers with a maximum price for the job; those looking for employment then underbid each other, and the winner was the person willing to work for the lowest wages.

People are becoming aware that the reverse auction is being extended to American college-educated workers. The impact of this bidding war is not just restricted to the size of an employee's paycheck, but it also includes longer working hours, inferior retirement provision, reduced health-care coverage, declining career prospects, and greater job insecurity. In a reverse auction, workers are expected to do more for less.

In the early stages of globalization, the reverse auction was limited to American workers with low skills. Today, four major forces are converging to create a price competition for expertise, forcing American students, workers, and families into a bare-knuckle fight for those jobs that continue to offer a good standard of living.

First, there has been an *education explosion* in the supply of college-educated workers in both affluent and emerging economies. Even when limited to affluent societies, this expansion poses a problem because widening access to a college education lowers the value of credentials in the competition for jobs. But of even greater importance is the educational explosion in emerging economies, including China, India, and Russia.

Harvard economist Richard Freeman points to a doubling of the global workforce, but our analysis also reveals a doubling in the number of university-level enrollments around the world in just 10 years.

China has more students at university than the United States and is also producing more scientists and engineers, sometimes of a superior quality to those found in the West.

Second, there has been a *quality-cost revolution* resulting in a rapid increase in productivity levels and quality standards following the application of "best practice" in emerging economies. The new competition is no longer based on quality *or* cost but on quality *and* cost, offering companies more strategic choices about their global distribution of high-skill as well as low-skill work. Western companies are developing more sophisticated approaches to outsourcing and offshoring more of their highly skilled jobs to low-cost locations. In financial services, jobs including client research and product development, as well as back office work, such as data entry or invoicing, are being undertaken in emerging economies.

The quality-cost revolution has also opened the door for Asian companies to compete higher up the value chain for goods and services by using their cost advantage to underbid Western competitors. Consequently, many of the things we only thought could be done in the West can now be done anywhere in the world not only cheaper but sometimes better. But the move to low-cost brainwork is not the end of the story.

Third, although much of the focus has been on the development of new products and services that highlight the demand for creative people exploiting clever ideas, few seemed to notice that the forces of creative destruction are followed by the destruction of the creative. The productive application of new ideas depends on standardization giving employers greater control over the workplace. Improvements in productivity for much of the twentieth century rested on the principles of scientific management outlined by Fredrick Winslow Taylor.

To date, the productivity of new technologies in offices and professional services has been disappointing in much the same way that it took decades to realize the potential of factory production. Companies have responded by trying to reduce the cost of knowledge work through a process of knowledge capture that we call *digital Taylorism*. The same processes that enabled cars, computers, and televisions to be broken down into their component parts, manufactured by companies around the world, and then configured according to the customer's specifications are being applied to impersonal jobs in the service sector—that is, jobs that do not depend on facing a customer.

In short, new technologies have increased the potential to translate *knowledge work* into *working knowledge*, leading to the standardization of an increasing proportion of technical, managerial, and professional jobs that raise fundamental questions about the future of knowledge work and occupational mobility.

The final trend relates to what is described within the business literature as the global *war for talent*.[4] Just as more individuals invest in their human capital and governments invest in increasing the national stock of skilled workers, the relationship between learning and earning is being called into question from within the business community. Leading consultancy companies assert that the relationship between learning and earning needs to be revised because it is less applicable in today's competitive world because it fails to reflect differences in performance, especially the productive contribution of a talented minority of top performers. This is viewed as a critical issue for global companies in Beijing, Shanghai, and Bangalore as well as New York, London, and Frankfurt.

Concerns about hiring the next generation of talented employees led corporations to gravitate toward global elite universities because they are believed to have the best and brightest students. This focus on attracting, retaining, and developing top talent leads to greater inequality of treatment, as companies seek to identify a cadre of high flyers across the globe. It also contributes to widening income inequalities within middle-class occupations and differences in career prospects among people with the same credentials, experience, or levels of expertise. Hence, those defined as the best are being treated very differently from the rest.

These trends result in many college-educated Americans becoming part of a high-skill, low-wage workforce.[5] Previously, differences in income were assumed to reflect a meritocratic pyramid of individual achievement. This relationship has never been straightforward, but it is now in crisis as the relationships among jobs, rewards, and entitlements are being reconfigured.

All affluent nations are witnessing the growth of a high-skill, low-wage workforce, but its extent will vary depending on national context, including labor market conditions, domestic supply of college graduates, and the strength of trade unions. Indeed, an important part of our argument is to show how the flexible labor market in America and Britain has left workers seriously exposed to the full force of the global auction. Although we focus on the political economy of these countries, this book has implications for almost every individual, business, and nation in the global economy.

Globalization from the Other Side

The sheer energy generated in Asia as barriers to personal gain, trade, and global market competition have been lifted is truly remarkable. Talking to Chinese and Indian managers is reminiscent of conversations heard in America or Britain in the 1950s. In India, there remains a strong sense of national renewal and individual opportunity despite potted roads and widespread poverty. When *The Times of India* launched "India poised: our time is now," it declared "we've gone from thinking small to thinking big," as Indian entrepreneurs and companies made a splash on the global stage. This feeling that India was on the move is also shared on the streets of Bangalore. As we passed a shopping mall, our taxi driver pointed out, "This is for the IT people; very expensive!" When we asked him more about the people who shopped there, he didn't feel part of the rising middle classes but believed his children would. He expressed considerable pride in the good grades his children received at school as they were striving for a better future.

But it is misleading to assume that Americans are the only losers in the global auction. Instead, there is uneven development where the preindustrial and the postindustrial share the same zip code. In India, almost a third of the population continues to live in abject poverty. Dharavi, one of the largest slums in the world, is home to a million people in the middle of Mumbai, India's financial capital.

Indian workers, including those employed by foreign companies, continue to struggle for decent wages and safe working conditions. Roy George, a human resources executive, was killed by disgruntled workers in a bitter dispute at Pricol, which makes auto parts for companies such as Toyota and General Motors. In reporting the "sickening regularity" of strikes in the Mumbai–Delhi industrial corridor, a leader column in the *Hindustan Times* concluded that "no country has developed without going through an industrial revolution and India's unlikely to be an exception. The scramble for investment can't be at the cost of a brutalized workforce."[6] Equally, although some Chinese university graduates have never had it so good, rural and industrial workers have been involved in riots as an expression of their frustration of not being part of the Chinese economic dream.

It makes less and less sense to think in terms of a national economy or average household income when talking about the fate of individuals and families because it misses what is important about knowledge capitalism. Complex webs of winners and losers that transcend national borders emerge as the global auction cuts across established ways of thinking about middle-class occupations and national economies. Titles such as accountant, professor, engineer, lawyer, and computer analyst no longer tell us as much as they once did about income, job security, or career opportunities because they are characterized by increasingly "winner-takes-all" competitions.[7]

Some American, Chinese, and Indian workers and companies have economic interests more in common with those living on the other side of the world than with those living on the opposite side of the street. Despite holding different passports, they may work for the same companies profiting from the competitive advantages that the global auction can create but at the expense of their fellow citizens.

Around the globe, elites in most occupations appear to be doing much better than everyone else. This is often true for those working in the public as well as the private sector, as many areas of public sector work are exposed to similar market forces that lead to those at the top earning far more than everyone else, even at a time when state budgets are being slashed.

The global auction creates mixed fortunes where a few will continue to be generously rewarded, but many others with advanced education will struggle to achieve the trappings of the middle classes alongside a working class that seems increasingly excluded through inferior education, declining occupational mobility, and wage competition. The result is an intense competition for the best colleges, jobs, and careers.

A Secret War

There is a secret war for positional advantage as people are forced to depend on a job market unable to cope with the rising tide of individual, social, and political expectations. How people are positioned in the global auction is of paramount importance. If they are not defined as top talent, they are likely to find themselves in a bidding war with high-skill, low-wage workers from emerging economies.

Competition begins almost at birth. Children with ambitious parents are forced into a relentless competition for the best prep schools, high schools, universities, and "branded" firms. Fueled by insecurity and moral obligations to do the best for their children, some parents adopt desperate measures to give their children a competitive advantage, such as remortgaging their homes to pay for private schooling or suddenly discovering a new faith to get their child into the local religious school with a good reputation. Competitive pressures become even more intense for adult workers as companies flatten their career structures, reexamine global sourcing options, and segment their workforce so that only a small minority are defined as indispensable to the future of the organization.

Personal freedom and intellectual curiosity become secondary to the requirements of the competition for a livelihood. Almost every facet of one's public life and private self are implicated in the battle to get ahead. The opportunity bargain has not extended individual freedom but has led to an *opportunity trap* that forces people to spend more time, effort, and money on activities that may have little intrinsic purpose in an attempt to fulfill one's opportunities. The trap is that if everyone adopts the same tactics, such as getting a bachelor's degree or working longer hours to impress the boss, no one secures an advantage.

Expectations of middle-class lifestyles, fueled by the rise of mass higher education, have sucked more people into already congested labor markets. Although not all expect glittering vocational prizes at the end of a college education, the supply of aspirants greatly outstrips employer demand for their services. At the same time, people are playing for higher stakes, as the price of failure has increased because the safety net that once caught the less fortunate is now threadbare.

The stark reality is that what the few can achieve the majority cannot regardless of how educated they are. Wage inequalities cannot be narrowed through better education or increasing skill levels because the global labor market is congested with well-educated, low-cost workers. Rather than enter an "age of human capital," where the economic successes of individuals and whole economies depend on how extensively and effectively people invest in themselves, human capital is subject to the laws of diminishing returns. The claim from neoliberal economists that the supply of well-educated workers would create its own demand as employers seek to profit from more productive employees seems fitting to a different world, such as in the second half of the twentieth century when America experienced educational expansion linked to a rising middle class and increasing social mobility.[8]

Today, when human knowledge is being taught, certified, and applied on a scale not witnessed before in human history, the overall value of human capital is likely to decline. For most people, it will take the form of a defensive expenditure: Education is a necessary investment to have any chance of fighting for a decent standard of living. But for the few, investments of effort, time, and money will continue to be handsomely rewarded.

Opportunity, rather than being the glue that bonds the individual to society, has become the focus of intense social conflict, raising the question of how to construct a new opportunity bargain that rebuilds trust and fairness within a sustainable economy.

A Window of Opportunity

The free market model driving government policies on both sides of the Atlantic was shaken to its foundations by the financial crash of 2008. This is more than another expensive lesson in the folly of market self-regulation that leads to irrational exuberance—which most of us would call greed. It also reinforces the fraying connections between the principles of merit, contribution, and rewards.

The problem this poses for governments of all persuasions is that the wealth of human capability nurtured within schools, colleges, and universities; the explosion of knowledge via new technologies and the Internet; and an exponential increase in the global supply of high-skill, low-wage workers challenge the legitimate foundations of how democratic societies have resolved questions of who does what and who gets what.

So how do we build a new opportunity bargain when the core means for delivering it is collapsing? To date, most Americans interpret these issues as a private matter of making the most of one's opportunities. Inevitably, this will become a major political issue because the high-skills, low-wages equation does not live up to the lifestyles most people want or expect. This book explains the true nature of the problem because there is little point developing good answers to the wrong questions.

America, along with other affluent societies, confronts stark choices. It is going to be difficult to avoid a return to greater protectionism as Americans and Europeans seek shelter from global competition, especially when unemployment rates are high. But such a response squanders the possibilities that now exist to shape American society and the wider world in ways that benefit future generations as well as our own.

Populist appeals and quick fixes will inevitably fail as industrial revolutions typically transform our understanding of individual and social possibilities along with a reordering of economic interests. Political attempts to rebuild the American Dream will equally fail unless there is a willingness to rethink the purpose of education, the nature of jobs, the distribution of rewards, and America's role in the world. How do we reconnect the socially excluded at both ends of the social spectrum—both the poor and the very rich—into a fairer competition for a livelihood? How do we reward achievement in ways that contribute to a shared prosperity rather than the enrichment of a few? It is difficult to exaggerate the scale of the challenge in creating a new opportunity bargain, but the challenge is doubly difficult because it will also require a global bargain no longer limited to the world's richest nations.

To move toward answers to these questions, we begin with an examination of the false promise that gave rise to the neoliberal opportunity bargain and continues to obscure the realities that workers in America and Europe now face.

CHAPTER TWO

The False Promise

The global economy imposes no particular limit upon the number of Americans who can sell symbolic-analytic services worldwide. In principle, all of America's routine production workers could become symbolic analysts and let their old jobs drift overseas to developing nations.

—*Robert Reich*[1]

THIS VIEW OF the global knowledge economy conjured up a world of smart people doing smart things in smart ways. Such an economy represented the high point of more than 200 years of Western industrial evolution, where the human side of enterprise slowly came to take center stage. Through investments in brainpower, it was thought that nations could deliver prosperity, justice, and social cohesion, companies could develop world-class employees, and individuals could secure a better future for themselves and their family. Increasing global competition served only to underline how the fate of American workers rested on their ability to outsmart economic rivals.

This faith in the endless potential to create middle-class jobs for those who invested in education resembles a secular religion. The hold of this faith over current thinking is difficult to exaggerate despite the fallout from the economic crisis.[2] This book explains why it would be more fitting in a fairy tale than in an account of reality. But first we need to see how the neoliberal opportunity bargain of individual freedom and national prosperity was supposed to unfold.

From Muscle Power to Brianpower

In the eighteenth-century world of Adam Smith, the wealth of nations was based on trade and plunder rather than increasing productivity. The founder of modern economics recognized that wealth could be created by improving the efficiency of the workforce, even if the price was to condemn most workers to jobs that in Smith's words made them "as stupid and ignorant as it is possible for a human creature to become." This was because the increase in productive capacity depended on sub-dividing the activities of workers, each performing the same repetitive task such as in the manufacture of pins where someone draws out the wire, another straightens it, another cuts it, and so on.[3] The dangers involved in creating a workforce of human automatons were not lost on Smith. He believed that although this was a price worth paying to increase national wealth, state-funded education should be developed to compensate for the mind-numbing work that a detailed division of labor imposed on the workforce.

Since Adam Smith, labor was treated as a homogeneous category. What counted was the number of workers or the size of the workforce, akin to the area of land for agricultural production or the number of machines in a factory. Well into the twentieth century, people were treated as expensive machines, and the personal costs of rising prosperity continued to be high. Fordist production lines—named after Henry Ford, who pioneered the mass production of Model T auto-mobiles in the early 1900s—were widely used in the manufacture of goods, including televisions, refrigerators, and washing machines that fueled the consumer boom of the 1950s and 1960s.

Although the families of production workers became more affluent, it required employees to leave their brains at the factory gate. As one car worker put it, "A man checks his brains and his freedom at the door when he goes to work at Ford's."[4] Equally, the growing numbers of white-collar workers employed in the offices of private and public cor-porations performed paper-pushing tasks every bit as routine as those found in factory production.

The possibility that differences in the skills of workers could have an impact on productivity and economic growth remained heretical within mainstream economics until the 1960s, when economists developed the theory of human capital which rejected the view of labor measured in number rather than quality.[5] They advocated a broader concept of capital that included the skills, knowledge, and know-how of workers. As Theodore Schultz, a leading proponent of human capital, asserted,

"Knowledge and skill are in great part the product of investment and, combined with other human investment, predominantly account for the productive superiority of the technically advanced countries. To omit them in studying economic growth is like trying to explain Soviet ideology without Marx."[6]

The protagonists of human capital argued that much of the unexplained increase in productivity, wages, and economic growth, which had puzzled economists at the time, could be explained by investments in human capital. Therefore, by investing in education and training, individuals could increase their lifetime earnings. In addition, governments could use such investments as a way of enhancing national economic growth.[7]

This offered a new way of thinking about economic progress and social justice. If quality of the workforce was the key to economic growth, companies and policy advisors needed to focus attention on the supply side of economic activities rather than such things as consumer demand or the cost of raw materials. It also changed the role of education and training. If they were vital to meet the needs of industry, it required major investments aimed at upgrading the skills of the workforce.

Human capital ideas not only changed the way people thought about skills and productivity but also had wider political appeal, as they suggested a new relationship between capital (money) and labor (minds). Investment in human beings was no longer solely a source of wealth creation for companies but also a source of earning potential for individuals. What people were paid did not depend on owning one's own business or result from collective bargaining that set employers against labor unions in a fight for a bigger slice of the cake. Rather, wages were based on a worker's contribution to productivity, as earnings were assumed to reflect value added to the organization.

Everyone could become a capitalist, whether or not people knew it (or liked it), by investing in themselves through learning. As Schultz suggests, "Laborers have become capitalists not from a diffusion of the ownership of corporation stock, as folklore would have it, but from the acquisition of knowledge and skill that have economic value."[8] In turn, this was believed to contribute to a broader commitment to social justice as people were rewarded on individual merit, and the growth in middle-class jobs offered the potential for rapid social mobility through investments in human capital.

Such ideas caught the mood of the time despite the realities of Fordist production. The growth of corporate bureaucracies and a burgeoning public sector accelerated the increase in white-collar employment, adding support to a model of technological evolution from a low-skill to high-skill economy. The growth of middle-class jobs was assumed to represent an ever-tighter relationship between human capital, jobs, and rewards, as it became more important to get the best minds working on the scientific and technological challenges of the age.

In his classic study *The Coming of Post-Industrial Society*, published in the early 1970s, Daniel Bell highlighted the link between a rising meritocracy and economic efficiency. "The post-industrial society, in its initial logic, is a meritocracy. Differential status and differential income are based on technical skills and higher education. Without these achievements one cannot fulfill the requirements of the new social division of labor which is a feature of that society. And there are few high places open without those skills."[9]

Bell's book appeared to confirm the growing importance of human capital and the need to find new sources of economic competitiveness as American and British manufacturers were struggling to compete with leaner and more flexible competitors from Japan and Asian Tiger economies.

There had been a power shift from muscle power to brainpower. In this new age of human capital, the prosperity of individuals, companies, and nations would rest on the skills, knowledge, and enterprise of all rather than the few that drove industrialization in the twentieth century. Smokestack industries had given way to California's Silicon Valley and Route 128 in Boston.

Working-class occupations were in decline as a larger share of the workforce joined the burgeoning ranks of knowledge workers. Peter Drucker, a leading management guru, wrote of another power shift from the owners and managers of capital to knowledge workers, as the prosperity of individuals, companies, and nations came to depend on the application of knowledge. Knowledge workers were gaining the upper hand because "the firm's most valuable knowledge capital tends to reside in the brains of its key workers, and ownership of people went out with the abolition of slavery."[10]

This required a new approach to management within a dynamic global environment. Management theorists reported a shift in the attitudes of business leaders who now recognized that human creativity and individual initiative were the keys to success. The new challenge was not to force employees to fit the corporate model of the past but "to build an organization flexible enough to exploit the idiosyncratic knowledge and unique skills of each individual employee."[11] This required a completely different approach for companies accustomed to focusing on managing machines, buildings, and balance sheets because their key asset was locked in the heads of knowledge workers with the power to walk away and take their intellectual capital with them.

Organizational success had come to depend on the utility of talent rather than alienated labor. Leading companies no longer depended on the mass production of standardized goods and services that are made, monitored, distributed, and sold by vast armies of blue-collar and white-collar employees. Rather, they depended on technological innovation, applied knowledge, and the intellectual capital of a highly skilled workforce. This gave rise to new opportunities for people to use their knowledge, initiative, and creative energies in a wide range of occupations reflected in the changing definition of occupational careers. Employees were no longer seen as reliant on the paternalism of corporate bureaucracies that previously controlled access to occupational careers.

Individual careers were redefined from a stepped progression within the same organization over an extended period to "boundaryless" careers that extended beyond any specific organization.[12] The bounded careers of the past subordinated individuals to the firm and "getting ahead meant being grateful for opportunities the firm brought your way," but the boundaryless career was believed to promote individual freedom and independence from traditional organizational arrangements.[13]

Rather than focus on how employers abandoned the psychological contract of loyalty for job security, changing career patterns were believed to reflect changing cultural values. Organizations had simply become more in tune with the shifting lifestyles of both younger and older workers who wanted jobs that offered new challenges. Unlike the baby boomers, Generation X "cannot and do not seek life-long employment, but they do crave life-long learning. They seek employability over employment: they value career self-reliance."[14] In a similar refrain, Generation Y, consisting of those born between 1978 and 1994, were seeking "a sense of purpose, work–life balance, fun, variety, respect, and the opportunity to do 'real' work that makes a difference. Arguably everyone wants these things from a job but the difference with Generation Y is they'll talk with their feet when their needs are not fulfilled."[15]

From Bloody Wars to Knowledge Wars

This evolutionary model of an inexorable shift from physical to mental labor is not limited to the changing occupational structure within North America or Europe. It extends to include the relationship between nation-states based on the principles of free trade and comparative advantage. David Ricardo, a nineteenth-century English political economist, argued the case for free trade, believing that rich and poor nations alike could gain from trading with each other as long as they specialized in products for which they had an advantage.

The rise of the global knowledge economy was believed to remove much of the source of conflict and strife between nations. Trade liberalization was presented as a "win-win" opportunity for emerging and affluent nations. The territorial disputes that drove nations to war in pursuit of land and material wealth became less important in terms of power, privilege, and wealth. According to Richard Rosecrance of Harvard's Kennedy School: "In the past, material forces were dominant in national growth, prestige, and power; now products of the mind take precedence. Nations can transfer most of their material production thousands of miles away, centering their attention on research and development and product design at home. The result is a new and productive partnership between 'head' nations, which design products, and 'body' nations, which manufacture them."[16]

This shift from bloody wars to knowledge wars marked a high point in international relations as nations put down their weaponry to concentrate on trade. Success in the knowledge wars rested on outsmarting economic rivals. Schools, colleges, universities, think tanks, design centers, and research laboratories stand on the front line in the search for competitive advantage. Although the competition is open to all nations, it assumed a competition between affluent economies because emerging economies were thought to lack the skills and technological know-how to compete at the cutting edge. The widely held view in the West was that the cost advantage of China, India, and other emerging economies would have a negligible impact on middle-class Americans as long as American workers continued to invest in marketable skills. This was again captured by Robert Reich: "Skilled labor has become a key barrier against low wage competitions for the simple reason that it is the only dimension of production in which existing capitalist powers retain an advantage. Technological innovation may be bought or imitated by anyone. High-volume standardized production facilities may be established anywhere. But production processes that depend on skilled labor must stay where it is."[17]

In this scenario, the knowledge and creativity of individual workers were crucial because there were no other sources of individual, family, or national welfare. Nation-states were seen as largely powerless to protect domestic markets from international competition. Routine production could be fulfilled in low-wage countries for a fraction of the cost of operating plants in North America or Western Europe. Gone were the days when national champions, such as Ford in America, ICI in Britain, and Siemens in Germany, offered high wages to low-skill workers as they did after World War II. These companies had little choice other than to exploit the global market for labor if they were to remain competitive. Accordingly, there are no American, British, or German jobs, only American, British, or German workers who must confront the ultimate judgment of the global market.

Although this presented a challenge to workers in affluent economies, the global job market also offered an unprecedented opportunity for America to become a magnet economy, attracting a disproportionate share of the global supply of high-skill, high-wage jobs.[18] If there was a global job market, the numbers of managers, designers, engineers, lawyers, and consultants in the American workforce could be rapidly expanded because they could be employed to service the global economy rather than be restricted to the requirements of the domestic economy. The numbers of high-skill, high-wage workers could dramatically increase by outsmarting workers from other nations, leading domestic and foreign companies to expand their high-value, knowledge-intensive activities in America, given the superior productivity that smarter employees can create.

As a consequence, there was no need to unduly mourn the loss of low-skill manufacturing jobs to Asia, South America, or Eastern Europe despite the short-term problems it caused for displaced workers. Better-quality jobs were being created to replace them, although there was bound to be a period of adjustment as workers retrained for more skilled positions.

The idea of a magnet economy recognized a global auction for jobs, but this was limited to low-skill jobs auctioned on price, resulting in manufacturing jobs migrating to low-wage economies in Asia, South America, or Eastern Europe. There was little understanding that price competition could ultimately reduce the bargaining power of America's professional and managerial workers. It was assumed that high-skill jobs would continue to attract higher wages because these jobs would continue to be auctioned on quality rather than price.

The view that American workers were the natural heirs, fated with the task of thinking for the rest of the world, reflected a legacy of empire and industrial heritage. The industrial revolution began in Britain and was later driven by the United States, notwithstanding the role of Japan in the 1980s. Unsurprisingly, Americans came to believe in their intellectual, technological, and commercial superiority. But there was also an awareness that leading nations were unlikely to supply all the talent they required from within their own populations.

The focus remained on lifting the skills and incomes of indigenous workers, but there was also a growing emphasis on attracting foreign workers to meet the needs of the national economy. The knowledge wars were extended from a competition for quality jobs to include a competition for the most talented workers. Pressures increased to attract, as well as retain, the global supply of international talent. This has long been a feature of the competitive strategies of the United States, but it now characterizes virtually all the affluent economies, including Canada, Britain, and France. It reflects demographic trends, a need to overcome skill shortages, and a global competition to be a net importer rather than exporter of inventors, scientists, and entrepreneurs.[19]

Again, this was not understood as a zero-sum game, robbing emerging economies of some of their most educated and, in some cases, essential workers, such as doctors and nurses, but as brain circulation rather than brain drain.[20] It is thought that workers from emerging economies could gain invaluable knowledge and experience while working in the West, which they could then use to contribute to the economic development of their country of origin when they eventually return home. The growth of the information technology (IT) industry in India is typically cited as an example of the beneficial consequences of such policies.

While clinging to the win-win scenario, there is a growing awareness, if not a culture shock, that Chinese and Indian workers are challenging American and European college-educated workers for knowledge-intensive jobs. There is a recognition that low-cost countries are developing their own knowledge workers capable of achieving global standards that were previously assumed to be out of reach by anyone other than Western workers.

Thomas Friedman's account of the "flattening" of the world economy has been widely debated. He sees little reason to worry about America's middle classes being embroiled in a global race to the bottom because he focused on the race to the top. The knowledge wars are, he believes, forcing Americans to raise their game in the competition for the best and most innovative ideas, leading him to conclude,

America, as a whole, will do fine in a flat world with free trade—provided it continues to churn out knowledge workers who are able to produce idea-based goods that can be sold globally and who are able to fill the knowledge jobs that will be created as we not only expand the global economy but connect all the knowledge pools in the world. There may be a limit to the number of good factory jobs in the world, but there is no limit to the number of idea-generating jobs in the world.[21]

Similar views are expressed in "official" policy. Gordon Brown, Britain's prime minister at the time of the financial crash, announced the beginning of a "global skills race" in which "Asian rivals" would not only compete on low-skill manufacturing but in hi-tech products and services. As a result, "we need to push ahead faster with our reforms to extend educational opportunities to all." This realization that the knowledge wars were no longer limited to affluent nations "heralds a worldwide opportunity revolution bringing new chances of upward mobility for millions. And Britain with its centuries old record of innovation, enterprise, and international reach, can be one of its greatest winners."[22]

This enduring faith in the global knowledge-driven economy to create upward mobility for Western workers, reflected the extent to which governments bought into a neoliberal agenda. To question the theology of the free market or the idea that it could destroy the opportunity bargain was almost a heresy. It is therefore not surprising that faith in human capital to resolve economic and social problems retains a powerful hold on American public policy. As President Barack Obama reaffirmed, "In a global economy where the most valuable skill you can sell is your knowledge, a good education is no longer just a pathway to opportunity, it is a pre-requisite."[23]

Naked Capitalism

The promise of a hi-tech future of highly paid knowledge workers was pivotal to the creation of a neoliberal opportunity bargain, which left individuals responsible for their employability through educational achievement and commitment to career development. Given that the knowledge economy now offered high-skill, high-wage jobs to those willing to invest in their human capital, the role of the state could be limited to improving educational standards, expanding access to higher education, and creating flexible job markets that reward talent, ambition, and enterprise.

Neoliberal reforms introduced by Ronald Reagan and Margaret Thatcher in the 1980s—subsequently pursued by governments of different political persuasion on both sides of the Atlantic—stripped away much of the safety net that offered security to individuals and families through the welfare state that characterized midcentury America and Europe. The pillars of prosperity, security, and opportunity embedded in the relationships among employers, trade unions, and the state were torn down in the belief that state control over the economy and the rigid regulation of people's lives were no longer appropriate or necessary in an age of consumer freedom, free trade, and market individualism.

Taking their cue from neoliberal economists like Milton Friedman and Friedrich A. Hayek, Reagan and Thatcher claimed that Western societies had run into trouble in the 1970s because of what was seen as unwarranted interference by the state.[24] Inflation, high unemployment, economic recession, and urban unrest were all believed to stem from the legacy of Keynesian economics and an ideology that promoted economic redistribution, equality of opportunity, and welfare rights for all.

In its place, a society would be built where individuals were encouraged to pursue their self-interest and where greed was treated as a virtue in the vain hope that the hidden hand of the market would miraculously benefit all through the trickle down of resources from the winners to the losers. "What I want to see above all," Ronald Reagan stated, "is that this remains a country where someone can always get rich." But Reagan was adamant that this could only be guaranteed by getting the state off the backs of the people, for "if the reins of government were removed, business would boom, spreading prosperity to all the people."[25]

The neoliberal opportunity bargain involved changing the incentive structures for individuals and the business community. If free enterprise was to be the motor of economic growth, everyone should be institutionally encouraged to pursue their self-interest by extending market competition, consumer choice, and shrinking the safety net provided by the welfare state. Getting the incentives right for business involved reducing all the impediments or rigidities to free market behavior. These included removing trade barriers and attacking the power of trade unions. In the global economy, barriers to entry were seen to protect inefficient businesses while trade unions kept wages artificially high.

At the same time, middle-class families were encouraged to believe that more consumer choice would give them greater control over their lives without government interference. Schools, hospitals, and pension plans were all now a matter of personal choice. In many cases, the promise of choice was and is illusory. Private health care in America has remained expensive and exclusionary, the attempt to persuade people to cash in occupational pensions and buy personal pensions in Britain has since been acknowledged to have been a disaster, and the idea that all parents can send their children to the school of their choice has proved to be a chimera.[26]

The empowerment of individuals to take greater responsibility for their own livelihoods was nevertheless reinforced by the rhetoric of the knowledge economy and celebrated as a final victory ending the conflict between individual aspirations for meaningful work and the demands of market efficiency. The outcome was a closer relationship linking education, jobs, and rewards as incomes grew in line with the market value of an employee's human capital.

The opportunity bargain reflected the inevitability (and desirability) of a more limited role for government, as it could no longer guarantee employment, given international rules on free trade, but only employability to gain marketable skills. This resulted in further investment in education at all stages at the same time governments encouraged individuals and families to fund their studies to take full advantage of the demand for a highly trained workforce. Those who showed themselves to be unfit due to unemployment and poverty had no one to blame but themselves and, with the right incentives, could reenter the workforce or invest in an education that would propel them into middle-class jobs.

This bargain was also touted as offering everyone an equal chance to become unequal in the competition for jobs, status, and income. Widening access to university was, for instance, presented as an extension of meritocratic competition giving all the opportunity to acquire knowledge and skills required in the new economy with credentials the currency of opportunity.

Changes in employer demands for talent also pointed toward a fairer society, as companies could no longer rely on the established stereotypes of managerial leadership based on the Ivy League or Oxbridge man. Going to a top university and living as part of a cloistered elite were no longer seen as sufficient in an increasingly multicultural and global economic environment. A greater diversity of talent was seen as integral to business success. Enlightened self-interest had led companies to develop policies aimed at widening their recruitment and the development of talent within the organization irrespective of gender, ethnicity, race, disabilities, or social background.

The opportunity bargain also traded on the idea that the inequalities and strife that surrounded early forms of economic competition could be resolved by developing the human capital of all Americans so that they can benefit from the middle-class jobs that the global knowledge economy has to offer. Although the rise in income inequalities posed a problem for American workers as they adjusted to the age of human capital, these inequalities were not viewed as an inevitable result of a free market economy. Rather, they were seen as the relative ability of workers to sell their skills, knowledge, and insights in the global job market.

In 1970, the chief executives of Fortune 100 companies in the United Stated received 39 times more that the average worker; by the end of the 1990s, this had increased to 1,000 times the pay of ordinary workers. Such spectacular increases at the pinnacle of the incomes pyramid were believed to reflect a wider trend toward a reevaluation of the value of human capital that saw the top 10–20 percent of earners pull away from the rest due to their ability to break free of the constraints of local and national job markets. The global labor market is seen to offer far greater rewards to knowledge workers precisely because the demand for their services has grown, whereas workers who remain locked into national or local markets, or who lack the appropriate skills or knowledge, are likely to experience stagnating or declining incomes. The solution is to reform the education system to give more Americans the employability skills to become part of a world-class workforce.

Keeping the Faith

Within this scenario of a free market, knowledge-driven world, the economic crash was never supposed to happen. We were often told by politicians and business leaders that rising prosperity was not debt driven but a result of smart people using smart technologies in smart ways, creating unprecedented prosperity for the most talented employees and enterprising companies in a burgeoning global economy. It was learning that was earning as the head nations supplied the ideas, technologies, and know-how, while the body nations manufactured a future for themselves. And we could all share in this prosperity if we invested in ourselves by gaining marketable qualifications, skills, and knowledge.

The political powers behind this faith in human capital, market competition, and technological innovation should not be underestimated. What is so fascinating is how pervasive such ideas have remained. Commentators from different disciplines and perspectives have bought into the underlying idea of economic progress and filled out the story line to provide a comprehensive guide to globalization, economic change, and the role of the individual within it. In reality, the interests of the powerful are presented as supporting those of the middle classes. Individually, no doubt, the super-rich will surf the highs and lows of political and economic waves, but the future of most Americans has an altogether different story line. Yet, governments have a mandate to deliver the American Dream and not to question its founding assumptions of efficiency and justice. For these reasons, every effort will be made to maintain the opportunity bargain, in part because America and Britain are politically bereft of alternatives.

While the U.S. federal government has taken some steps to control the irrational exuberance of the financial markets, the opportunity bargain via education has become even more important as schools, colleges, and universities are called upon to drive America's recovery from recession. Virtually all the books written about the competitive challenges confronting the U.S. economy and the future of social justice conclude with a restatement of their faith in the powers of learning to deliver the promise of a better life for American workers and families. Yet although it is believed that America's problems can be solved through the powers of learning, American education is often presented as not fit for this purpose.

In setting out his road to recovery and how America must regain the lead in key areas of the global economy, including renewable energy and clean technologies, President Barack Obama observed, "Right now, three-quarters of the fastest-growing occupations require more than a high school diploma. And yet, just over half of our citizens have that level of education. We have one of the highest high school dropout rates of any industrialized nation. And half of the students who begin college never finish. This is a prescription for economic decline, because we know the countries that out-teach us today will out-compete us tomorrow."[27]

Such comments are not without historical precedent when times are tough. In the 1980s, when America confronted mounting competition from Japan and the Asian Tiger economies, the widely publicized report *A Nation at Risk* declared, "If an unfriendly foreign power had attempted to impose on America the mediocre educational performance that exists today, we might well have viewed it as an act of war. As it stands, we have allowed this to happen to ourselves.... We have, in effect, been committing an act of unthinking, unilateral educational disarmament."[28]

The next chapter explains why concerns about America's education system in delivering the opportunity bargain are well founded, as there has been a rapid global expansion of college-educated workers entering the global knowledge wars.

CHAPTER THREE

⌘

Knowledge Wars

Having been to China and been aware of what's going on there—the speed at which the high skills work is being developed is something of a threat I think, and something of a shock . . . totally gone is the comfort of it's just low wage jobs and cheap labor.

—*Head of Education Policy, American Industrial Trade Association*

The Multinational Companies are our schools.

—*A Leading Chinese Economist*

IN SOUTHERN CHINA, an entire island has been developed into a Higher Education Mega Centre with its own metro line connecting it to the city of Guangzhou. It is home to 10 universities with 120,000 students and the potential to accommodate another 80,000 students, with 20,000 faculty and 50,000 support staff. It took only 18 months to construct and includes state-of-the-art information technology (IT) and science labs, world-class libraries, and an Olympic-standard stadium and sports facilities. In addition, there are more than 50 research centers in fields ranging from engineering, medicine, IT, advanced manufacturing, and business management.[1]

The sheer speed and scale of this project demonstrate China's ambition to create a world-class workforce. Expansion plans are also being repeated across emerging economies with major financial investments in countries like India, Russia, Brazil, Hungary, Lithuania, Ukraine, and the United Arab Emirates. In Saudi Arabia, the King Abdullah University of Science and Technology has an endowment fund of over $10 billion with ambitious plans to join the ranks of the world's leading universities. All of this presents a major challenge to the idea that the knowledge wars would remain restricted to head nations in North America, Western Europe, and Japan.

Although leading-edge knowledge was supposed to trickle down to emerging economies traveling the evolutionary path to development, in reality it has taken the form of a tsunami of ideas, knowledge, and technologies flooding over national borders. This has contributed to a massive increase in the global supply of college-educated workers armed with the latest scientific ideas, software applications, and management techniques, along with the lingua franca of economic globalization, English.

The explosion in the global supply of college-educated workers is, however, only part of the story. Increasing the supply of educated workers rarely generates the kinds of learning or business innovation necessary for competitiveness. Unlike the pundits of neoliberalism who assume the supply of human capital creates its own demand in the job market, policy makers in China understood that more is required if investments in education are to translate into economic gain. China has not only expanded its education system but actively tried to link it to national economic development. Here, Western universities and companies have played a key role in taking best practice to emerging countries, offering a crash course in what it takes to globally compete on brainpower.

The Globalization of High Skills

In the club of rich nations, a college education is no longer the preserve of an elite.[2] The view that a large proportion of the workforce requires a college education led to a rapid increase in participation rates.[3] Whatever the merits of the economic case for this expansion, it is hard to be unimpressed by the rise of mass higher education in these countries. Canada was the first country to achieve the target of over 50 percent of people aged 25 and 34 to enter the job market with a college education, followed by Japan and then South Korea, which has engineered massive growth in higher education since 1991.[4] Figure 3.1

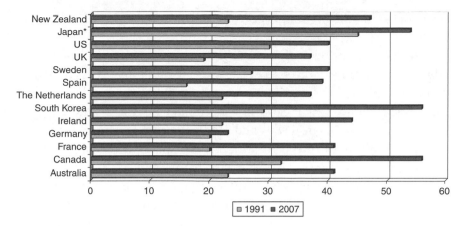

FIGURE 3.1 Trends in educational attainment at college level (1991 and 2007), aged 25–34. *Japan 1997 instead of 1991. *Note*: The OECD uses the term tertiary rather than college education. It consists of both study leading to a Bachelor's degree in preparation for post-graduate study or for entry into professions that require high skills such as medicine, dentistry or architecture (International Standard Classification of Education 5A), and also the equivalent to studying at a junior college which includes technical and more practical vocational programs that are at least two years full-time equivalent at the tertiary level (International Standard Classification of Education 5B). For more details see http://stats.oecd.org/glossary/detail. asp?ID=1436. *Source*: OECD, *Education at a Glance*, 2003, 2008.

shows that the United States, had one of the highest participation rate in the early 1990s, but has since been overtaken by several countries, with others in close pursuit.

Whether this expansionary phase will continue remains to be seen, but as most countries benchmark themselves against those with the highest participation rates, it is likely to encourage further expansion. The United States will try to close the gap on its economic competitors, as will France, Australia, and Britain. Enrollment at degree granting colleges and universities in the United States is projected to rise above 20 million by 2016, a 43 percent increase since 1991.[5] This does not take into account responses to economic recession, but there is a tendency for governments to increase college participation as a way of reducing youth unemployment. When students cannot find the jobs they want, they often feel compelled to invest in a college education in the hope of gaining a competitive advantage over other job market hopefuls. Indeed, the Democrats have pledged to regain America's status of having the higher proportion of college graduates in the world by 2020.[6]

The fact that other nations are seeking an advantage in the knowledge wars is often forgotten in debates about widening access to higher education and upgrading the marketable skills of the workforce. But this game of educational leapfrog is no longer restricted to the league of rich countries. In the 1980s and 1990s, there was considerable surprise, on both sides of the Atlantic, at the speed at which the Asian Tiger economies of Hong Kong, South Korea, Singapore, and Taiwan grew their economies in ways similar to Japan (which joined the club of rich nations in 1964).[7] Indeed, the lesson received by policy makers in America was that much of the success of the Asian Tigers resulted from investing in the human capital of the workforce.[8] What nobody predicted was the educational mobilization of the largest countries on the planet. China and India with populations over a billion people along with others, including Brazil (199 million) and Russia (142 million), all entered the global knowledge wars.

Figure 3.2 shows that China had over 7 million more students than the United States and 10 times as many students as Britain. But perhaps the most extraordinary statistic on education in China was enrollment in high school, which witnessed an increase from 26 percent to almost 60 percent since 1990. To achieve this expansion, more than 250 new teacher-training colleges were established, and qualified graduate teachers were offered better housing, remuneration, and

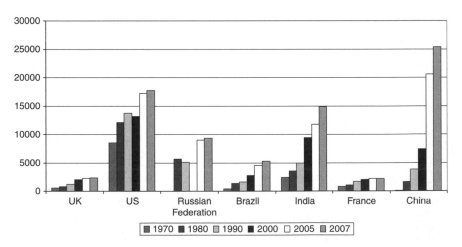

FIGURE 3.2 The expansion of higher education in selected emerging and developed economies (enrollments), in thousands. *Source*: Compiled from the Worldbank data.

health care by the Ministry of Education.[9] Equally, participation in higher education increased from a little over 3 percent in 1990 to 22 percent in 2006.[10] These figures reflect a broader strategy presented in an official policy statement on employment prospects to 2020 that recognized the need to "make efforts in improving education quality, so as to train millions of high-caliber workers, thousands of special talents and a large number of outstanding innovative talents for the socialist modernization drive."[11]

In 1995, as part of this strategy, the Chinese government launched Project 211 aimed at strengthening over 100 institutions of higher education and key disciplinary areas as a national priority for the twenty-first century, with the mission of "training high-level professional manpower to implement the national strategy for social and economic development, accelerating economic progress, pushing forward the development of science, technology and culture, enhancing China's overall capacity and international competitiveness... Establish international prestige and position of Chinese universities among the top universities of the world with teaching and research excellence."[12]

The expansion of higher education in India is following a similar path, although with a less spectacular growth rate than achieved in China. Following independence in 1947, there were only 27 universities. By 2006, this had increased to 367 universities and 18,000 colleges with a population of 13 million students. More than a million of these students were in technical and professional studies, and another million were undertaking graduate studies and research degrees. Despite this expansion, at 13 percent enrollment levels in India are low compared to America. Yet there are still a significant number of students to lead research and innovation in India, as 220,000 students study at the Indian Institutes of Technology and the Indian Institutes of Management, which are reputed to have tougher admissions policies than Harvard or Oxford.

Further plans for expansion have been implemented as part of India's Eleventh Five-Year Plan (2007–2012), which includes a major increase in central government support for education, representing what Prime Minister Manmohan Singh viewed as "an unprecedented increase in allocation for education in the history of our country."[13] This includes funding for thirty new Central Universities, five new Indian Institutes of Science, Education, and Research, eight new Indian Institutes of Technology, seven new Indian Institutes of Management, and twenty new Indian Institutes of Information Technology.[14] Mr. Singh, suggested that a fivefold increase in education expenditures was required because "it is through universal literacy, access to education and knowledge based agricultural and industrial development that India must henceforth march ahead to join the front ranks of the great nations of the world."[15]

In India along with China, there is a long cultural heritage that bestows social status on the educated person regardless of its economic value. But in a more market-driven era, education is viewed as a route to social mobility that could liberate the poor and disadvantaged. One of a number of people we met who was now a senior manager for an international IT company understood the pent-up demand for widening access to educational opportunities, as all the benefits of the latest technologies only come to the people who are well educated. "What," he asks, "about the people who don't have that education?" He thought this had become a more important issue as the communications revolution has "brought a lot of ambitions in the minds of people. Even poor people, when they see things on television, they also dream why shouldn't I have a car, why shouldn't I fly all around; they dream about it, so when they don't find the opportunities, it breeds resentment." And this sense of resentment is what a senior government policy maker described to us as socially "explosive material" that is now leading the Indian authorities to invest in a new ladder of opportunity to meet the growing demand for education.

The view that there was a real chance to make a better life through opportunities for education had resulted in an intense competition being felt by India's middle classes. In Delhi, we received an invitation by the Indian human resources (HR) director of a successful international company to celebrate the Holi festival with his family friends. We were advised to wear a T-shirt and shorts because on arrival we were sprinkled with brightly colored powders, and this was repeated as each guest arrived. On the streets, it was also fair game to be bombarded with brightly colored water bombs as the whole idea is to break down social barriers at least for one day a year. One of our host's close family friends arrived without his wife and daughter. Despite being a national celebration, his teenage daughter had an important examination the following week, and it was decided that she shouldn't be disturbed or waste valuable revision time. There wasn't a hint of surprise from the other guests that the wife had been left to supervise her daughter's studies or the necessity for this additional revision as the conversation focused on the importance of education for personal and national success as India takes its place alongside the world's leading economic powers.

Without firsthand experience of the social hunger for education and a better life, it is difficult for Americans to comprehend the scale and intensity of the education explosion. We have noted how Richard Freeman highlighted the importance of what he called "the great doubling," referring to the increasing size of the global labor pool from around 1.46 billion to 2.93 billion workers.[16] But there is another great doubling. Based on our analysis of enrollment figures for 113 emerging and developed countries, we found that undergraduate and postgraduate enrollments virtually doubled within a decade from 72.5 million in 1996 to 136.1 million in 2007.

These data should be treated as indicative because it is difficult to assess their reliability. Equally, enrollment figures do not tell us how many actually enter the global job market on an annual basis due to high levels of dropouts in some countries. But it does show that the expansion of higher education has not been limited to Organisation for Economic Co-operation and Development (OECD) member states or the BRIC nations of Brazil, Russia, India, and China. Ukraine and Mexico have more people enrolled in higher education than the United Kingdom, with Poland and Turkey making rapid gains, almost doubling their participation rates between 1996–2007. Diana Farrell and colleagues at the McKinsey Global Institute also found that "Poland has nearly as many suitable engineers as does much more populous Russia. The Czech Republic, Hungary, Poland, and Russia together have as many suitable generalists as does India, which has 5 times their total population, and nearly as many suitable engineers. As a result, many countries besides China and India will play a role in the emerging global market for high skilled workers."[17]

Leveraging Learning

The rapid increase in college-educated workers in emerging economies is intended to make a great leap forward, but it requires more that a veritable army of well-qualified workers. It also requires engineering a link between education, learning, and economic development.

In neoliberal economies, we've seen an almost exclusive emphasis on generating a supply of highly qualified employees, given an assumption that this will motivate employers to use these skills in new and innovate ways. But the Chinese government understood that the benefits of education were limited unless it could be used to drive its entry into the global competition for high-value goods and services following its success in becoming the "factory of the world." Educated labor needed to be put to work because China could not politically afford to have large numbers of well-qualified young people waiting for employers in run-down state industries to discover the benefits of human capital.

The Chinese authorities had studied the recent history of economic development which had unfolded around its borders. In virtually all cases, with the possible exception of Hong Kong, national governments performed a leading developmental role in turning a growing supply of education workers into a globally competitive workforce. In terms of gaining access to productive knowledge, there are three aspects that require further consideration. First is the focus on expanding numbers of young workers with knowledge of engineering, scientific, or technological subjects. This included sending large numbers of students to the United States and elsewhere in the developed world to learn about the latest ideas, software, and management techniques, which could be repatriated at a later date. Second, there was a drive to attract Western universities and companies as a source of knowledge transfer. Many leading transnational companies were used as schools for Chinese state and private enterprises in exchange for access to China's growing and lucrative markets. This was extended to using government-owned sovereign funds to acquire knowledge through taking an equity stake or buying Western companies. Third, the limitations of relying on foreign companies to deliver knowledge innovation led China to develop its own research and development (R&D) capability, including research in frontier fields such as nanotechnology.

Engineering the Future: The Focus on Science, Engineering, and Technology in Asia

When we look behind the headline figures of educational expansion around the globe, it's important to consider what subjects are being studied in pursuit of a college diploma. In America, the rhetoric of learning is earning led to the view that it does not matter what is studied because interesting and well-paid jobs were available across the economy. But no matter how a knowledge economy is defined, it is difficult to produce an account that does not include the centrality of science and technology, given that these are major fields of innovation.

If America has been engaged in an act of "unilateral educational disarmament," it stems from large numbers of students attracted to celebrity careers and the lure of big prizewinners at the top of industries like finance, law, business, fashion, and the media. This has been reinforced by proponents of the knowledge economy who portrayed manufacturing as part of yesterday's economy, overtaken by knowledge economy jobs in financial services and other creative industries. In response, talented students turned their backs on what are viewed as less exciting or financially rewarding careers in science, technology, engineering, or math (STEM subjects). Even before the financial crash the governor of the Bank of England, Mervyn King, was sufficiently concerned to speak out against the social and educational distortions caused by inequalities in material wealth, working conditions, and cultural prestige in the financial markets in London, which applied equally to Wall Street. "I do think it is rather unattractive that so many young people, when contemplating careers, look at the compensation packages available in the City and think…it is the only place to work in. It shouldn't be. It should be one of the places, but not the only one."[18]

In the early 1970s, there were four times more bachelor's degrees awarded to American students studying engineering than communication and journalism. This picture dramatically changed as more students now graduate in journalism or related programs than engineering.[19] The picture for mathematics and statistics is especially perilous because, although the numbers of students in colleges and universities significantly increased, those studying mathematics and statistics fell from 24,801 to 14,770 during the same period, representing a fraction of the bachelor's degrees awarded in psychology (88,134) or business (318,042).[20] In the United Kingdom, we find a similar picture. There are now twice as many students studying business and administration than engineering and technology.[21] Even in computing, a discipline that stands at the heart of hi-tech industry, there has been a significant decline. The number of students studying computing fell by 22 percent between 2003 and 2006, a decline of more than 30,000 students, which may reflect concerns about future employment prospects as high-skill computing jobs are offshored.[22]

But it is not only a problem of getting high-caliber students to study in STEM subject areas; it is also a problem getting those who do study these subjects to enter or stay in STEM-related employment. Based on U.S. data, Harold Salzman concluded that the "education system produces a supply of qualified STEM graduates in much greater numbers than jobs available. If there are shortages, it is most likely a demand-side problem of STEM career opportunities that are less attractive than career opportunities in other fields…standard labor market indicators do not indicate any shortage."[23] This conclusion is based on evidence showing that the STEM workforce in the United States totals about 4.8 million, which amounts to less than a third of the 15.7 million workers who hold at least one STEM degree. The fact that large numbers of STEM graduates have entered jobs in non-STEM-related occupations is a timely reminder that solutions to wider economic issues can rarely, if ever, be solved through education alone.[24]

In Asia, the study of science, technology, and engineering is viewed as crucial to national economic development and the route to a worthwhile career in the way a liberal arts degree is in North America. We were made aware of this during a visit to a high-achieving school in Singapore in the late 1990s. Students told us how mathematics was the core subject because it offered the flexibility to take different routes into higher education and the job market. This was reinforced by a strong steer from government based on the view that you could make a manager out of an engineer but you couldn't make an engineer out of a manager.

The Singapore government has relaxed this approach as it strives to diversify its economy. But the focus on science, technology, and engineering remains a major facet of the educational explosion across Asia. When we compare national differences in the proportion of students studying engineering for their first degree, the scale of the transformation in the global distribution of expertise in key areas of the knowledge economy becomes obvious. In China, around 37 percent of students are studying engineering compared to 27 percent in South Korea, 22 percent in Germany, 7 percent in the United Kingdom, and 5 percent in the United States.[25]

Figure 3.3 reveals the regional composition of students being trained in areas of science and engineering. It again shows that Asia is producing more engineers and physical scientists than Europe and North America combined. These trends not only relate to undergraduate study in different parts of the world, as America's capacity for innovative research in engineering, mathematics, and information science has been "hollowed out," given its reliance on foreign expertise. Figures from the National Science Foundation found that 41 percent of science and engineering doctorates from U.S. universities were awarded to foreign students in 2005, the same proportion as in Britain. In the field of engineering, more than 60 percent of engineering doctorates were awarded to foreign students in both countries.[26]

A significant share of foreign scientists and engineers educated in America would previously have chosen to stay after graduation, but more are returning home and contributing to the capacity for industrial

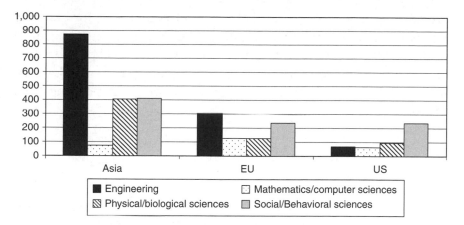

FIGURE 3.3 First university degrees in science and engineering fields in Asia, Europe, and North America, by field: 2006 or most recent years (thousands). *Note*: Natural sciences include physical, biological, earth, atmospheric, and ocean sciences. *Source*: Science and Engineering Indicators 2010.

innovation in emerging economies including China and India. Around two-thirds of foreigners with science and engineering doctorates from U.S. universities in 2005 remained 2 years after graduation. Anna Lee Saxenian has documented how in the initial phase, doctoral graduates from Taiwan and India often headed to jobs in Silicon Valley and Route 128 on the eastern seaboard, building up business know-how, industry contacts, and an understanding of the innovative process. In Silicon Valley, companies founded by immigrants produced $52 billion in sales and employed 450,000 workers.[27] This experience led them to explore opportunities to link up with entrepreneurs or set up businesses in their home countries. In the case of China, Taiwan was the springboard. These trailblazers created the conditions under which those who have qualified in the United States can return to develop their own businesses. Economic retrenchment and tougher visa restrictions have accelerated the number of foreign workers leaving the United States, a trend also being driven by new business and research opportunities closer to home.[28]

The extent of what Saxenian calls "brain circulation" rather than "brain drain" should not be exaggerated. Academics of Asian heritage continue to make up 35 percent of computer science and engineering faculty, 30 percent in mathematics, and 20 percent in the physical and life sciences in American universities. But when the increase in research capacity in Asia and the networks into American universities are taken into account, it is possible to understand how, for example, China could successfully participate in the Human Genome Project in the 1990s. Chinese scientists and engineers who had been educated abroad were recruited to 20 institutes in Beijing and Shanghai, which formed the expert base they needed to be involved in this cutting-edge research.

Innovative Learning: Crouching and Leaping Economies

The expansion of higher education in countries like China and India is not only intended to improve the quality of jobs linked to inward investment from foreign companies. It is also intended to serve as a springboard to lift productivity and competitiveness across the whole economy. As Kent Hughes reflected in his testimony before the U.S.-China Economic and Security Review Commission, "Every high-technology factory and every R&D facility is a learning opportunity for China."[29]

The same could also be said for collaborations between American and Chinese universities. Although these are intended to build mutual understanding and overcome cultural barriers, Western universities have been enticed by the potential for new pools of tuition-paying students, funded research programs, and university endowments, such as the $50 million gift Yale University received from two U.S. foundations to develop research collaboration in China. There has been an "educational gold rush" as American universities have competed to set up outposts in countries including China, India, and the Gulf states.[30] Most of China's leading universities have joint research programs or student and faculty exchange programs, which now number around 700 according to official figures from the Chinese government.[31]

A similar story of mutual self-interest is evident in the way China has systematically used foreign companies to learn how to develop sophisticated organizational capacity, such as international supply chains, and to provide access to the latest technologies essential for indigenous companies to become "national champions" as they gear up to compete in the global marketplace. Rubbing shoulders with leading foreign companies served as a benchmark for their own developmental learning and performance.

In this sense, we might see learning rather like a person who is crouching and watching before having the knowledge to leap from a position of disadvantage to one of advantage. A leading Chinese economist, with expertise in the area of state-owned enterprises, described to us how foreign companies had brought China a "school" in which they were "good teachers" in the management and organization of state-owned enterprises. These enterprises were recruiting senior executives in the global marketplace and were especially interested in Chinese-speaking personnel who had experience working in international companies, including those working in South Korean and Japanese firms.

A healthy supply of college-educated workers was important for Chinese companies, whether big or small, to take advantage of technology transfer, which leaks across corporate boundaries as employees move between companies. It is obviously something that the Chinese authorities wanted to encourage because foreign companies were required to enter joint ventures with Chinese companies as a condition for access to its domestic markets. Following China's entry into the World Trade Organization (WTO), it has been easier for foreign companies to trade independently, but the issue of safeguarding intellectual property is inevitably sensitive.

A young corporate lawyer we interviewed from a leading European electronics company thought the Chinese government was demonstrating an increasing willingness to police violations of corporate intellectual property rights (IPRs) compared to the early days when they entered the Chinese electronics market. Although a European expatriate, he demonstrated a degree of empathy, pointing out that weak policing of intellectual property enabled technology transfer, while keeping costs low for Chinese manufacturers whose margins were already being driven down to rock bottom. If they had to pay for IPRs, they would be driven out of business. He explained how access to knowledge was intimately related to the expansion of the Chinese job market. "Anything that may threaten the employment situation in China would conjure up this picture of unemployed workers, you know, going on the streets, striking, rioting, whatever. So we do appreciate the difficulties that the Chinese government faces in licensing issues [IPRs] and there was in fact…a direct and logical correlation between licensing and people going out of jobs."

Conflict over access to such learning opportunities has a very long history, but there are also plenty of recent examples of what is called *reverse engineering*, where countries such as South Korea developed the business and technological acumen to thrive in the global economy. At its most basic, leading products from the West were dismantled to see how they were designed and constructed. Korean conglomerates then improved on them and exported the products at a far lower price than the originals, exploiting the low cost of Korean labor.

In China, this process has been taken to new levels of sophistication, largely through the speed at which high-quality copies can be manufactured. There is an apocryphal story told by a German auto manufacturer about a bus company which it set up in southern China. As the German plant was being constructed on one side of a highway, a Chinese plant was being constructed on the other side. Within a week of the German buses rolling off the production line, the Chinese company across the street was producing almost identical buses at a fraction of the price, highlighting the speed at which Chinese companies can leverage new technologies to compete with foreign competitors.

The Chinese strategy of crouching, learning, and leaping is no longer limited to home study. They have globalized the learning process by buying knowledge, technologies, and the expertise of foreign firms through strategic alliances, equity stakes or wholesale acquisitions. The Chinese government has encouraged approximately 50 global champions, many of them state owned but not state run, to take a stake or acquire American and European companies. They include Lenovo's acquisition of IBM's personal computer business; ZTE, a telecom company, has strategic alliances with companies including Motorola and Alcatel and has set up 13 R&D centers in China to learn from the experience; and Nanjing Automotive acquired MG Rover in Britain. This enabled Nanjing Automotive to acquire key technologies and engineering knowledge along with the production line that was shipped back to Nanjing. MG Rover engineers, production managers, and technical staff were also hired to help improve production and strengthen their design and innovation capabilities.

The China Development Bank (CDB) and Temesek Holdings from Singapore, both state-owned corporations, bought into Barclays Capital, originally to support its takeover bid for the Dutch investment bank ABN AMRO. Luckily for them, the bid failed and Royal Bank of Scotland struck a deal with ABN AMRO and subsequently lost 96 percent of its share value following the credit crunch. In our interviews with some of the leading players and commentators in this bid, it is clear that the China Development Bank had linked up with Temesek because it had far wider experience in this area and because of the learning and experience that the CDB would acquire with positions on the board of Barclays.

There has also been increasing use of state "sovereign funds" that have enabled countries including China, Russia, Singapore, and the Arab states to accumulate large reserves of U.S. dollars, giving them the financial resources to buy into overseas companies. The China

Investment Corporation has, for example, bought stakes in Blackstone and Morgan Stanley. The financial crisis has accelerated this process, and China's access to the technologies and expertise it requires, as Anthony Leung, managing director of Blackstone Group Greater China, has suggested, is "a one-time-in-100-years chance for China's Sovereign Wealth Funds to invest in good companies and acquire more shares." It also gives Chinese companies a strategic opportunity to take "stakes in advanced overseas companies so that Chinese companies can learn how to move from the low end of the production chain to the high end."[32] Germany is a particular focus for China, and here their interest appears to be in the Mittlestand engineering companies. So concerned was the German government that it considered legislation to protect strategic German companies from mergers and acquisitions.

Research and Development Capacity

But these strategies for the next great leap forward in China's economic development have their limits. Continuing to rely on the transfer of expertise and technologies from foreign companies would keep China in the status of an economic follower rather than leader. Achieving global standards is important, but the real profits stem from defining global standards, such as Microsoft's dominance in computer software or Intel's processing chips that allow PC users to work with several applications at a time.

This led the Chinese government to inject vast funds into R&D in an attempt to develop a national innovation system capable of competing with the best in the world. As in many countries, including the United States, Russia, and India, most of its previous research was geared toward national security. As Zeng and Williamson note, "In the central-planning era, Chinese government institutions developed strong capabilities in basic research and development, especially in advanced technology related to military applications. As late as 2003, they still accounted for 78 percent of total investment in basic research."[33] But since the 1980s, it has decentralized and broadened its research activities with an emphasis on commercial applications. Several areas of high technology were identified for investment, including biotechnology, photoelectric materials, and high-performance computers. In 2006, the medium to long-term plan for the development of science and technology from 2006 to 2020 was launched and aimed to make China an innovation-oriented nation.[34]

Cong Cao, from the Levin Institute, has asked whether China, "once considered one of the more backward developing countries," is now "poised to become a global leader in science and technology."[35] Significant problems remain, as we will go on to see, but the scale of their ambition is revealed in the attempt to catch Japan and the United States in the field of nanotechnology. This involves the manufacture of nanoparticles which are incredibly small, as 1 nanometer (nm) equals 0.000000001 meters. The Web site Nanotechnology Now listed 803 products or product lines in January 2009 in its consumer products inventory, a 279 percent increase from 212 in March 2006.[36] Many of these are related to health and fitness, but they also include a wide range of other uses such as self-repellent clothing that never needs cleaning and the potential for computers to be incorporated "into next-generation nanostructured materials in much the same way color is incorporated in the materials with which we now make clothing, appliances, motor vehicles, and aircraft."[37] In some areas of nanotechnology, China is already ahead of the United States, as the Chinese Academy of Science has a nanotechnology program involving at least 20 academic institutions and around 1,200 scientists leading different projects along with 2,000 graduate research assistants. The Shanghai Nanotechnology Promotion Center has trained more than 1,500 scientists and engineers in molecular manufacturing and related equipment.[38]

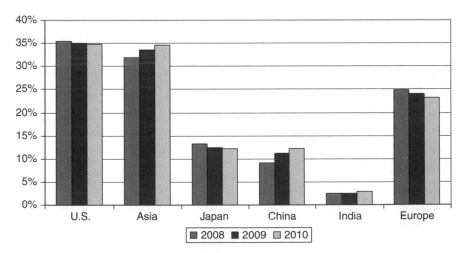

FIGURE 3.4 Share of total global R&D spending, 2008–2010 (percentage). *Source*: *R&D Magazine* (2009), http://www.rdmag.com/Featured-Articles/2009/12/Policy-And-Industry-Global-Funding-Report-Emerging-Economies-Drive-Global-R-D-Growth/

Figure 3.4 shows the shift in global distribution of R&D. Europe and the United States experienced a decline in their share of global R&D spending while China's share rose from 9.1 percent to 12.2 percent. It also shows a major difference between China and India; India has remained fairly static with a relatively small global share of 2.9 percent. Although China has a long way to go to catch the United States, such trends appear to be supported by a rapid change in the global distribution of patents that grant intellectual property rights to individuals, companies, and universities. Eve Zhou and Bob Stembridge of Thomson Reuters found that if current trends continue, China will patent more inventions than any other nation by 2012.[39]

Conclusion

If knowledge is power, we are witnessing a shift in its global distribution. Since the early days of the Industrial Revolution in the 1750s, it has been Europe and the United States that drove innovation through new ideas and technologies. This gave them global economic dominance that many in America and Europe believed to be unassailable as economic activity became more knowledge based. Today, this dominance is under threat because the knowledge and technologies that were thought to create "smart" barriers to late economic entrants have enabled some emerging nations to leapfrog decades of development to compete shoulder to shoulder on a number of economic plateaus, notwithstanding vast inequalities in terms of social infrastructure.

This chapter shows early signs of America losing some of its advantage in the knowledge wars through a retreat from STEM subjects, through knowledge transfer from American and European companies and universities to Asia, and through the sale of Western companies and know-how. Undoubtedly, there will be gains for America and the West from economic advancement in China and the rest of Asia. There are already 10,000 American students studying in Chinese universities, and much of the advanced research in emerging economies will benefit American companies, consumers, and citizens. It may also force Americans and Europeans to up their game as the complacency of past decades evaporates, but there is a major shift in power away from America and Europe that will have profound implications for rich economies.

We have described a process in which China is rapidly closing the gap in technological know-how in key fields, including nanotechnology, supercomputers, genomics, and stem cell research. Some universities in Asia now rival the capabilities of those in the West, and no doubt more will do so. We are likely to see more partnerships between American universities and those in Asia develop technologies that may not benefit U.S. workers as much as those in China or India. This applies equally to American corporations, as we will go on to discuss in the next chapter.

The speed of change will in part depend on the quality of graduates in East Asia and across the developing world. There are important quality issues and challenges confronting the education systems in China and India, which together will account for 40 percent of the world's workforce by 2030.[40] Diana Farrell and her team at McKinsey's have argued that only 13 percent of the university graduates from the 28 low-wage nations they studied were suitable for jobs in mainly American and European companies due to what HR managers perceived as poor team-working skills, too much emphasis on theory, lack of cultural fit, and poor grasp of English.[41]

There can be no doubt that the quality of university graduates outside high-prestige institutions in emerging countries will be highly variable, but this is a problem not restricted to emerging economies. Moreover, what the McKinsey team appears to overlook, given its focus on the potential for offshoring to low-cost locations, is that these countries are not only creating high-skill workers to serve the needs of foreign transnational companies. They are also creating homegrown companies where team-working skills are likely to take a different form, where the emphasis on theory could provide the foundations for further learning, where there is likely to be a good cultural fit, and where there is less need to communicate in English on a day-to-day basis.

We must also caution against lumping countries such as China and India into simplistic categories such as "emerging" or "Chindia." We have focused on China because it exhibits a more systematic approach, driven by a dirigiste state that shares some features common to the economic strategies previously pursued in Japan, South Korea, Taiwan, and Singapore. In many respects, the economic development in India, especially its spectacular achievements in information and communication technologies, were achieved despite, rather than due to, the role of the federal government.

India has not expanded its system of college education as rapidly as China, and its economic takeoff has been fueled by concentration on its elite Indian Institutes of Technology and Management. To put the challenge facing India into context, it has been estimated that to achieve the levels of enrollment in India that are current in the United States for the 18–23-year-old cohort, India would need an additional 2,400 universities in the next 25 years.[42] Its crumbling infrastructure and unrelenting poverty will add to the problem of creating a world-class workforce despite the rising ambitions of Indian workers and families and their command of the English language, which is a major advantage in today's global economy. Most of the Indians we spoke to thought the country was doing things its own way. They contrasted what is sometimes called the "Hindu pace" with the breakneck "Shenzhen speed" of China. Shenzhen is a city located near Hong Kong which experienced a 30 percent annual increase in GDP from 1979 to 2006.

Global recession creates serious problems for the political system in China due to rapid industrialization and urbanization. The reduction in growth rates in 2008 to 6.8 percent, while enviable in the West, was not sufficient to absorb the supply of young workers entering the job market. With more and more of these young people being educated to university level and with memories of Tiananmen Square still alive, the threat of graduate unemployment forced the authorities to institute emergency measures designed to contain the potential political threat. The closure of factories, leaving workers with unpaid wages and no welfare resources to fall back on, resulted in riots, some including university students. In November 2006, students at Shengda Economics, Trade and Management College, in central China, rioted because the title on their degree certificate was changed to include the name of their college alongside Zhengzou University, which is a prestigious university to which the college was affiliated. This was seen to devalue the quality of their graduate credentials at a time when students confronted increased competition for professional and managerial jobs. According to the Ministry of Public Security, there were 10,000 "mass incidents," in 1994. By 2005, the latest available published figures show this rising to 87,000.[43] Faced with a mounting series of such problems, which inevitably threaten the faith of workers in the ability of the system to deliver better living standards, the legitimacy of government economic strategy may be cast into doubt.

But what is not in doubt is the globalization of high skills.[44] This poses a significant challenge to America's middle classes whose livelihoods depend on increasing the value of their human capital within employment. It raises issues of what kind of educational experience could enable American workers to regain their bargaining position as many confront the prospects of being outsmarted in key sectors of the global economy. But the global auction is more than a competition for knowledge and ideas; it is also a competition based on price. What is revolutionary about the globalization of high skills is that it has been combined with low-cost innovation, challenging many of our cherished beliefs about the social foundations of economic success.

⌘

CHAPTER FOUR

The Quality-Cost Revolution

Twice as well at half the cost. Everybody has to live it.

—U.S. Bank, Mumbai

O N A RESEARCH visit to the engineering heartland of Baden-Württemberg in Germany, we interviewed a senior corporate executive from the auto industry about his company's global operations. When asked if they could make their luxury models anywhere in the world, his response was an emphatic "No!" He explained that the quality of engineering required in the production of their luxury models, given the complexities of combining mechanic and electronic components, meant that they could only be produced in Germany. This was in the late 1990s. When we returned several years later, we met up with the same executive and posed the same question. This seemed to take him by surprise, not because we'd asked it before but because the answer was obviously "Yes!" They were building the entire product range not only outside Germany but in an emerging economy. This was consistent with what we had been told by the head of human resources for a Japanese automaker near New Delhi, "You have to make an effort to make bad quality products."

Through a combination of rising skill levels, new production technologies, and international industrial standards, transnational companies have overcome many of the problems that hampered previous attempts to create high-quality goods and services in lower-cost economies. Although quality issues remain, virtually all the companies we studied reported rapid improvements in quality standards across their global operations. An automaker headquartered in Detroit told us, "If you had asked me 5 years ago, I would have said that the skill sets probably are still in the advanced economies, but I think that is changing very, very quickly." He was equally quick to understand how this was transforming the relationship between quality and cost. "The advantage from our perspective is that you are paying those guys anywhere from sort of $12,000 to $15,000 a year versus, say, a European or a U.S. engineer at anywhere from $75,000 to $95,000 a year, with a whole bunch of benefits as well."

Americans were led to believe that the country faced a choice between two futures: a high road to high-skill, high-wage work based on quality products or a low road to low-skill, low-wage work based on price. Today, competition is based on quality *and* cost, increasing competitive pressures to improve quality and reduce labor costs at the same time. Bill Ford while CEO of Ford Motor Company captured this new reality in his remarks to shareholders when he announced that changing business conditions "represent a turning point unlike anything we've experienced in our history. The auto business has shifted completely and permanently to full-scale global competition."[1] This observation was made before some leading American automakers were forced to seek a $23.4 billion bailout from the federal government.

The rapid improvement in quality standards achieved in emerging economies such as China and India was not limited to manufacturing but has extended to a broad range of service industries. Occupations under the definition of services include everything from shop workers, schoolteachers, lawyers, tourist guides, university professors, and management consultants. Clearly, only some service sector jobs are tradable, given that it is difficult to look after the sick in Minnesota or Manchester if you live in Mumbai or Mongolia. However, in the service sector, there are more workers in jobs that could potentially be offshored than those who remain working in manufacturing.[2]

But because services are "weightless," they can be moved with extraordinary speed. Research on the transfer of back-office functions from the United States to India shows that services are different from manufacturing because it takes a lot longer to close factories and set up elsewhere; in services, where the objects are pixels and electronic pulses, they are "easily transmitted by photons and radio waves."[3] An executive at a leading European bank agreed, noting that their decision to globalize many of their functions involved little more than moving knowledge around, "whereas if you are a car manufacturer you have to move steel and parts of engines, and so you need a big plan of logistics of how you globally integrate your manufacturing plants." In contrast, "We can overnight change everything," and in many respects, they did transform their global operations. Ten years ago, there were no global teams "but now we have 2,000 managers who have their teams sitting in all time zones and I have my directors reporting…in to me sitting in New York, London, Sydney, Singapore, or Frankfurt, and their teams are also spread all over the world."

One of the most striking things about financial services, including retail and investment banking, insurance, and brokerage, is the way new technologies have enabled companies to globally integrate complex activities such as research, financial analysis, regulatory reporting, accounting, and human resources work as well as the more routine activities such as customer services, invoicing, and payroll. Within a major American bank, there was no strategy to shift jobs to India from New York or elsewhere within the group, but a discussion between senior staff in Mumbai and sponsors in New York led to a "handshake for a few operations jobs." This was in 2002, when the company began engaging in a number of pilot projects in response to increasing cost pressures. The experiment with back-office functions reflected the growth in offshore call centers and business process outsourcing (BPO). There was little point using staff in New York or London to process invoices or very basic data-entry jobs when it could be done in real time in India or Vietnam at a fraction of the price.

Although the company was in the early stages of developing wealth management and investment banking within the country, there was rapid growth of the middle office that includes research and analytical jobs for its New York and London offices. "For five analysts in New York or London, you could have at least fifteen in India." Before 2000, business process and analytical work were done close to the main business centers, but with the rapid development of Internet capability, secure networks, and standardized software, they have drawn a clearer distinction between work and place. Differences in time zones also facilitated the need for investment bankers and brokers in North America and Europe to make a pitch to a client based on quick and accurate information that could be packaged overnight in Asia.

A young woman of Indian descent based in Mumbai, with work experience in New York and London, told us that she believed Indians are often viewed as "smart, intelligent, and being able to put their head down and do the job." However, she thought that colleagues in North America were "surprised at the extent and the kind of work they are doing—the speed at which we are delivering and the fact that some of these individuals are actually moving into front-line jobs and competing with them in their sphere as well." Her senior colleague added that what was really different was the quality of the research they were generating for the front line to use—that is those who actually negotiate the deals with clients. "These are the areas that we find that talent is delivering to an even higher standard than expected. We're not doing those menial call center type jobs. It's global work and that's where we think we've been able to add a lot more value than what was initially expected and that will continue."

Quality: From Local Adaptation to Global Markets

We have already seen how Western companies have played a key role in the transfer of knowledge in China and India. The opening up of new markets to more than 2 billion potential consumers led them to follow the market. Some of these companies had a presence across Asia decades before the creation of the World Trade Organization in 1995, but trade liberalization in both China and India proved irresistible to many other companies.[4] American household brands where among those quick to recognize how the extension of global trade gave them access to new consumer markets and gave them the potential to revolutionize their global operations. This will be examined in a later chapter, but first we need to investigate the role of these companies in moving price competition up the value chain by achieving global quality standards in low-cost locations.

In less than a decade, there has been a fundamental change in the attitudes of transnational companies. They often began by experimenting with their own captive operations in low-cost countries or by using third-party providers such as Wipro, Tata Consultancy Services (TCS), or Infosys, which are at the forefront of India's IT revolution.

While following the market, they were also assessing how far they could move a low-cost model of production and routine services, such as sales and marketing through offshore contact centers, up the value chain of knowledge, skills, goods, and services. This led to increasing investment in research centers intended to adapt Western technologies and know-how to emerging markets. The Volkswagen Passat built for the Chinese market is 10 centimeters longer than that sold in North

America and Europe because managers in China like to sit in the back passenger seat and be chauffeur driven. Philips toasters in India have an extra lift lever for removing bread from its toasters because of differences in the size and shape of breads found across India. The sound quality of televisions for the Indian market is enhanced to meet consumer demand for good sound quality. The color is also varied between the north and south of the country because people in the south prefer a reddish tinge.

After meeting requirements to adapt existing Western technologies to local markets, they began to engage in global work. Take one of the major North American producers of mobile phones that started with basic manufacturing in China but, realizing the potential, rapidly moved their Chinese operations up the value chain to include designing both hardware and software. The company now has over 3,000 research engineers working in China who design and develop products for the global marketplace. We were told how the company had initially invested in manufacturing as part of plans to expand its global supply chain, but when senior American executives realized there were many talented engineers, they rapidly moved into leading-edge R&D. A Chinese manager based in Beijing observed how they moved from "coding work" and "customization" to research "fundamental architecture development, so we've created a lot of IPR [intellectual property rights] here in China."

The speed at which transnational companies included China in their blue-skies research that may not have immediate commercial application can also be seen from the example of a major Korean electronics company. In 2004, we visited its impressive research center outside Seoul. At that time, the company was adamant that it would not situate basic research in China because of the fear of losing their research intelligence to Chinese competitors. Two years later, we visited their research center in Beijing, from where they now pitch for blue-skies research projects. The Korean manager who headed the center believed that Chinese researchers were able to think outside the box because they were more egalitarian in their willingness to speak up and share ideas. This is perhaps a legacy of China's communist past and ironic because it is now fueling commercial enterprises. Concerns about intellectual property being smuggled to Chinese competitors remained, but the company decided it was a trade-off worth making precisely because it was forced to reduce the cost of innovation.

This drive for low-cost innovation is reflected in patterns of corporate investment monitored by the United Nations Conference on Trade and Development (UNCTAD). They identified a major shift in the way corporate foreign direct investment (FDI) has been deployed since the 1970s. Initially, developed-country foreign direct investment was geared toward natural resources and market seeking. In the 1980s and 1990s, investments were also made to "take advantage of cost differences in different production locations by building up global production networks to produce for regional and world markets (efficiency-seeking FDI). In recent years, another kind of trend in FDI from developed countries has emerged as companies also engage in R&D activities abroad."[5] This is reflected in the fact that value added per employee of foreign affiliates continued to rise as technically more complex activities such as design, testing, and R&D are increasingly shifting to China and India.[6]

By 2005 there were 315 new FDI projects in R&D in Asia, of which 80 percent were in China and India. Motorola has invested around U.S.$3.8 billion since it entered the Chinese market in 1987, including U.S.$1 billion in R&D. The company has over 10,000 employees, with more than 3,000 in R&D in the country.[7] In the auto industry, Shanghai GM and Shanghai VW were expanding existing centers. Nissan, Daimler, Honda, and Hyundai, together with local partners, were establishing new centers. Toyota established a Technical Center Asia Pacific in Thailand and an R&D center in Tianjin, China.[8] Companies including Microsoft, Nokia, GE, IBM, Siemens, DuPont, General Motors, Philips, and Toshiba also have significant research capability in the country.[9]

In the current phase of global capitalism, there is a relentless process of raising quality and reducing costs, leaving little room for complacency. In Beijing, a Chinese senior manager told us how they could increase production simply by employing more people because there was a plentiful supply of cheap labor. "But now, we are becoming much, much more expensive, so the only way for us to justify investment here rather than India, Vietnam, the Philippines, or Eastern Europe is to ensure our productivity is, you know, appropriately increasing."

In Mumbai, employees working for an American bank that expanded its Indian workforce from 12 to 9,000 in 6 years constantly felt under pressure to reinvent themselves and demonstrate their worth. "I need to demonstrate to head office that I can do the job better than the guy in Singapore, and that is my worry every day. I need to be able to deliver a job as good as London, if not better than them. That is how the value chain is going to change, and that is the really scary factor. There is no rest...you take a pause and others will say, 'Make way, I'm coming in.'"

Cost: Best Practice for Less

As differences in quality narrow between operations in different parts of the world, the cost and working conditions of Western employees are no longer the global benchmark. In moving offshoring up the value chain of products and services, companies are not only following the business into rapidly expanding emerging markets. They are also adopting a deliberate strategy of establishing leading-edge operations in parallel to those in the developed economies. This not only gives them global flexibility if there are industrial relations problems or problems of underperformance in a specific regional center. It also enables companies to point to the cost advantage of their overseas operations when negotiating with employees.

The gravitational pull of global competition for most American workers takes salaries in a downward direction, especially when companies are under competitive or market pressures to increase profits or reduce debt. The same market logic not only applies in the context of price competition from emerging economies but it applies equally to differences in labor costs within domestic economies, as autoworkers in Detroit are well aware. Before contracts were renegotiations in the autumn of 2008, the differential between United Auto Workers members employed by the big three Detroit automakers and the nonunionized workers in international auto firms such as Toyota and Honda was between $25 and $30 per hour in wages and benefits. This differential has disappeared as workers are forced into a reverse auction in a desperate bid to keep their jobs.[10] For entry-level jobs in Detroit's auto industry, workers previously earning $28 an hour are now on $14 an hour.[11]

The Competition for Profit

The quality-cost revolution was initially driven by American, European, and Japanese corporations, but it led to new forms of low-cost innovation increasingly driven by Chinese and Indian companies. In much the same way that workers in emerging economies were assumed to lag far behind on the evolutionary path to knowledge work, Chinese and Indian companies were also assumed to stand little chance of competing against the technological superiority of American enterprise. Yet Chinese and Indian companies are using state-of-the-art technologies, business processes, and management techniques combined with low-cost innovation strategies that enable them to compete for profits with American corporations for the full length of the value chain.

The growing capacity of companies from emerging economies to move up the value chain and compete in world markets was described by an Indian executive working for an American consultancy company. He suggested that most of the jobs offshored to India in the 1980s and 1990s did not require "tremendous talent," but things had changed as Indian companies were "scaling up very fast," especially in the software sector. In this sector, companies had gained confidence and were saying,

> We will now design the software ourselves....It is just that in India we did not have the right processes, we did not have the right type of environment that we could tap the talents of our population, but luckily now thanks to the Internet, to the changing world order, I think we have more opportunities...to come up to a higher level...it is possible to do any type of activity in India and pass on the information anywhere else in the world.

Infosys started as an IT outsourcing firm for foreign companies and grew from 3,000 employees in 1999 to 104,000 in 2009. The scale of expansion is mind boggling, as this was one of several companies hiring up to 10,000 university graduates a year. Another Indian software company has offices in 33 countries as well as global research centers with 60,000 employees, of which approximately 80 percent are in India. During our research, we encountered a number of such Indian IT firms who set up offices in major cities, including New York and London, with the aim of competing with U.S. and European companies as they moved up the value chain into consultancy.[12] This global reach gave them the chance to successfully bid for projects because they were frequently more cost competitive. They could ship the full range of IT services, including software development and consultancy, back to India.

The same processes are at work in other industries like pharmaceuticals where Indian companies such as Dr. Reddy's have moved from the development, manufacture, and sales of generic drugs into the more lucrative marketing for innovative drugs. Already one of the largest drug companies in India, it now has wholly owned subsidiaries in United States, United Kingdom, Russia, Germany, and Brazil and joint ventures in China, South Africa, and Australia. It spends 12 to 14 percent of annual revenue on its R&D centers in Atlanta and Hyderabad. According to its Chief Executive G. V. Prasad, it is "a global generics player on the way to innovation." The company is transforming itself into a discovery-led pharmaceutical company. In 2006, it sealed one of India's largest overseas deals with the $627 million purchase of Betapharm, Germany's fourth-largest generic drugmaker. The company is partnering with other pharmaceutical companies to share the huge costs of research and development for new drugs. It does the initial research and then finds partners such as to ClinTec in the United Kingdom to help share the cost of clinical trials. Overall, the costs of development are reduced significantly thanks to the research done by India's pool of highly trained but inexpensive scientists.[13]

Such companies represent a rapidly growing phenomenon. There were only 19 companies from the developing world in the Fortune 500 in 1990, by 2009 the number had risen to 65.[14] Some of these have already achieved important global positions in industries such as automotives, chemicals, petroleum refining, steel and in services including banking, shipping, telecommunications, and construction.

There can be little doubt that the combination of well-qualified, low-cost staff will see many more such companies achieve global reach. As a senior policy advisor in New Delhi observed, the costs of producing are higher overseas, and Indian investors see an opportunity for taking over Western companies, "initially produced there by Indian management style of low cost, and at some time relocate here in India." Therefore some commentators still talk of a technology gap between the older industrial countries and emerging economies, but the combination of leading-edge research and low-cost skilled labor is the new benchmark against which workers and companies from the older established economies must compete.

Ming Zeng and Peter Williamson, in their salutary book *Dragons at Your Door*, suggest, "The cost-innovation challenge presented by Chinese companies is disruptive because it strikes at the heart of what makes many businesses in high-cost countries profitable."[15] They illustrate their argument with the example of China International Marine Containers Group (CIMC), which now dominates the world of shipping containers. It is worth retelling the story of CIMC because it demonstrates a further consequence of the quality-cost revolution for Western workers and businesses.

China International Marine Containers Group started by cutting its competitive teeth in the Chinese market that demanded well-honed skills and consistent cost reductions while delivering quality products in competition with 20 other container producers within China. This proved to be a useful capacity-building exercise before taking on established global players in the shipping container industry. Zeng and Williamson found that when Chinese Dragons, as they called companies like CIMC, started to expand abroad, they used cost innovation as a tool to identify loose bricks—that is "those market segments where existing players are potentially most vulnerable."[16] It was helped by intense global competition in the container industry in the late 1990s that drove down prices and forced competitors out of the industry as profit margins evaporated. China International Marine Containers Group survived because it squeezed costs and still made a profit as it expanded to the point where in volume terms it became the biggest global producer in 1996. In 1997, the Asian financial crisis hit competitors and enabled CIMC to break out of the low end of the container market. Asian competitors wanted to divest out of containers, and German companies' business was threatened because Asian customers could not pay the premium for their products.

China International Marine Containers Group bought patents from its German competitors and improved on them. It also bought up German production lines, repatriated them to China, scaled up, and lifted productivity. By these strategies, they became global leaders in refrigeration, state-of-the-art electronic tracking, and folding mechanisms to flat pack empty containers for which it brought a majority shareholding in a British company and then introduced customized features. The strategies of buying up others' innovations, improving on them, and then gaining from economies of scale enabled CIMC to become the world leader in container technology and production. And it is not the only Chinese company engaging with global competitors in this way.

Here's the rub, which is captured by Zeng and Williamson: "because the Chinese are using their cost advantage across a broad swath of activities, including R&D, design, and customization, not just in volume manufacturing, moving to successively higher-end segments is just as likely to result in bankruptcy as it is in salvation."[17]

Hence, the widely touted view that American workers and companies can prosper in the global economy by moving up the value chain fails to understand the realities of today's quality-cost revolution. Simply moving upmarket is based on the same residual thinking that assumed it would take China and India decades before they could compete with the West on brainpower. Whatever strategies are developed in response to this kind of disruptive innovation, they must begin from a shocking truth that in the global auction there are few places to hide from price competition.

Sustaining Asia's Low-Cost Model

A key question is whether the quality-cost equation is sustainable in the medium term; there are also questions about its impact on the jobs and incomes of American workers. One view is that even if emerging economies are now competing for knowledge work, their cost advantage is due to temporary differences in wage rates. These differences will disappear as laws of supply and demand come into play to bring salaries of the expanding middle classes in countries including China and India into line with those of older industrial countries.[18] Such arguments rest on what economists call "factor price equalization." Free trade will lead to an equalization of the price of goods between countries, which will result in similar wages paid to workers doing the same jobs anywhere in the world. The key issue is how quickly incomes in China and India will rise and how far those in America and Europe will fall before they are harmonized. Such an equilibrium remains a long way off, and as John Maynard Keynes famously put it, "in the long-run we are all dead."

The World Bank predicted that the speed of convergence between developing and developed countries incomes will be modest. Based on an international standard measure of purchasing power, the income of an average resident living in a developing country is about 16 percent of the average of high-income countries: $4,800 versus $29,700. This ratio is predicted to rise to 23 percent in 25 years. Of course, such averages do conceal considerable variations. Chinese incomes are predicted to rise from 19 percent of the average of high-income countries to 42 percent in 25 years.[19]

Wage rates in the new member states of the European Union, including Poland, Hungary, and Romania, were about 70 percent lower than those in the E.U.-15 countries, including Germany, France, and the United Kingdom, in 2005 and were expected to remain at this level.[20] International comparisons on the relative costs of employing a chip design engineer also show that a chip designer in the United States costs over four times more than a designer in South Korea and ten times or more than the costs associated with the same worker in India and China.[21]

Although wages in China and India increased, especially in the economic hot spots such as Shanghai or Bangalore prior to the global economic downturn, a well-informed Indian CIO observed it would "take until 2022 before we touch U.S. salary levels. So we still have 15–20 years." The same view was expressed by the head of an automotive research center also based in Bangalore. This center engaged in global product development where one might expect to find comparable wages due to high levels of expertise, but we were informed that "tremendous differences" remained in labor costs for researchers as "the highest paid researchers here would be a third of an American."

Indeed, regardless of the prevailing economic climate, there are limits to wage hikes if emerging countries are to continue to take advantage of a low-cost model. In Bangalore, there were shortages of IT professionals. These shortages led to increasing attrition as people jumped jobs to take advantage of new opportunities created by companies such as Accenture, IBM, HP, and Dell, which were all offering salaries 25–30 percent higher than those offered by Indian companies. This led salaries in the IT sector to increase at a rate of about 15–20 percent every year prior to the economic downturn. But as we were told by an Indian IT executive, "There is a limit to which these salaries can increase. Beyond a certain level, it becomes unviable. After all, why are people outsourcing: because it is cheaper."

The wage hikes in Bangalore were fueled by pressure on American corporate managers to show greater profitability leading to a reduction in the number of people in the United States and hiring people in India. This was at a time when American and European corporations were making record profits—before the financial crash. At the time of writing, it is difficult to accurately assess the future scale of offshoring, which will inevitably be driven by both political and economic considerations.

Nonetheless, financial services companies are being advised to balance short-term cost cutting, such as head count reduction, with longer-term strategic initiatives, including "the outsourcing of non-core functions like learning, HR and finance and accounting. If done correctly, companies can lower overall costs by up to 20 percent without compromising their organizational strength and capabilities to gain competitive advantage once the market turns."[22]

Whether companies take this advice remains to be seen, but we do know that in an attempt to maintain a low-cost model, China and India have a huge reserve army of labor. China has over 661 cities whereas it had only 13 in 1978, and of these, 49 have a population greater than a million.[23] Most people have heard of Beijing, Shanghai, and Guangzhou, but there are many more low-cost locations such as Tianjin in northern China that has a population of more than 10 million and an economic technology development area that already houses 3,300 foreign companies. Many other countries are also engaged in similar developments, as previously mentioned. It is irrelevant if high-value economic activity is based in Chennai or Ho Chi Min because it will do nothing to reduce the pressure on American incomes.

Equally, competition based on cost as well as quality will intensify for the reasons outlined in this chapter. Using low-cost labor will enable Chinese and Indian companies to eat into markets that would otherwise have been met by production based in the developed world. Together, these represent substantial forces at work to sustain the availability of low-cost labor and the pressure that will be exerted on the incomes of those in the advanced industrial countries. The few hot spots in the developing countries where wages were rapidly increasing have temporarily cooled. However, this is not necessarily good news for American workers because, although their own incomes have stagnated or fallen, it does little to narrow the gap with low-wage competitors.

Inside-Out Economic Development

It wasn't supposed to be like this. Emerging economies where expected to concentrate on the bodywork and slowly evolve toward more heady activities moving through the stages of economic development.[24] But the quality-cost revolution challenges established ideas about the evolutionary model of economic progress and comparative advantage, lending support to Alexander Gerschenkron, a Russian-born economic historian at Harvard University. He argued against much of the literature in development economics in the 1960s by claiming that relative economic backwardness may not prevent emerging economies from leapfrogging more established economic competitors by finding substitutes for what are often seen as the prerequisites for achieving global quality standards.[25] One of the advantages of backwardness is that there is no legacy of industrialism, as companies, regions, and nations can rapidly incorporate new technologies and business practices while taking advantage of low labor costs.

New technologies appear to hasten this process. On a taxi journey to the international airport in Mumbai, the cell phone of the taxi driver rang. It was the kind of conversation you hear on train journeys that offer few clues to their real purpose apart from demonstrating a need to stay in touch with family and friends. At the end of the call, he said, "I wish I could shake the hand of the person who invented the mobile phone; it's transformed my life." It was not difficult to understand why because he was now able to coordinate fares more easily as many of his customers did not have access to a landline. He was also able to stay in regular contact with his extended family living in a rural area outside the city.

In another conversation on the same visit to India, we were told that "the concept of a mobile phone from something being seen as a status symbol to being a common status has taken 4 years." This has enabled them to leapfrog all the developments in communication technologies, avoiding the expense and time it takes to cable vast cities and rural expanses, as erecting cellular towers is faster and cheaper. But the trends described in this chapter can't be explained simply in terms of new technologies; otherwise, virtually all developing economies could match the growth rates of India and China, which is something other countries have spectacularly failed to achieve.[26] Why we have witnessed these changes in China and India rather than sub-Saharan Africa requires a complex answer that is beyond the scope of this book. But there is no doubt that the pace of change in a number of emerging economies has been fueled by Western companies seeking to leverage the productive and profitable advantages of globalization, new technologies, and the ambitions of the nation-states to rapidly modernize.

Our studies show that the assumption that hi-tech economic development depends on social sophistication in the form of democratic politics, welfare provision, and high GDP per capita fails to capture the extreme forms of uneven development where, as already mentioned, the preindustrial and the postindustrial share the same zip code. On a trip to an electronics plant outside New Delhi, the perimeter fence delineated more than company property. It defined two worlds: insiders and outsiders. On the inside, plate glass buildings housed the latest production technologies able to build high-definition televisions and other electrical products for the domestic and international market. At the time of our visit, it was winning plaudits as one of the most productive plants in the global group. On the outside, derelict land and slum settlements house families with little access to the education that could qualify family members to cross the company threshold. They are forced to live in the rubble of modernization, under highways, on scrap land, or on the roadside. As we left this factory, we drove past two young men trying to balance industrial cable on a rusty old bicycle that was being taken to a local construction site, resembling a scene more suited to a period of early industrialization. In Mumbai, India's financial and commercial capital, around 7 million people live in slum conditions.

There seems little sense in talking about the Indian or Chinese economy as if educated workers inside this plant and those locked out of it share a common fate. This is not to say that employees on the inside were getting things easy. They were expected to work long hours and constantly admonished to achieve higher performance targets. As the CEO for the company made clear, "I hate to hear people say [our company] is a comfortable place to live. I want it to be tough." In part, an assumed sense of common fate associated with national economic development reflects the experience of the developed economies of the past, where economic innovation and social progress were assumed to march to the same beat.[27] As we will show, the economic fates of those living in America and other developed economies have also diverged, perhaps in a less visible way, but its consequences are no less problematic.

National economic performance in much of the expert literature is explained in terms of path dependence. This highlights historical, social, and institutional sources of comparative advantage to explain differences in national economic performance.[28] Differences in social foundations are believed to explain why, for example, Germany has maintained a competitive advantage in high-end engineering. The high quality of its technical education is organized through the dual system of workplace and college training, and high trust relations within the Mittelstadt sector of small and medium-sized family-dominated companies encourage sharing ideas, technologies, and organizational know-how that contribute to competitive advantage.

Built into this way of understanding economic development is the assumption that achieving the same quality standards would be difficult, if not impossible, to duplicate.[29] Again, we find an evolutionary logic which in a context of twenty-first-century globalization, technological development, education explosion, and knowledge diffusion may no longer hold. In short, the quality-cost revolution described here has turned business inside-out.

We had been struggling to explain the quality-cost revolution when, at the end of an interview at a European electronics company in Mumbai, a senior Indian manager told us, "We have an 'inside-out' model which is very clever. It gives us more flexibility over what to do where." The company focuses on creating a corporate culture inside the company's facilities as well as with key companies in the supply chain. It carefully hires well-educated and motivated employees, often with a college or university education. They invest in training both in soft and hard skills and impose a corporatewide system of performance management. There is a regular ratcheting up of performance targets, with staff expected to do whatever is necessary rather than keep to fixed hours during a 6-day week. This is all combined with access to the latest technologies and product range, set up by global operational teams who travel the world establishing new production facilities and training local staff to deliver global productivity standards.

There is little relationship between what lies inside company premises and what lies outside in the wider society. The inside-out approach still requires a decent infrastructure in terms of transportation to ship supplies and finished products, stable power supply, good communication networks, and a source of well-educated workers, but companies are able to set up "oasis operations"—hi-tech factories, offices, and research facilities—in low-spec neighborhoods that leave the rest of society largely untouched by their existence.

Although this raises profound questions concerning the source of comparative advantage in the older developed economies when similar quality standards can be achieved in emerging economies, it also poses the question of quality at what price. Can the fruits of economic development be spread beyond oasis operations, some of which exploit the vulnerability of employees that may have few realistic opportunities of finding alternative employment? Although the focus of this book is on the implications for those living in affluent societies, it raises equally important questions about the benefits of economic growth in developing economies. For if high tech and no tech can exist side by side, then most of the assumed connections between economic efficiency and social justices no longer hold unless there is the political will to move toward shared prosperity.

CHAPTER FIVE

Digital Taylorism

Industrial revolutions are revolutions in standardization.

—*Jay Tate*[1]

Standardization in terms of IT has become huge . . . not only standards for a single customer but across countries . . . technology is the ultimate equalizer . . . it will drive globalization, drive change . . . I hope that people don't get reduced to the state of drones . . . but I think increasingly employment will shrink.

—*Chief Information Officer, Financial Services*

T HE OPPORTUNITY BARGAIN rests on an upbeat view of the future of work where a growing number of Americans will do clever and complex things to earn a living in the global economy. Much of the business literature has focused on how companies should develop their human capital to create innovative ideas, products, and services to take American companies forward. Peter Drucker, a highly respected management guru, argued that the source of productivity in a knowledge-driven economy was different from an earlier age of mass production. Then the revolution in productivity, which he credited to Fredrick Winslow Taylor's system of scientific management, was achieved through the application of knowledge to work.[2] It was the organization of factory production based on the moving assembly line that created the mass production of autos, TVs, and washing machines and fueled the consumer boom of the 1950s and 1960s.

In today's knowledge economy, Drucker believed that competitive advantage has come to depend on the productivity of knowledge—using existing knowledge to create new knowledge.[3] The use of existing ideas to create new ideas also required a change in the role of management from responsibility "for the performance of people" to responsibility "for the application and performance of knowledge."[4] This is why knowledge management has become a key business issue. Thomas Friedman adds weight to the idea that America's competitive advantage depends on creativity, innovation, and a highly skilled workforce, as the full force of the hi-tech revolution remains nascent. In *The World Is Flat*, he suggests that "the last twenty years were just about forging, sharpening, and distributing all the new tools with which to collaborate and connect. *Now* the real IT revolution is about to begin, as all the complementarities between these tools start to really work together to level the playing field."[5]

This chapter will show that there has been an IT revolution, but Freidman along with many others have failed to understand its full significance, especially for college-educated workers. Corporate survival will depend on the creation of new markets through innovative products and services, but the global IT revolution has presented companies with new tools, of a digital rather than mechanical kind, to improve performance in much the same way that it was applied to mass production through the application of knowledge to work.[6] Companies may continue to pay a premium for outstanding talent, however it is defined, but they are increasingly segmenting their knowledge workers in an attempt to know more for less. Although some are given permission to think, increasing efforts are being made to translate *knowledge work* into *working knowledge* where what is in the minds of employees is captured and codified in the form of digital software, including online manuals and computer programs that can be controlled by companies and used by other often less skilled workers.[7]

This follows a well-established trend where the gale of creative destruction is followed by the destruction of the creative. Today's innovations are tomorrow's routines, which is why Jay Tate's observation that "industrial revolutions are revolutions in standardization" is a telling insight into the source of productivity. The productive potential of steam engine technology took 200 years to realize after Thomas Savery patented the first steam powered pump in 1698.[8] It was the development of the factory system that brought together workers, supervisors, machines, materials, and steam power into an integrated unit of production based on the introduction of standards of time, behavior, and techniques that led to rapid improvements in productivity.[9] The same process of rationalization is now taking place in many of the industries currently associated with the knowledge economy, such as information technology, financial services, legal services, and pharmaceuticals. Although the rationalization of knowledge work may increase the productivity of knowledge, it will also have profound implications for the relationship between education, jobs, and rewards.

When considered in its historical context, this should come as no surprise. Productivity has not come from giving people permission to think but from imposing barriers to individual initiative and control through a detailed division of labor. Dating back to Adam Smith, there was a view that the prosperity of workers and nations depend on breaking down jobs into routine activities that did not call upon even a rudimentary intelligence. Although this was presented as a choice between prosperity or poverty for ordinary workers, it can also be viewed as a conflict between capital and labor because the issue of employee discretion and power is closely related to that of rewards—how the spoils of productive growth are to be distributed, especially among shareholders, executives, managers, and the rest of the workforce.

There is an assumption that the more companies depend on knowledge workers, the greater share of profits will go to these workers, ending the age-old struggle between the interests of capital and labor. This is not the first time this has been proclaimed, as we shall see in the following discussion of Taylorism. But the growth of knowledge work creates new tensions, if not outright conflict, between the many sides of industry because it has the potential to transform existing patterns of ownership and control. The key assets of knowledge-intensive companies shift from the ownership of physical assets such as land, factories, or machines, where property rights are clearly defined, to intangible knowledge-related assets, where property rights are less clear cut.[10]

In a system where the interests of shareholders are given priority over all other interested parties, including employees, questions of who controls, owns, and profits from knowledge work are paramount. While companies depend on driving up productivity, corporate executives eager to maximize their bonuses and shareholders eager to maximize their dividends are given priority over corporate profits. The role of management is to ensure a return on investments made by the owners of the company. This requires elaborate accounting systems and mechanisms of control that safeguard property rights. It is these concerns that are shaping the direction of technological and organizational change.

If the profitability of companies depends on the productivity of knowledge, companies confront the problem of imposing their property rights over intangible assets and of how to manage what resides in their employees' heads. This is a variation on the age-old issue of how to convert an individual's capacity to think and act into added value for the company. For this reason, some management scholars, including Barbro Anell and Timothy Wilson, argue that the question of how to extract and distribute knowledge efficiently will not be answered by relying on the initiative and intellectual capital of knowledge workers, as it is difficult to control, standardize, or profit from ideas that remain in the heads of individual workers. "The solution resides in the ability of knowledge firms to extract and translate more or less tacit, personal knowledge into explicit, codified knowledge," moving away from the individual nature of knowledge work.[11] In short, if knowledge has become a key economic asset, the task of business is to capture and control as much of it as possible without undermining the organization's capacity to innovate and compete in global markets. In celebrating the rise of the knowledge worker, its protagonists have neglected that "the loss of control over production violates the profit-making objectives of a firm."[12] To understand how companies are standardizing knowledge work into digital software, we need to begin with Taylor's ideas on scientific management.

Mechanical Taylorism

Fredrick Winslow Taylor thought he had found a solution to both raising productivity and the conflict between employers and employees over the distribution of profits. At the turn of the twentieth century, Taylor argued that American industry was inefficient because it failed to apply the principles of "scientific management" which could be used to ascertain the "one best way" of organizing production. He believed that the benefits of adopting a scientific approach to management were so large that both employers and employees would prosper, ending the squabble about who gets what, which Marx viewed as the Achilles heel of the capitalism system.

Taylor drew a distinction between scientific management and management by initiative and incentive. He believed the principles of scientific management "can be applied absolutely to all classes of work, from the most elementary to the most intricate," although most of his work focused on elementary tasks, such as shoveling pig iron or laying bricks.[13] However, it was the application of knowledge rather than muscle power that Taylor recognized as the source of productivity.[14]

He argued that both sides of industry had to replace the old individual judgment or opinion with exact scientific investigation and knowledge."[15] Managers had to assume new burdens, duties, and responsibilities "never dreamt of in the past."[16] This involved the scientific study, analysis, and measurement of each job to raise production standards and to work in collaboration with workers for these standards to be achieved. In his book *The Principles of Scientific Management* published in 1911, Taylor outlined the major problem for what he called "ordinary management" (as opposed to scientific management) in the following way:

> in the best of the ordinary types of management...foremen and superintendents know...that their own knowledge and personal skills falls far short of the combined knowledge and dexterity of all the workmen under them. The most experienced managers therefore frankly place before their workmen the problem of doing the work in the best and most economic way. They recognize the task before them as that of inducing each workman to use his best endeavors, his hardest work, all his traditional knowledge, his skill, his ingenuity, and his good will—in a word, his "initiative" so as to yield the largest possible return to his employer.[17]

For Taylor, trusting workers to do a decent job was no way to run a business. Social relationships needed to be replaced by a system that gave managers a monopoly of knowledge and expertise. This involved the separation of mind and body to achieve common standards. Herbert Stimpson, one of a growing number of efficiency engineers in 1911, was asked by a congressional committee investigating the dehumanizing consequences of Taylorism whether workers and machines could be classed in the same category for the purposes of industrial organization. Stimpson replied that he looked upon the worker "as a little portable power plant...a mighty delicate and complicated machine...The physical body of the man is constructed on the same mechanical principles as the machine is, except that it is very much higher developed." He argued that it was possible to scientifically measure the limits of these human machines by employing "specialists" that became known as time and motion experts, as they calculated "what the human frame can stand."[18]

This mechanized, clockwork view of the worker not only required the separation of mind and body but also an unprecedented process of knowledge transfer. In the transfer of the knowledge, techniques, and know-how of workers, including those in craft trades to company bosses, "The managers assume...the burden of gathering together all of the traditional knowledge which in the past has been possessed by the workmen and then of classifying, tabulating, and reducing this knowledge to rules, laws, and formulae which are immensely helpful to the workmen in doing their daily work."[19]

In reality, a lot of this traditional knowledge was not captured but ignored because Taylor's ultimate goal was the introduction of a new system rather than the use of historical precedent as a starting point.[20] In concentrating knowledge with managers, it not only transformed the way work was organized but also entailed a loss of power and autonomy from craft workers that was bitterly resisted. At Watertown, a U.S. government arsenal, striking workers had a rare and notable victory. It was judged that Taylor's principles were an abuse of the welfare of workers, and the principles were banned on all government-funded work until 1949.

Yet it was the rise of mass assembly-line production associated with the name of Henry Ford that ensured Taylor his place in economic history. Ford drew on a range of innovations that were prevalent at the time, although he denied that scientific management had influenced the creation of the moving assembly line that employed mass ranks of low-skill workers responsible for carrying out the same monotonous tasks. Craft skills were broken down into their most rudimentary form, reduced to a series of simple repetitive operations of the order of punching a hole in metal plates thousands of times a day without moving from the machine. In the case of General Motors' Vega, two young women jumped on and off the assembly line and slid grilles behind the headlights; this was one of the more active roles available.

The inspiration for Ford's continuously moving line was watching butchers in Chicago use an overhead chain to move beef during the dressing process. Describing the principle of the continuously moving line in 1922, Ford wrote, "Every piece of work in the shop moves; it may move on hooks on overhead chains going to assembly in the exact order in which the parts are required; it may travel on a moving platform, or it may go by gravity, but the point is that there is no lifting or trucking of anything other than the materials...No workman has anything to do with moving or lifting anything."[21]

The goal was to mechanize everything, including human beings. In his description of factory life, he talked of "men and machine united in production" in a fashion similar to Herbert Stimpson but recognized a major difference between the two. While both men and machines need repairs and replacements, "machinery wears out and needs to be restored. Men grow uppish, lazy, or careless."[22] Despite such human glitches, the moving assembly line gave management a new weapon in the struggle to impose the techniques and disciplines of mass production on workers. The key challenge for management now became combining materials and humans to produce quality goods at the maximum speed possible.[23]

The pros and cons of scientific management and Fordist mass production have continued to generate heated debate. But in the present context, it's worth noting Taylor believed that what was truly revolutionary about scientific management was not time and motion studies or even increasing productivity but what he called a "mental revolution." This changed the way both workers and managers understood the division of the surplus resulting from their joint efforts: "under scientific management . . . both sides take their eyes off of the division of the surplus as the all-important matter, and together turn their attention towards increasing the size of the surplus until this surplus becomes so large that it is unnecessary to quarrel over how it shall be divided."[24]

The introduction of the $5 day in Ford's Highland plant in 1914 more than doubled the average wage for production workers, which led the *Wall Street Journal* to denounce it as "an economic crime." It gave some credence to Taylor's optimism, but this was short lived as other companies quickly improved on Ford's production techniques. Ford was soon forced to compete on cost, which was achieved by increasing the speed of the production line. This led one of Taylor's disciples to conclude that rather than maximizing harmony between man and machine, it was achieved at the cost of the "destruction of the workers."[25] J. K. Galbraith also concluded that in the mid-nineteen twenties, Ford's River Rouge plant "was a machine-age nightmare."[26]

By the 1980s, scientific management and the Fordist assembly line had been discredited. In a dynamic knowledge-intensive economy requiring customized products and services to meet the exacting demands of sophisticated consumers, new models of work organization were developing that required the workforce to act as more than expensive machines. The initiative, trust, and discretion that were anathema to Taylor's view of organizational efficiency were now seen as a source of competitive advantage. Equally, the distinction between thinking and doing was now viewed as an impediment to innovation, which depended on the creative insights of employees. Thirty years on, however, some of Taylor's key ideas have been given a virtual new lease of life.

Digital Taylorism

If the twentieth century brought what can be described as *mechanical Taylorism* characterized by the Fordist production line, where the knowledge of craft workers was captured by management, codified, and reengineered in the shape of the moving assembly line, the twenty-first century is the age of *digital Taylorism*. This involves translating the knowledge work of managers, professionals, and technicians into working knowledge by capturing, codifying, and digitalizing their work in software packages, templates, and prescripts that can be transferred and manipulated by others regardless of location. It is being applied to offices as well as factories and to services as well as manufacturing. Unlike mechanical Taylorism, which required the concentration of labor in factories, digital Taylorism enables work activities to be dispersed and recombined from anywhere around the world in less than the time it takes to read this sentence.[27]

Paul Romer uses a broad definition of software to include all the knowledge that has been codified and transmitted to others. He suggests that "it can be stored on paper, as images on film, or as a string of bits on a computer or laser disc."[28] But as long as companies were limited to knowledge capture in the form of physical manuals or mechanical devices, its application to the office and service industries was limited because senior managers lacked the digital equivalent of mechanical drills, jigs, or presses used in manufacturing. However, the impact of typewriters and calculating machines in the late nineteenth century office should not be underestimated. William Henry Leffingwell was an early advocate of applying scientific management to routine office functions. In *Scientific Office Management* (1917), he observed, "Many businessmen, after analyzing the remarkable results secured by applying Frederick W. Taylor's system of scientific management in factories, have asked whether or not similar betterments could not be obtained in offices with the system. Their question can now be answered, for the main principles of the Taylor system have actually been adapted and applied to office work."[29]

This conclusion was an exaggeration because today's managers have the major advantage of the Internet, networked computers, and workflow software. Although Leffingwell and others were inspired by mass-production techniques, it is, as Simon Head notes, "the modern-day re-engineer who has come much closer to reproducing in an office setting the rigor and disciplines of scientific management. The re-engineer owes this to information technology's prodigious powers of measurement, monitoring, and control, unavailable not only to Leffingwell but to all office managers of the pre-digital age."[30]

One of the difficulties identified by Leffingwell when applying Taylor's ideas to the office was that service industries often required greater flexibility because it was difficult to judge the requirements of customers or to standardize the way they ordered goods or services. Requests were usually received by letter in different formats that lacked the standardization of online applications or order forms. Leffingwell attempted to solve this problem of diversity by applying what he called the "exception principle." This was the process of weeding out difficult cases and channeling them to experts for handling, thus reducing the need for extensive training to only a handful of employees.[31]

The exception principle has now been digitalized. Indeed, it represents the organizing principle of today's call or contact centers, where customers are digitally routed to different teams depending on the nature of the inquiry, reducing the need for job training beyond the requirements of a specific customer inquiry, such as purchasing vacation insurance. We have become so used to online applications and digital payment software that we barely notice how they require us to complete forms in ways that reduce the need for any human interaction, let alone human initiative. When we call our bank or after-sales providers on toll free 800 numbers, we are invariably asked to "select from the following options," repeated several times to narrow our range of possible questions, and only after failing to identify the exact inquiry are you connected to an exceptional employee.

In investment banking, the exception principle was applied to selling over-the-counter (OTC) derivatives. To reduce its operational costs, a major American bank offshored as much as possible to India. It examined the various features of the selling process and decided to offshore initial telephone or Internet contact with customers "while the more experienced resources based in London processed exceptions." Using this model, the bank was able to "minimize their investment in knowledge transfer and training of the India-based staff while reaping as much as 40 percent savings in operating costs."[32]

Customer contact centers are the office equivalent of the Fordist production line. There is an extensive use of scripts which instruct employees about what to say, often with online instructions on what to do depending on a customer's answer to each prescribed question. Those employed as cold-callers have the unenviable task of trying to sell us everything from kitchens, mobile phones, financial advice, and charitable causes. They also have their pace of work determined by an autodialer that selects and dials numbers giving managers complete control over the pace of work. Some autodialers do not have a pause button, making it difficult to take a break, even to visit the restroom.[33]

Television monitors also adorn the walls of contact centers that give supervisors minute-by-minute information about the number of calls answered or in a queue waiting to be answered. The performance of individual operators is monitored on displays with smiley faces for those meeting appropriate performance targets and sad faces for those who are not. Although the level of surveillance and the nature of the work vary considerably within contact centers, new information technologies give employers the tools to micromanage through the use of software programs that monitor e-mails and telephone conversations. There are also electronic manuals that prescribe various aspects of the job that are easy to update to meet changing business circumstances.

We were told how executives in an automotive company had introduced digital monitoring software that gave them real-time information about the productivity levels being achieved by any of their factories around the world from a laptop. Over a slice of toast and mug of coffee, the company's CEO would breakfast watching these performance figures before making a few calls to plants where production targets were not being met. Digital Taylorism has given companies a powerful tool for employee surveillance and remote control to compare the performance of plants, offices, suppliers, managers, and workers located anywhere in the world. Its application has become more widespread with consequences for employees in a wide range of industries and occupations.

The Industrialization of Knowledge Work

Leading consultancy companies are playing an important role in applying digital Taylorism to a range of service industries, including retail, health, and finance, that typically focus on business processes, including receiving orders, marketing services, selling products, delivering services, distributing products, invoicing for services, and accounting for payments. Digital Taylorism enables innovation to be translated into routines that might require some degree of education but not the kind of creativity and independence of judgment often associated with the knowledge economy. To reduce costs and increase control, companies are eager to capture the idiosyncratic knowledge of workers so that it can be codified and routinized, thereby making it generally available to the company rather than being the property of an individual worker.

There are many ways digital Taylorism can be applied; for example, a leading company producing and selling software handling credit card transactions and credit rating expanded very rapidly over the last decade, both within Britain and overseas, mainly through acquisitions. In an interview with the CEO in 2006, we were told that the company's major problem was how to encourage staff—mostly college graduates—to be innovative. The CEO thought this was essential for the continued success of the business as they developed products for new markets and customers. Today, the problem has changed dramatically. The company has achieved an annual growth rate of 25 percent and opened offices across the developed and developing world, including China, India, and Bulgaria. There has been a change in CEO, and the major issue is no longer defined as innovation but of how to align business process and roll out software products to a global market. The creative work in producing new platforms, programs, and templates has been separated from what they call routine analytics. Permission to think is restricted to a relatively small group of knowledge workers currently still in Britain, and the more routine work (that is, customizing products to different markets and customers), also referred to as the grunt work, is offshored to their offices in Bulgaria and India, where college graduates can be hired at a third of the cost.

A business relations manager for wealthy clients at a bank that was brought to its knees due to disastrous speculation told us how his discretion over the amount of money he could lend to a customer had declined well before the financial crash. The bank previously respected his expertise and judgment in making decisions, but loans where increasingly authorized by a credit controller. This credit controller is a software package that automatically assesses a loan application according to specified criteria. Only in appealing against the controller's judgment does the manager have a role, but even in these cases, he was often overruled. From a position of authority and respect, he described himself as a salesperson armed with a series of software manuals instructing him how to sell particular kinds of products, which now meant that "a junior with a ready smile could now do my job."

If we think of the way this manager's job has been reclassified, then digital Taylorism has become central. Its effect is intended to increase the decision-making power of those at the top of the organization, reduce inconsistency in performance, and reduce costs. As we were told by another leading main-street banker, "We have to drive the business on a mass scale; we cannot have . . . files being checked on an individual basis. It's a mass game . . . we have to run that kind of a model." As a result, "analytical power is something which employees are losing out on because previously they used to analyze a lot on their own. Today it is format driven."

The separation of conception from execution (thinking from doing) that is a trademark of scientific management represents more than another attempt to shift the priority from human creativity to behavioral control by prescribing conduct through technological means. It reveals why the modular corporation is a revolution at work. Companies are not only reexamining where to think but are also using new technologies to redefine the nature of work itself.

The Modular Corporation

Accenture Consulting uses the term *industrialization* to highlight the way functions within service industries can be broken down into their component parts. It is almost exactly the same way that Adam Smith described the division of labor in the manufacture of pins in the eighteenth century. But today, components can be "recombined in a tailored, automated fashion—to non-manufacturing settings."[34] Hewlett-Packard's motif is "invent," yet it has put standardization at the center of building a modular organization. It wants to reduce complexity across its global operations to reduce the cost—both in time and money—of implementing change.

Here standardization is no longer embraced to create bureaucratic routines but to increase flexibility by combining and recombining reusable components. When companies are attempting to globally integrate their operations, they need to develop common standards across the organization. A building-block, or Lego, approach using platform architectures and reusable IT components is now seen as a more efficient way of making organizations more adaptable to change, which can be applied to systems, processes, and people. As Hewlett-Packard's Nora Denzel suggests, "Jobs, business processes and technology are beginning to be standardized, virtualized and integrated into an IT 'supply chain' that delivers services on demand—where, when and precisely how much the customer requires."[35] The idea is to break everything down into its most basic components, including work roles. These components can then be translated into reusable software so that they can be reconfigured in response to changing customer requirements, strategic initiatives, or competitive pressures.

In response to global competition, IBM decided to reengineer its global operations to raise productivity and lower costs with 250,000 employees in 80 delivery centers around the world. It adopted the joint strategy of automating areas of repetitive work and "turning repeatable processes into software" that could be used with different clients.[36] Along with many other companies, it attempted to manufacture or industrialize services so that assignments could be carried out using the same software applications in Vietnam and Venezuela in much the same way that identical autos or iPods can be built to the same standard anywhere in the world. As Mike Daniels, head of global technology services at IBM suggests, the real advantage "comes out of doing the work in a codified way." This required asking the key question of how you do the work using base-level components that do not rely on the tacit knowledge of employees that may lead them to undertake the same assignments in different ways. To help IBM achieve this, it has over 500 efficiency experts "to scrutinize its operations and apply disciplines from 'lean' manufacturing."

Likewise, Suresh Gupta from Capco Consulting foresees the arrival of the "financial services factory" because as soon as banks or insurance companies begin to break tasks into a series of procedures or components that can be digitalized, it gives companies more sourcing options such as offshoring. If these trends continue, "tomorrow's banks would look and behave no differently to a factory."[37]

This is part of a new vocabulary of digital Taylorism that includes components, modules, and competencies. The way these are combined to create a new model of the modular corporation was revealed to us in an interview with the female head of global human resources for a major bank with operations in 85 countries. Until 2000, the bank adopted a country-based approach with little attempt to integrate its operations globally. It then set up a completely separate business to manage its high-volume, low-value transactions using operations in

China, India, Malaysia, and the Philippines. She commented, "So what we were doing is arbitraging the wage costs," but this initial approach to offshoring based on "lift and shift" did not go according to plan. "We had errors, we had customer dissatisfaction, all sorts of bad stuff."

She recalled that it took time to realize it is not easy to shift a process that has been done in the same place and in the same way for a long time. When people are asked to document what they have been doing for many years, there are inevitably going to be blind spots because they know it so well. As a result, "The semidocumented process gets shunted off while the process itself is dependent on long-term memory that is suddenly gone, so it really doesn't work."

Thus, the bank recognized the need to simplify and standardize as much of the company's operations as possible before deciding what could be offshored. "So we go through that thinking process first, which means mapping these processes, changing these processes." She also thought that this new detailing of the corporate division of labor was in its infancy "because you need the simplicity that comes with standardization to succeed in today's world."

The componentization of functions, alongside the modularization of jobs, reveals the growing importance attached to behavioral competencies. Reminiscent of Taylor's mental revolution, she argued that demand for a competence-based approach was coming from employees as well as the company. Speaking before the financial crash, she believed that the biggest change during her 20 years with the company is that employees today want choice—"what they do, when they do it, where they do it." But as she explained in this part of our discussion, which is worth repeating in full:

> If you are really going to allow people to work compressed hours, work from home, then work needs to be unitized and standardized; otherwise, it can't be. And as we keep pace with careers, we want to change; we don't want to stay in the same job for more than 2 years max. They want to move around, have different experiences, grow their skills base so they're more marketable. So if you're moving people regularly, they have to be easily able to move into another role. If it's going to take 6 months to bring them up to speed, then the business is going to suffer. So you need to be able to step into a new role and function. And our approach to that is to deeply understand the profile that you need for the role—the person profile, not the skills profile. What does this person need to have in their profile? If we look at our branch network and the individuals working at the front line with our customers, what

do we need there? We need high-end empathy; we need people who can actually step into the customers' shoes and understand what that feels like. We need people who enjoy solving problems…so now when we recruit, we look for that high-end empathy and look for that desire to solve problems, that desire to complete things in our profiles…we can't teach people to be more flexible, to be more empathetic…but we can teach them the basics of banking. We've got core products, core processes; we can teach that quite easily. So we are recruiting against more of the behavioral stuff and teaching the skills stuff, the hard knowledge that you need for the role.

Whatever the merits of her argument about the future of portfolio careers, it is diametrically opposed to how pundits of the knowledge economy have portrayed the future of work, within loosely defined occupational roles and high levels of employee discretion. In the modular corporation, there is a different kind of flexibility that requires clearly defined roles that are simplified and codified to enable plug-and-play even for highly qualified employees. This is what is at the heart of digital Taylorism—the digital documentation of business process and job descriptions, linked to electronic databases of individual competence profiles, based on human capital metrics.

Human capital metrics involve the numerical measurement of individual performance through software programs that are used to assess individual, team, or organizational performance. Writing for *CFO Magazine*, Craig Schneider observed how chief financial offices were behind attempts to measure the value added of the workforce because established HR measures, such as head count, turnover, or the cost of compensation and benefits, "no longer cut it in this new world of accountability. They don't go far enough to create shareholder value and align people decisions with corporate objectives."[38]

The implications for employees were highlighted in our discussions with a senior manager working for an international bank in India. The bank had developed "staff league tables" to measure both hard performance, such as meeting sales targets, how many times they had visited customers, and so on, and soft performance, such as relationship management or customer satisfaction. The creation of these league tables gave senior managers control over what is to count as performance. There is also nowhere for employees to hide because anyone within the organization across the country is able to compare the performance of individuals, teams, and branches. As we were told, "If a particular person in the banking hall needs to know where he or she stands in the country in her particular function, she can just go and open the league tables, and she will get to see where her position is."

We were assured this did not mean that people where constantly being judged: "I am underperforming or you are overperforming because they may all be performing to a high level." The reality is that employees are constantly under pressure to raise their performance, as companies use software tools such as the customer relations management modules used by this company to codify performance alongside a worker's job description.

The Future of Knowledge Work

Economic history shows that the power to both innovate and standardize has increased over time. It also shows, at least in America and Britain, a proclivity toward managerial control over employee discretion. But it is important not to emphasize control for its own sake as in Harry Braverman's classic study of Taylorism because it should be seen as the latest attempt to boost productivity and corporate profits.[39] The economic landscape is also strewn with historical examples of how highly skilled workers have found that their skills are not as unique as they assumed or have been rendered redundant by technological innovation. Today, the extent to which companies can capture the knowledge of those trained to think for a living is difficult to judge, although there is little doubt that this has become a corporate "holy grail."

The prospect of work organization being restructured by digital Taylorism was recognized by Harold Wilensky nearly half a century ago. He envisaged a time when the distinction between conception and execution would move farther up the occupational hierarchy as new technologies offered senior managers and executives great control of their white-collar as well as blue-collar workforce.

He predicted that all but a cadre of top managers would lose most of the discretion they had previously enjoyed, as new technologies permitted "the top to control the middle, as scientific management in the past allowed supervisors to control the workers." Innovation and planning would be centralized with top executives, surrounded by programmers, efficiency experts, and other staff experts, more sharply separated from everybody else. As Wilensky predicted, "the line between those who decide, 'What is to be done and how' and those who do it—that dividing line would move up. The men who once applied Taylor to the proletariat would themselves be Taylorized."[40]

The distinction between thinking and doing in a period of mechanical Taylorism also helped shape class relations between blue-collar and white-collar workers. Digital Taylorism is not only deskilling many white-collar workers, but it also incites a power struggle within the middle classes, as corporate reengineering reduces the autonomy and discretion of some but not all managers and professionals. It encourages the segmentation of talent in ways that reserve permission to think to a small proportion of elite employees responsible for driving the business forward, functioning cheek by jowl with equally well-qualified workers in more Taylorized jobs.

Many knowledge workers may disappear off the talent radar screen. This process is at an early stage in many organizations, as we've already indicated, but we can distinguish three types of knowledge worker: developers, demonstrators, and drones. Developers include the high potentials and top performers discussed in the next chapter. They represent no more than 10–15 percent of an organization's workforce given "permission to think" and include senior researchers, managers, and professionals. Demonstrators are assigned to implement or execute existing knowledge, procedures, or management techniques, often through the aid of software. Much of the knowledge used by consultants, managers, teachers, nurses, technicians, and so forth is standardized or prepackaged. Indeed, although demonstrator roles may include well-qualified people, much of the focus is on effective communication with colleagues and customers. Drones are involved in monotonous work, and they are not expected to engage their brains. Many call center or data entry jobs are classic examples, where virtually everything that one utters to customers is prescribed in software packages. Many of these jobs are also highly mobile as they can be standardized and digitalized. They are increasingly filled by well-qualified workers either attracted by relatively high salaries in emerging economies or those in developed economies who are overqualified but struggling to find a job that matches their training or expectations.

If the translation of knowledge work into working knowledge is once again the price the workforce has to pay to increase productivity, the context today is very different from that of the early days of scientific management. Peter Drucker argued that it was the application of knowledge to work which "created developed economies by setting off the productivity explosion of the last hundred years."[41] What Drucker ignored was Adam Smith's insight into the human cost of such working practices. Today, the question is how will a much better educated workforce respond to work that does not fulfill their expectations, given that there is little prospect of rising incomes to compensate for the new realities of work. There is little incentive for companies to raise wages to compensate for a loss of intrinsic satisfaction in the context of a high-skill, low-wage workforce, as we will go on to show, but first we need to consider the global war for talent.

❧

CHAPTER SIX

The War for Talent

If it is to count in the corporate career, talent, no matter how defined, must be discovered by one's
talented superiors. It is in the nature of the morality of corporate accomplishment that those at the
top do not and cannot admire that which they do not and cannot understand.

C. Wright Mills[1]

The Rise of Talent Management

FastTech is a manufacturer of car interiors that supplies the big auto
companies in Detroit. In the mid-1990s, most of its 35,000 workforce
were American, but this all changed within a decade. While its U.S.
workforce stagnated, its global workforce increased to 115,000 across
33 countries. This transformed the way they understood managerial
talent. As their global head of human resources recollected, we had
to "get on the stick pretty quickly and learn how different countries
operate and build cultural sensitivity." They built a new management
team "with a global mind-set as opposed to what we had 10 years ago,"
as they met some resistance to developing managerial talent outside
America. They wanted managers that had lived and worked in a country other than that in which they grew up as well as demonstrating
the high levels of performance expected of managers wherever they
happen to work. They undertook a systematic review of all staff and

came up with a list of 400 to 500 individuals they thought "had what it takes."

They divided staff between A, B, and C players. The A players were considered crucial to the future of the company. Every effort is made to retain this group through generous compensation, interesting assignments, and career development. "You have just got to decide that those people are our future, and whether they are kind of A players or they are kind of high-potential people lower in the organization, those are the people that we are going to pay, you know, whatever." The B players are the engine house of the company; they get things done and need to be treated with dignity and paid at a competitive rate. It includes engineering talent with extensive experience, but "they usually are folk that don't really want to lead the charge." The C players are the underperformers. "You don't see a C player in this organization for too long; you either shape up or ship out." They don't spend much time on helping the Cs shape up because the problem is rarely seen as a lack of skills but about attitude, commitment, and getting along with colleagues. "It usually isn't as much about technical skill; it is about sort of chemistry, attitude, ability to see the bigger picture, prepared to roll your sleeves up and get stuck into things, so it is usually for those reasons that it falls apart."

In the early days, he believed they made an error in not sending their A players on overseas assignments. "We would send B and C players and guess what? You send a B and C player, but they don't actually help you at all; in fact, if anything, they make things worse because the local nationals that get receipt of this hairy arsed American look at him and say, 'this is the best they have got, you know.'" But when they started to send their A players, a mutual respect developed because then people say, "Hey, this guy really knows what he is doing," which made the fact that it remains an American company less of a contentious issue.

That a talented few matter more and that talent remains in limited supply despite the rising skills of the workforce were commonly held views in other companies we spoke to, which helps to explain why learning isn't earning for many college-educated workers. We've seen how companies are reducing the cost of knowledge work by shifting it to low-cost locations and by capturing it in our discussion of digital Taylorism. But the war for talent is another strategy that provides an explanation of the divided fortunes of America's middle classes, as companies reevaluate the productive value of a college education.

In the past, the ordering of blue-collar and white-collar jobs reflected a hierarchy of academic achievement. Those with more credentials were often in better-paid jobs based on the often dubious assumption that they contributed more to productivity. But as large numbers of employees have a college education, the relationship between credentials and performance has been called into question. Many companies, including FastTech, have introduced talent management strategies aimed at ranking the individual performance of managers, professionals, and executives. These rankings are then used to create a cadre of top talent based on a belief that they contribute most to the bottom line and should be rewarded accordingly. Therefore, at the same time that companies are trying to reduce their labor costs, they are also trying to attract and retain top talent, so a larger share of the wage bill is going to those judged as top performers.[2]

This process of white-collar stratification is evident in a number of professions, such as legal services. Daniel Muzio and Stephen Ackroyd, who have undertaken detailed studies of the reorganization of law firms, reveal how senior partners defend their salaries and status. As more people enter the legal profession and pressures mount on fee income, they construct new barriers to achieving partnership status. Law firms have also expanded the ranks of salaried professionals who have few decision-making powers and inferior employment conditions. These authors conclude that the traditional relationship of colleagueship has been transformed into one of top-down control.[3]

The business literature suggests that these inequalities in treatment are justified because the demand for talent far outstrips supply. Consultants at McKinsey, who popularized the idea of a "war for talent," argued that talent management has assumed greater strategic importance since the 1980s with the growth of the knowledge economy.[4] They also suggested that as the numbers of knowledge workers increased, "it's more important to get great talent, since the differential value created by the most talented knowledge workers is enormous."[5]

Consequently, being good is no longer good enough because much of the value within organizations is believed to be contributed by a minority of employees. John Chambers, CEO of Cisco, is reported as saying, "A world-class engineer with five peers can out-produce 200 regular engineers."[6] A Corporate Executive Board (CEB) study also found that the best computer programmers are at least 12 times as productive as the average.[7]

Globalization, market deregulation, and rapid advances in technology are also cited as explanations of why companies need to distinguish top performers from the rest of the workforce. McKinsey's Ed Michaels and colleagues suggest that companies "need managers who can respond to these challenges. They need risk takers, global entre-preneurs, and techno-savvy managers. They need leaders who can re-conceive their business and inspire their people...over the coming two decades...companies will be competing intensely for the limited supply of very capable managers."[8] They conclude that far more atten-tion needs to be given to hiring, developing, and retaining the top 10–20 percent of employees—the A players who are key to global success.

The war for talent originated in America but has become global. In Bangalore, a company in financial services had developed three bands conforming to the rhetoric of A, B, C players. The company's senior manager for operations across southern India told us,

> if I do a bell curve, you've the top performers, you have the average performers, and you will have the underperformers. The risk is to sustain top performers and also a certain amount of average perform-ers...we want the talent to be retained with us for the next 3-year period to contribute to our growth aspirations. And the challenge will be to retain...a combination of the top 20 percent and also the top 40 percent of the average performing band.

The head of HR within the same company in London told us, "We have segmented our employees brutally just in terms of talent. They've gone through quite a tough assessment process over many years now. So we have the group that is recognized as talent, and sadly, there is this group who are recognized as not talent. I don't know how I fix that; that's next year's problem." The group recognized as talented are actively managed in terms of current and future assign-ments and move around the world quite a bit. "They get stretched and out there." They look for about 15 percent of employees to be in the talent pool, which is divided into the global talent pool that is expected to go anywhere and basically do anything, and the business talent pool, which is the management cadre of top performers in dif-ferent regions or countries.[9]

A widely heard explanation of the war for talent in interviews with senior managers and executives was that in a highly competitive world, there is no time for people to learn any more. This had led to a dearth of managerial talent able to "hit the ground running." The head of a major body responsible for the employment skills in financial services recollected that when she entered the industry in the 1970s, there were entry-level schemes for college graduates "where you were nurtured for a year or 2, and you went through the various motions, and then you were airborne, whereas now that doesn't exist any more." What now matters is how long it is going to take before a new hire is productive, as CEOs are looking at margins as the competitive threat is no longer domestic but global. Today, she believed that if someone comes in who's got to be trained for a year or 2, then unless it's a specialist role, "the chances are they will go for someone who has an existing track record."

Corporate impatience was also contributing to a war for talent in economic hot spots such as Beijing, Shanghai, Mumbai, and Bangalore, although there was a significant cooling following the global recession. When asked about the war for talent, the immediate response from Indian managers working for an American bank was, "It's a complete war!" But they then explained that a major cause was trying to get enough people to undertake analytical financial research in the time expected. "It is not that there are no people, but time expectation for them to execute is so short that you can't deliver…that is the war for talent."

Globalizing the War for Talent

Premier League soccer in the United Kingdom offers an outstanding example of how the war for talent has become global. In the 2007–2008 season, only 170 of the 498 players who started matches were English, a little over a third of the total. It is difficult to find comparable data for transnational corporations, but our analysis of the 38 companies that retained their position in the top 100 companies based on assets between 1995 and 2007 (excluding companies in the finance sector) shows that the proportion of foreign workers increased from 47.5 to 60.1.[10] Unlike Premier League soccer, which includes some of the best players in the world, information published by companies tells us little about where the A players are based. Yet there is little doubt that many companies have been forced to reexamine their cultural assumption about the pool of talent in much the same way that national governments in the West are being forced to rethink a world divided between head and body nations.

American and European banks have traditionally recruited from elite universities, including the Ivy League and Oxbridge Universities, but a European bank that we interviewed was engaged in a major push to globalize the company. The head of global sourcing told us that they have now adopted an "extremely global" approach to talent acquisition. "We share candidates…we hire from everywhere." This includes hiring in India for jobs outside India: "our MBA and higher graduate level entry is completely global." This resulted from her being persuaded to visit some of the Indian Institutes of Technology (IITs) and the Indian Institutes of Management (IIMs).

At that time, she was only looking to hire two or three for the London office but found that she could hire "40 fantastic people" capable of "wiping the floor with all the grads here in the U.K. Perfect English! They can work anywhere and be part of our global team." But she quickly added that they are not going to populate the bank with 100 percent Indian expats because they need "a culturally diverse workforce which reflects our client base...but from a pure talent point of view, I could easily find the 250 people for the global market that we need out of India in terms of pure technical skills." She also visited Beijing and found some outstanding people but "a tiny, tiny minority can speak English, and the competition for these people is unbelievable...because everybody wants them." In financial services, she believed this gave India a massive talent advantage but only in the short term, "not necessarily in the long term."

This story is typical of many we heard, although it is difficult to assess the extent to which corporations are talent spotting for managers, professionals, and executives to work in the West. But American and European corporations also played a role in creating a war for talent in the major cities of emerging economies such as Mumbai. A senior Indian manager working for an American company thought the paucity of talented managers was similar to that confronting colleagues in the United States as "there are limited places where you can find the talent." For more routine process-driven jobs, there was believed to be a bit more room to maneuver, but when it comes to business analytics and research, "You're still looking for people to deliver very high-end work" and capable of interacting with colleagues around the world. This led them to hire from leading institutes and universities, but the difference is that "while in Europe and the United States, your competitors are based in the same geography...here our competitors are multinationals sitting anywhere in the world because they are all coming to India to recruit and set up shop here...so everyone is trying to hire from a very small pool, so it is a war for talent."

The same was true in Beijing. "As you know, in China the economy develops very quickly and there is a war; the war is a talent war. This means that our people can work today for us and tomorrow for others, so how to retain them is very important for us." This Chinese manager, working for a foreign bank which had been a front runner in developing its operations in China, also believed that the war for talent had been created by other banks coming to China. "So our people are quite valuable for other companies who are coming here, so we need to think about it, and it is very important to retain them..."

In the IT sector in Bangalore, the foreign demand for talent was believed to have far-reaching consequences for smaller Indian IT companies that lacked the resources and brand value of companies such as IBM. The Indian chief information officer running a shared services operation for a number of leading American companies observed,

> companies like IBM are Hoovering up people with implications for local firms... people go in for brand value so all the small companies today in India—the small IT companies and middle-sized companies—are finding it very tough. I don't see how they can sustain themselves over the next 5–7 years; either they'll merge and grow up in size or they will perish... they can't sustain themselves in India in the current environment... I predict that within 5 years there will be only eight to ten India IT companies and U.S. companies and they will compete with each other. The small companies will not be able to hold on to the talent.

Following the global recession, this remains to be seen, but there was also evidence of some senior managers operating with ethnic hierarchies that undervalued the talent of highly qualified Indians. This was not restricted to the arrogance of some Western managers, as it was also found within Asia. One of the European managers we interviewed was worried about the level of racism that remained in assuming that Indian university graduates would be happy working in a call center if it was for a European or American company. "The top talent can compete on a global stage; we've already proved that, but you can't expect these people to go and work in a call center. But some people seem to believe that is going to happen; it's bizarre... this is just racism parading by some other name. They are going to be really grateful for the chance to work in a call center." A Chinese banking executive also told us that an ethnic hierarchy worked in his bank because there was widespread resentment of a glass ceiling for local Chinese employees, as all the talent that had been fast tracked appeared to come from Western countries.

Competitive pressures may break some of the glass ceilings associated with ethnic hierarchies. One major bank had little doubt that the globalization of talent would have implications for workers in Europe and the United States, as they moved a lot of work to India that was previously undertaken by college graduates in New York, London, or

Frankfurt. In corporate finance and banking, "We're looking at off-shoring a lot of the evaluation, pitch-book writing; that's all stuff that traditionally new grads did." So I think,

> we'll see a decline in the number of new graduates that they take in because the model there has always been to take in analysts, put them in a cellar for 3 years, and they come out and do an MBA and then come back as associates and they make a lot more money. If you move the cellar somewhere else, you have to change that whole supply chain. It needs to be redefined and rethought, and we're in the process of doing that.

If more of the cellar jobs previously undertaken in America and Britain are being exported, it is going to have major implication for the supply and development of talent within the industry. But the globalization of talent was not only driven by major corporations; it was also driven by governments from affluent economies.

National Competitiveness and the War for Talent

The opportunity bargain espoused by the U.S. federal government asserts a need to draw on the talents of all American citizens to create a magnet economy for high-skill, high-wage employment. Although such views are intended for domestic consumption, governments in affluent economies bought into the corporate rhetoric of the global war for talent and the idea that competitive advantage cannot be sustained by relying on the talents of the national workforce. Upgrading the skills of the existing workforce needed to extend to attracting the most highly skilled and talented workers from around the world.

Richard Florida is a leading proponent of this line of argument. He states that the United States now confronts its biggest challenge since the dawn of the Industrial Revolution, "the *new global competition for talent*, a phenomenon that promises to radically reshape the world in the coming decades." Gone are the days when the economic might of nations depended on their natural resources, manufacturing excellence, military dominance, or scientific and technological prowess. According to Florida, the competition now revolves around "a nation's ability to mobilize, attract, and retain human creative talent. Every key dimension of international economic leadership, from manufacturing excellence to scientific and technological advancement, will depend on this ability."[11]

The apparent need for nations to target foreign talent implies that the domestic working and middle classes could no longer be relied on to supply fresh talent to fuel America's or Britain's knowledge economy. The focus on foreign talent was justified on grounds of an aging workforce, skill shortages in key areas such as engineering and science, or the benefits of rubbing shoulders with the best of the best as a way of lifting everyone's game. Again, the analogy of Britain's Premier League soccer has been used by British politicians to demonstrate the value of foreign-born talent to the national economy. Attracting superstars like the Beckham's of science to the country "can only help take our world-class domestic research to the next level.... To be the best you have to work with the best."[12]

And to work with the best justified radical changes in national policy, especially the reform of immigration policies that opened borders to the highly skilled and offered attractive tax benefits to make a country more competitive and attractive to top-level professional and managerial workers. Immigration reform in the global war for talent involves the market-based liberalization of national borders, removing barriers to the entry of foreign talent. Although states have long used market criteria to shape immigration policy, the trend across OECD nations over the past two decades has seen a rise in immigration levels overall, with a growing bias toward the highly skilled.[13]

The scale of high-skill migration can be shown in some of the available evidence.[14] Globally, high-skill migration increased at a rate two and a half times faster than low-skill migration between 1990 and 2000. By 2000, the college educated made up 35 percent of immigrants to OECD countries, up from 30 percent in 1990 and far exceeding the 11 percent of the world's overall labor force that they represent.[15] Over a 10-year period from 1986 to 1997, Canada saw its flow of immigrant computer scientists increase 15-fold, the flow of engineers increase 10-fold, the flow of natural scientists increase 8-fold, and the flow of managerial workers increase 4-fold.[16] In Britain, it is estimated that 80 percent of all new doctors and 73 percent of all new nurses hired between 1997 and 2003 were foreign born, and 22 percent of all new college graduates hired in the financial and business services sector prior to the financial crash were foreigners.[17]

One of the problems with importing skilled workers is that it may reduce the incentive for companies to invest in the training of indigenous workers and may encourage employers to reduce labor costs, given that migrants, irrespective of skill level, typically do the same jobs for fewer rewards and inferior contracts of employment. Even in areas where there is increased demand for high-skill workers, there is a growing propensity to import qualified labor rather than invest in the skills of the less qualified and socially disadvantaged. This has led to political pressure to reduce the numbers of H-1B visas issued to foreign workers in the United States, and political pressure has grown in the United Kingdom with increasing unemployment. Indeed, the Lords Select Committee on Economic Affairs concluded that "we have found no evidence for the argument, made by the Government, business and many others, that net immigration—immigration minus emigration—generates significant economic benefits for the existing UK population." The report goes on to state, "We do not support the general claims that net immigration is indispensable to fill labor and skills shortages."[18]

The brain drain of talent from emerging countries, such as doctors, nurses, teachers, and IT workers can also have negative consequences for the countries they leave behind. This is far from a win-win scenario for many emerging economies, although in the medium term, there may be some advantages if they receive advanced professional training and return to their home countries to work.[19] But for many emerging economies, the negative consequences of the human trafficking of skilled workers are clearly evident. There was a shortfall approaching 40,000 nurses in South Africa in 2008, but they were losing 300 nurses a month before the global economic crisis. This situation led Thembeka Gwagwa, chief officer of the South African Nurses' Association, to conclude that the overseas recruiters know they are going too far but are ultimately driven by profit: "As long as they make money they don't care what they are doing to the health care of our nation."[20]

This brain drain can leave emerging economies with a lack of the critical skills required to attract foreign inward investment. At least 40 percent of Filipinos live on less than $2 a day, and unemployment stood at 22.7 percent in 2007.[21] Remittance accounts for around 13 percent of the Philippines GDP, but it tends to encourage consumer spending rather than create the conditions for export-driven growth. The brain drain to the developed economies, at least in part, accounts for the lack of skilled workers in health, aviation, mining, shipping, and port operations. The problems in the health sector are stark, as 85 percent of the country's trained nurses are overseas Filipino workers (OFWs). David Llorito, a journalist based in Manila, observes that "what really alarms health policy makers is the new trend of doctors becoming nurses—the so-called 'nursing medics' phenomenon—so they can more easily leave the country and work abroad."[22]

Hiring the Brightest and the Best?

If there is a political tension between hiring foreign talent rather than nurturing the skills of American citizens, there is also a tension between the corporate rhetoric of employee diversity—widening access to non-white Americans, women, or those from poorer social backgrounds—and how talent management is understood in many leading companies. This is evident in the way companies define talent. In the corporate bureaucracies of the past, there were distinct entry routes and career structures that reflected differences in academic performance, as only a small minority entered the job market with a bachelor's degree. Today, as many more graduate with a bachelor's degree, HR managers talked with authority about the robust nature of their hiring methods aimed at assessing a broad range of competencies beyond being book smart. But the main protagonists of the war for talent find it difficult to define what companies are supposed to be fighting over. Ed Michaels and his colleagues at McKinsey suggest that talent is often seen as "the sum of a person's abilities—his or her intrinsic gifts, skills, knowledge, experience, intelligence, judgment, attitude, character, and drive. It also includes his or her ability to learn and grow."[23] They then concede, "defining great managerial talent is a bit more difficult. A certain part of talent eludes description: You simply know it when you see it."[24] Ultimately, talent is a "code for the most effective leaders and managers at all levels who can help a company fulfill its aspirations and drive its performance."[25]

Self-reflection provides a useful proxy for managerial talent, as senior managers tend to think of talent while looking in the mirror. It reflects social judgments alongside hard measures of bottom-line potential. But these social judgments have become trickier because the war for talent is not simply the latest excuse for excluding candidates that lack the appropriate pedigree. They now require a second glance in the mirror as judgments are required between "people like us," as more get access to a college education.

This has led companies to artificially limit the pool of talent by targeting elite universities and ignoring graduates from less prestigious universities and colleges, who are written off as having subprime credentials. They recruit from elite universities because their students are regarded as the best of the best and most likely to exude the personal chemistry and social fit required for success. A global head of HR in financial services told us, "We are very keen to get the best talent, so we go after the elite…in other words, we want to get the top half percentile of university students…we're not interested in the rest." She went on to explain that the company set the bar extremely high because what makes the company earn any money at all is its intellectual hardwiring. "There is no other asset. There's no cars; there's no pharmaceuticals. We're not selling anything but our brainpower of providing financial solutions to clients. That's it, and the way that we win over our competitors is having smarter people in the firm."

Although there was a greater focus on technical knowledge from firms in the electronics and engineering fields, we heard similar stories of how they targeted top-notch universities. A global engineering company confirmed that they were in the business of selling jobs. "Our basic understanding of recruiting is of a marketing process; it's not a purchasing process. The basic idea behind this is we are selling jobs and trying to find customers for the jobs." Along with other leading companies, they target a small number of reputed universities in each of their designated countries. As another HR director explained, they only invest in top-tier universities where they give presentations, sponsor clubs or societies, and spend their scholarship budget. "Everything that's going to enhance our brand at those universities then we'll do it."

The decision to target elite universities was in part intended to deter those in other universities and colleges because leading corporations receive thousands of applications for a relatively small number of positions. A major problem confronting many of these companies was that "there's this massive population which we've got to get down to a manageable pool." This HR director recognized that while there may be some good candidates in lower tier universities, the numbers are tiny, as those at elite universities have already gone through a rigorous selection process. "It's a total numbers game; it's very frustrating but it's a total numbers game." But by choosing to fish in such a small pool of college graduates, companies are strengthening the barriers to entry. It is as if they are putting a sign out: "Those who are not at top-notch universities need not apply." What may be considered extraordinary about this strategy is that despite the demand for increased numbers of young managers who can work across the globe, they remain focused on recruiting from the elite universities in each country. The consequence is that many able students will not have the opportunity to get their foot in the door to demonstrate their worth.

The same logic applies globally as companies seek to internationalize talent management. In hiring their future talent pool, corporations have benchmarked leading universities around the world, often based on their own formulations in conjunction with public rankings of the world's top universities. Such rankings are compiled by Jiao Tong University in Shanghai and the World University Rankings by the *Times* newspaper group in the United Kingdom that has Harvard, Yale, Cambridge, Oxford, and the California Institute of Technology as their global top five. A leading financial services company illustrates this trend as it targets just eight globally ranked universities, including Columbia, Wharton, and Harvard. The London Business School was the only British institution to appear on the list despite the company having major operations in London.[26]

While corporations gravitate toward a global elite of universities, such a strategy is actively promoted by leading universities, as higher education has also become a global business. The branding of universities and faculty members is integral to the organization of academic inquiry. Claims to world-class standards depend on attracting the best academics and forming alliances with elite universities elsewhere in the world, while recruiting the right kinds of students. Universities play the same reputational games as companies because it is a logical consequence of global market competition between universities. Leading corporations and elite universities have engaged in a tango that enhances each other's brands.

In reality, the war *for* talent is best understood as a war *over* talent. When many more people have access to knowledge that was previously restricted to a minority and when more companies have access to the technologies, techniques, and management tools that had previously defined competitive advantage, how talent is defined is something worth fighting for. Talent is not simply about being the most productive in the sense of making or delivering more of something. Whether the winners in the war for talent achieve higher productivity is debatable, but the value of a company is not only determined by the objective value of what it produces but also on its reputational capital, or what is commonly referred to as "branding."[27] As Samsung, a leading global electronics firm, has observed, "In the digital era, a product will be distinguished by its brand more than by its functions or by its quality." Today, many companies and their employees create nothing tangible such as trains, planes, or automobiles; they sell information, ideas, or solutions that are difficult to price. Value depends on market judgments that are shaped through image management, marketing, and public relations.[28] Value added in knowledge-intensive industries, such as management consultancy or financial services, stems from branding the company to maximize the price of its professional knowledge.

But the value of corporate branding is not restricted to the image of goods or services sold to consumers around the world. It also relates to the workforce. Work is not measured by performance; it *is* performance. For many, it has become a real-life drama where impression management is critical to the brand value of a company. When meeting clients, company employees are expected to look, talk, and act "expensive" to convince clients that they are the best and therefore worth their eye-watering consultancy fees. This is why the more corporate value is embodied in the people who work for it, the more companies want to be seen to hire the best.

Hiring to enhance the brand of the company also has implications for the market value of employees. The quality of new appointments at all levels of the organization reflect the labor market power of those already in the posts. Fierce competition from high-caliber applicants is seen to enhance the bargaining power of those employed, who may be keenly aware of the need to optimize their job prospects beyond their present employer. Attempts to increase diversity are often resisted by existing employees when they are seen to dilute their labor market status. Greater diversity may "be bad for the wallets of senior managers and executives but also bad for their egos."

The Mismanagement of Talent

The opportunity bargain was supposed to take the poor out of poverty and take the middle classes to within touching distance of the truly wealthy by educating the workforce. Mass ranks of knowledge workers were envisaged doing clever things in interesting and well-paid jobs, where profits would be widely shared to reflect productive contribution. The corporate response to this new wealth of talent was to initiate the war for talent—a Darwinian view of exceptional people, educated at exceptional universities, working for exceptional companies, achieving exceptional performance, and deserving exceptional rewards.

Although it sounds radical, the war for talent conforms to the gut instincts and vested interests of many executives that see themselves as part of a breed apart no matter how many Americans pour onto the job market with college credentials. Its emphasis on outstanding talent is an attempt to legitimate a new hierarchy of professional jobs based on a corporate power elite responsible for finding innovative ways of extracting value from the organization through labor arbitrage and digital Taylorism aligned with the short-term interests of shareholders, as we will go on to show in the following chapter.

The war for talent is also cheap management. It is not cheap in terms of cost, where the compensation going to top performers is racing away, but in terms of the real art of management, which is getting the best from the whole workforce. Not all companies subscribe to the war for talent. Some set their talent radar closer to the ground where much of the productive value is created. Charles O'Reilly and Jeffrey Pfeffer, who are leading experts on organizational behavior, have observed that "the unfortunate mathematical fact is that only 10 percent of the people are going to be in the top 10 percent. So, companies have a choice. They can all chase the same supposed talent. Or they can...build an organization that helps make it possible for regular folks to perform as if they were in the top 10 percent."[29]

Therefore, a key issue is not what proportion of the workforce is capable of thinking for a living but how people are assigned to occupational tasks within a highly stratified structure of rewards. What is offered to a few is denied to the many regardless of how knowledgeable or talented they are. The war for talent is presented as an attempt to more accurately relate rewards to performance. But in many respects, it rewards success in a positional competition for senior posts that also serve to legitimate widening inequalities that privilege a minority at the top of organizations or those being nurtured in elite universities to join them.

The war for talent is a battle for money, status, and power within the ranks of professional workers. At stake is not simply the reproduction of existing divisions but a power struggle that is reshaping productive and unproductive inequalities at work and beyond, transforming the trading position of America's middle classes. Those defined as top talent are able to draw on their personal and reputational capital to leverage the American Dream for themselves, whereas other equally well-qualified employees find themselves in a reverse bidding war as companies try to reduce the cost of knowledge.

CHAPTER SEVEN

Managing in the Global Auction

People have become the value chain of the future.

—*Global Head of HR, European Electronics Company*

S O FAR, WE have described how a global auction for high-skill as well as routine jobs has been created in little more than 30 years. This has challenged much of the existing thinking about the future of the global economy and the dominance of Western workers employed to do the world's thinking. It has challenged the idea that wealth and power would flow to individuals with the knowledge, skills, and insights that could be sold within an increasingly global marketplace.

It has also challenged the global win-win which assumes a race to the top. We have shown how such ideas fail to understand how transnational companies have shaped the global auction in ways that threaten the trading position of college-educated Americans, undermining the promise of the neoliberal opportunity bargain. The same free market policies that were supposed to lift the demand for American brainpower have in reality removed the constraints on American corporations to maximize returns to shareholders through increasing corporate profits, irrespective of its implications for American workers.

The assumption that national champions such as Ford or DuPont shared the interests of American workers lost much of its political credibility in the 1980s when American corporations were moving production jobs to low-cost countries, leaving a rust belt of deindustrialization symbolized by the cities of Detroit, Pittsburgh, and Cleveland. These early stages of globalization were not widely seen to undermine the opportunity bargain because it was believed that the same global forces would increase the demand for high-skill Americans. As long as knowledge workers could not be sourced more cheaply elsewhere, companies remained limited in their use of offshoring. Trade barriers and low levels of investment in college education in emerging economies offered few prospects for cut-price expertise. This gave companies little option other than to recruit from domestic job markets and pay the going rate along with their industrial competitors.

This situation did not last as the global auction brought millions of high-skill, low-wage workers onto the international job market, leading companies to denationalize or globalize their HR strategies. In turn, this has led to a bidding war that economists sometimes refer to as labor arbitrage: playing off different groups of workers or suppliers by taking full advantage of the new supply of high-skill, low-cost employees.

Companies no longer need to divide their human resource strategies between high-cost "head" nations and "body" nations restricted to low-skill, low-wage employment. This gives companies much greater control over their sourcing options from the mundane to the most complex aspects of the business. They can now take advantage of advances in communication technologies, the globalization of high skills, and state-of-the-art factories and research facilities in emerging economies. The corporate home base remains a key location for developing and coordinating business strategies, but companies have questioned the role of the aptly named head office as the primary source of corporate brainpower.

Indeed, a defining feature of the shift from multinational to transnational companies is the growing importance attached to the way companies are restructuring their global division of labor. Transnational companies are developing modular capacity for high-, medium-, and low-skill work that connects across national borders and have a growing proportion of high-value work located in low-cost countries. In these circumstances, the global auction for labor becomes a potential source of competitive advantage because companies can (re)configure their global workforce in distinct ways that increasingly impact on corporate profitability. The problem for American workers is that the country's corporations have used these sourcing options to reduce the labor costs of college-educated workers in an attempt to capture the best ideas delivered at the lowest cost.

Leveraging HR

A company's human resources have typically been understood as the firm-specific stock of human capital—that is, the sum total of individual knowledge, skills, and know-how that an organization has at its disposal within national economies. This approach is derived from classical economics where economic activity rests on an analysis of the three factors of production—land, labor, and capital goods (for example, machinery, tools, plant). As a result, each is treated in isolation, which is why human resource management was defined as administrative rather than strategic. It is worth remembering that is was not until the 1960s that economists began to take seriously the idea that human initiative, knowledge, and skill could lead to increasing productivity. The role of human resources was to deliver enough bodies on the line or bums on seats with the appropriate skills and training to fulfill the organization's business in specific national locations. The emphasis was on procedures, including the hiring, training, and firing of individual employees.

The corporate stock of human capital was locked into national pyramids with little connection between them. However, the global integration of human resources into modular components and behavioral competencies has become the latest weapon in corporate efforts to achieve competitive advantage through people. Value is derived from the creation of innovative linkages that connect individuals, technologies, and suppliers scattered around the world; it is how these components are put together and reconfigured at short notice in response to changing market conditions that is key. The issue is not the amount of knowledge individual employees command or the amount of knowledge organizations control but the corporate capacity to connect employees, software, and suppliers to increase performance and the profitability of knowledge.

Nicholas Donofrio, executive vice-president for innovation and technology at IBM, describes the company as a globally integrated on-demand enterprise capable of responding locally to rapid shifts in demand for integrated IT and business solutions. This not only requires breaking down organizational silos but also a globally integrated workforce "unencumbered by geography, processes or structure, a workforce that can effectively operate across boundaries, sharing the knowledge and skills needed to bring new value to our clients." And he sees this capacity as "a crucial competitive differentiator" in today's global economy.[1]

Modular corporations have become adept at looking beyond those on the company's payroll to extend their range of strategic options despite some firms continuing to directly employ hundreds of thousands of people around the globe. Some of this is driven by the rapid pace of technological change. The blurring of the boundaries between different companies and product markets and the disintegration of knowledge, product, and service boundaries have all contributed to the growth of the modular corporation. Research and development activities offer an example because it is often difficult for companies to undertake blue-skies research and platform developments in isolation. It is not only prohibitively expensive and risky to develop new products, but the pace of change in key sectors such as telecoms, automotive, and biotechnology makes it increasingly unlikely that companies have access to the knowledge and know-how that is required, especially given the trend toward focusing on core competencies.

As the boundaries between products such as telephones, cameras, computers, and audio systems collapse, as with cell phones and with similar trends in mechanical and electronic applications (mechatronics) in robot technology, hospital equipment, and autos, much of the knowledge that companies need must be accessed outside the formal boundaries of the organization through strategic alliances and outsourcing.

There is also more pressure on companies to reduce the time from innovation to invoice, reflecting the growing importance of mass customization in virtually all industrial sectors. This customization requires both innovative ideas and the flexibility to reuse standard components to meet the specific requirements of customers. More than 80 percent of BMW Minis produced in Britain for the global market are built to customer order, offering a range of over 250 factory-fit options and dealer-fit accessories that make every Mini uniquely similar. In the United States, the Toyota Tundra has 22,000 possible configurations, and the Chrysler Dodge Ram is available in 1.2 million variations.[2]

The use of build to order, where products are only made to the specific requirements of customers, is not restricted to the auto industry. Dell computers has established a sophisticated made-to-order business that gives customers the opportunity to build a computer based on a choice of the 20 or so product features that go into a computer, including memory (RAM), disc space, modem, processor, screen, and software. The same processes are being applied to clothes, watches, sneakers, cosmetics, window frames, and houses. Nike offers customized sports shoes with a vast range of uppers and soles and with the option of have your name embroidered on the back of each sneaker. Customatix, an Internet company, allows you to design your own shoes based on almost limitless combinations of colors, graphics, logos, and materials.[3]

The use of 24-hour design teams, working around the clock moving through time zones across Asia, Europe, and North America, offers another example of how companies are trying to reduce the time between invention, application, and market launch and also to reduce costs by taking advantage of lower salary levels in much of Asia. An American auto manufacturer, for instance, set up a new research center in India specializing in the virtual modeling of the production process because they were able to recruit talented IT and math college graduates. When asked whether they worked in virtual teams on the same projects, we were told by the head of operations in India that they "followed the sun."

We found most manufacturing companies operated in this way not only with research but also with design. A leading German automaker explained how they followed the sun in various areas of design by operating in "Stuttgart, Mumbai, and Los Angeles in a 24-hour cycle, so we have round the clock." They have a design studio at Los Angeles and a major design center in Stuttgart. In India, they have a center for electronic and other design activities, and in Italy, they have a design team working on automobile interiors, but "they are connected and they are working 24 hours a day. In India, people are working when it is night in Germany, and German employees pick up the direction in the morning and continue."

Companies not only have more choice about where to think but also have greater choice over what to *produce* themselves, what to *purchase* from suppliers, third-party vendors, or even competitor firms, or whether to *partner* with other companies in the form of shared services or R&D. The modular organization is not limited to the formal organization giving them greater options in regard to what is done, how it is done, and where it is done because what is different now is not only the global supply of highly educated workers but also a growing number of low-cost providers able to deliver more for less.

What corporations produce themselves, for instance, will depend on the degree to which they focus on core competencies over trying to do everything for themselves within vertically integrated organizations. The fashion within American business literature is to focus on a narrow range of core competencies. This has encouraged corporate executives to virtually disintegrate rather than vertically integrate their organizations because it was assumed to offer a competitive advantage in areas of business for which they are best suited, with all other activities purchased or partnered. A senior manager for a British bank spoke of the "fever" among companies to stick to core competence, increasing the use of outsourcing. "Essentially, why are you outsourcing is because you find somebody can do it cheaper, and that's not just it, can also do it better, and that's not just it, can do it in a faster time than you can."

The business literature has celebrated companies such as Dell Computers, ABB, or Li & Fung that purchase rather than make anything themselves, relying on an extended use of outsourcing and offshoring to third-party providers. It was this focus on core competencies that gave Indian companies such as WIPRO and Infosys the opportunity to enter the global market as they expanded to service the IT requirements of Western companies.

But the focus on core competencies can lead to the hollowing out of companies, as they outsource profitable areas of business activity that they could feasibly do themselves. It can also lead to a loss of control over quality standards and limit their internal knowledge capacity. Boeing's Dreamliner 787 aircraft offers a salutary example as the company outsourced various parts of design, testing, and production using state-of-the-art technologies to reduce fuel consumption. As a result, it led to the longest air travel delay in history, taking its maiden test flight from its factory near Seattle two and a half years late. This led Richard Aboulafia, an aerospace analyst, to suggest that the idea of placing a high level of trust in the design and responsibilities for coordination with their suppliers would have initially "sounded great to executives. 'We can fire lots of engineers, give the money to shareholders, and I can go and buy a yacht.' Except it needed a greater degree of oversight and more in-house resources."[4]

It is for these reasons that some companies, especially those based in South Korea and Japan, continue to keep a broad range of activities in house, although they were not immune from the consequences of global recession. Today, a key issue for all companies is how to connect profit centers, business units, product markets, design teams, suppliers, franchisees, research centers, universities, licensees, business start-ups, and strategic alliances with competitor companies wanting to share the costs of research or business processes. The calculation of the costs and benefits associated with building these linkages, whether within the core business, through alliances, or through outsourcing or offshoring, is now an integral part of the corporate drive to competitive advantage. So how do companies create and leverage these connections?

Empty Suits

In the same way that digital Taylorism enables companies to translate knowledge work into working knowledge to achieve more control over the work context, the global auction has given companies more strategic choices about how to create a new global division of labor. Although this offers the potential to develop the creative energies, trust, and wealth of talent that now exist globally, the dominant response of American corporations has been to exploit the bidding war to reduce costs and maximize profits.

The competition strategies of American corporations are therefore playing a crucial role in creating the reverse auction for high-skill workers. Time and again, companies told us that costs had to be driven down because of intense international competition. Just as the breakdown of national barriers exposed workers to the full force of the global auction, erstwhile national champions were similarly exposed to foreign competition. When one firm acts to take advantage of lower costs offshore, it often leads their competitors to follow, unless they can create a particular niche advantage by remaining at home.

Those corporations that exist just for profit—maximizing returns to shareholders—are more likely to strip out costs within global operations by taking advantage of differences in wage rates and cultural differences in social expectations. As we were told in more that one company interview, "In China, they're hungry to work." Such companies are at the forefront of the trends toward offshoring high-value activities to low-cost locations. According to Japanese management guru Kenichi Ohmae, the value of global networks is giving companies the freedom to drive down costs while maintaining quality through the threat, or use, of exit strategies, given a choice of providers.

He argues that the source of competitive advantage that derives from business networks of individuals and companies comes from exploiting the capabilities and cost differentials that exist within the network itself. As he suggests, "Arbitrage simply means the playing off of one supplier against another, to continually bring the price of goods and services down, and the quality up—not through control or negotiating, but simply through choice." Rather than build trust relations and work closely with suppliers to address quality issues, Ohmae advises corporate executives to eliminate these difficulties "by finding new partners that operate in a less fettered way." He admits that this is likely to make some people unhappy, but "the savings are so great that the new choice is necessary. No business can justify refusing the advantages of an arbitraging choice."[5]

This extends the reverse auction from individual employees to suppliers and subsidiaries located in different parts of the world. Rather than work together to improve productivity as a means to reduce costs, it has encouraged just for profit companies to disregard loyalty and trust in favor of contractual relations and service agreements, alongside a top-down approach to management with a radical separation between financial planning and service delivery.[6]

This is not without historical precedent as Robert Hayes and William Abernathy remind us in their acclaimed essay on how modern management principles, which they called "management by the numbers," destroyed the productive vitality of the American economy in the 1970s.[7]

Management by the numbers values analytical detachment and "short-term cost reduction rather than long-term development of technological competitiveness."[8] Planning takes the form of financial targets within corporations broken down into cost centers subject to global arbitrage; subsidiaries, suppliers, and even head office functions are frequently market tested.

In such a context, it is hardly surprising that American and British top managers "driven by bonus schemes and fear of stock-market reaction, set ludicrously short pay-back periods, effectively disqualifying all but short-term schemes...and cost-cutting."[9]

The CEO of a leading auto supplier we met in Detroit referred to those people who understand the numbers but not the human skills, knowledge, and relations that generate productive organizations as "empty suits."[10]

> The fundamental flaw that I have seen occur in my 41 years in this business is that we get these incredibly bright, well educated people, and we take them up through positions and never teach them the core business. They become what I call the empty suits, and all of a sudden

they are running these divisions or groups or companies and they really don't know the fundamentals of people engineering that you learn on the factory floor with your people.

But learning these fundamentals is redundant when the focus is on transactional or contractual relationships. Employees are judged on current performance targets, and a free agent mind-set encourages short-term interests rather than loyalty. When companies are run by empty suits in the interests of shareholders, the strategic importance of people as a source of competitive advantage is reduced to meeting performance targets at low cost.

Reflecting on the fate of HR over the last decade, another experienced manager who has been the HR director for a number of American companies around the world believed there had been a missed opportunity, given a shift from a high-touch employee relations HR model to a transactional operations delivery model driven by the competitive demand to reduce the cost of corporate human resources.

"The drive was to ensure the essentials get delivered in a world class manner—that meant speed of transactions with high quality—all very good but with no resources to do anything in the soft 'people' side of HR that then slipped into the twilight." The result was more HR functions added to already overburdened line managers. Employees (including senior executives) no longer went to HR to obtain the benefit of compensation information. They now have an 800 number to call the outsourced supplier with requests channeled through a call center in Indian or the Philippines. "No longer does an HR representative 'walk the floor' and know everyone in their designated patch—that role no longer exists." The longer-term impact of global recession is too early to judge, but in a recent discussion with senior HR managers, there was little sense that this model was about to be abandoned. We were told that no one is safe, and at least one company admitted to sweating its talent pool to justify existing salary levels.

Hit and Run

Although many American and British companies have used the global auction to reduce labor costs and maximize profits, others are struggling with the tension between competitive demands to cut costs and longer-term commitments to their workforce to maintain their loyalty, skills, and experience. In part, the differences between the tooth-and-claw cost cutters and these other companies reflect differences in product markets and industrial sectors. They also reflect differences in corporate traditions, cultures, and governance because not all companies define their main purpose as maximizing returns to shareholders. Some are trying to balance the interests of different stakeholders, including employees, shareholders, suppliers, and national governments. Japanese transnational companies often emphasize the importance of products and services for the global good, however vague this aspiration, whereas German companies have traditionally traded on quality engineering built on high trust relations between managers and workers.

The head of human resources for a major German company in the telecoms sector took great pride in discussing its long history of international operations and good global citizenship. It has 70 percent of its employees outside Germany and emphasized the need for a sustainable approach based on quality, innovation, and business performance. He was highly critical of the Anglo-Saxon hit-and-run approach to globalization, where companies offshore solely as a cost-cutting measure.

He believed that productive gains may come from the exploitation of the global auction, but for him, there were other factors that needed to be taken into account. While labor arbitrage has become a key strategic option for companies, it has to be balanced by other intangible considerations, such as trust relations with employees and suppliers, which are often related to commitment and loyalty.

The emphasis was on building the company's competitive capacity that required it to go beyond contract in its commitment to workers, suppliers, customers, and overseas operations. He observed how the company tried to engineer relationships likely to foster long-term commitment by developing trust relations throughout their global operations. In other words, he was acutely aware that cost reduction may come at the price of increasing what economists call transaction costs—that is, the cost of getting things done.

Having said that, the imperative to reduce costs and prices remained, given a need to ensure that costs are compatible to the price level they were getting from the market. And although cutting costs and jobs in Germany was a politically sensitive issue even before the global recession, he observed that German consumers don't pay his company a price premium because, like everywhere else, people want the best goods at the lowest price. Yet in the longer term, he recognized that the company could not survive by cost cutting alone. Innovation was the key, but the cost of innovation had to be reduced, leading to major investments in research and design facilities in Eastern Europe and Asia. As we were told, "We cannot in the long term be successful just with low-cost products. We have to focus on innovation...we have to drive innovation. We have to be at the leading edge at reasonable cost...that's it. And this can be transferred to the labor market. Most of all, we have to try to get higher skills at reasonable cost and high flexibility."

After the financial crash, this company has come under more pressure to reduce labor costs across the organization, as it experienced a dip of more than 80 percent in profits. The attempt to maintain breakthrough innovation at the same time as reducing costs is leading them to make greater use of offshoring, "as people have become the value chain of the future." Today, even companies that don't believe in hit and run are reexamining their whole organization to define which parts of the process can be outsourced and which parts can't be done in an offshore location. "This engineering of the value chain, this will be quite a tough thing." But it is a tough thing that many other organizations have already undertaken, as offshoring moves up the value chain.

Evidence of Offshoring Moving Up the Value Chain

We can identify two waves of offshoring. In the first wave, it was low-skill work that was offshored, where companies move some of their operations to reduce costs. But in the second wave, it is more highly skilled work that is relocated. It is difficult to gain an accurate picture of offshoring activities because companies are reluctant to divulge how they are restructuring their global operations, arguing that they are simply following the market when investing in emerging economies. Despite such difficulties, the widely held view that offshoring would be largely restricted to low-skill, low-wage workers in manufacturing industries such as apparel, toys, and footwear has been shown to be hopelessly flawed.[11]

Robert Scott attempted to assess the employment implications of the trade imbalance between America and China. By examining the types of goods and services being imported and exported, he calculated that 2.3 million jobs were lost or displaced in the United States from 2001–2007. This not only included routine manufacturing and clerical jobs but also 561,000 jobs in computer and electronic products—a sector that has also been successfully targeted by India. There were also 128,000 jobs lost or displaced in professional, scientific, and technical services, along with a similar number in administrative support services.[12] Scott found that Western economists had assumed America would export knowledge-intensive goods and import labor-intensive goods from China and other emerging economies, but the opposite was found. Hi-tech goods were being exported to the United States rather than being exported to China.[13] Moreover, 90 percent of hi-tech imports into the United States are produced by foreign-invested firms located in China.[14]

The protective barrier that offered respite from global offshoring to America's middle classes has been breached. In Alan Blinder's widely cited study, he developed an index of "offshorability" to calculate the number of service-sector jobs that could potentially be offshored from the United States.[15] He distinguishes between jobs that are personally delivered (janitors, child-care workers, and surgeons) from jobs that are impersonally delivered (call-center operators and scientists). Using a comprehensive U.S. database, he calculates that between 22 percent and 29 percent of all U.S. service sector jobs could be offshored with little or no degradation in quality.

Of course, not all these jobs will be offshored in the same way that not all manufacturing jobs moved outside America. But there remains real potential for a growing proportion of good jobs to disappear overseas. Blinder's study shows that in the global auction, there is "little or no relationship between an occupation's 'offshorability' and the skill level of its workers (as measured by educational attainment or wages)."[16] Similarly, an international report on offshoring from the OECD found that skilled jobs were no longer safe from being sent offshore as it spread to technology-intensive industries such as software, computer services, and other information technology services.[17]

Evidence on offshoring knowledge-intensive jobs also comes from consultancy firms such as A. T. Kearney, who found that offshore relocation of financial services began with back-office functions such as data entry, transaction processing, and account reconciliation. It now includes "a wider range of high-end internal functions...including financial analysis, research, regulatory reporting, accounting, human resources and graphic design." They concluded that "any function that does not require face-to-face contact is now perceived as a candidate for offshore relocation."[18]

Studies that point to the rapid offshoring of skilled jobs are consistent with our own investigations not only in financial services, where we found evidence of high-level actuarial risk assessment being undertaken in India for international banks, but also in legal work. We might expect complex legal work that commanded an annual salary of around $200,000 in New York or London to remain onshore because of the knowledge required of specific national legal systems. But an American legal firm, closely involved in litigation related to the collapse of a high-profile corporate bankruptcy, offshored much of the work involved in sifting through thousands of commercial documents to Manila, where there is a cadre of highly qualified lawyers in American and British legal systems willing to undertake this work at a fraction of the cost.

The implications of offshoring for the global auction are not limited to the numbers of jobs that are physically relocated. For almost all categories of workers, there is a price to pay for concessions they need to make in terms of wage levels and working conditions. High-profile employers such as Siemens and Volkswagen in Germany threatened to move investments abroad if trade unions did not make significant concessions. Volkswagen achieved concessions from unions after it threatened to move production of a new sports car to Portugal, agreeing that under a new deal, wages would be 20 percent lower than for existing workers, allowing the company to save 850 euros per car.[19] Employees at all levels are being forced to accept cuts to compensation packages across America, Europe, and Asia as occupations that offer little protection from being offshored are paid significantly lower wages.[20]

Conclusion: Knowledge without Power

Regardless of all the talk of increasing power accruing to knowledge workers, economic globalization has allowed employers to regain the upper hand in relations between capital and labor. The global auction gives companies an opportunity to rethink their strategic capability by leveraging the auction for clever people. In companies that exist just for profit and where the incentives are for senior executive to line their own pockets through short-term increases in share prices linked to bonus payments, it leads to the mass degradation of middle-class jobs.

This should caution against the idea that talent has been freed from the constraints of knowledge capitalism. Likewise, human capital assumptions about the returns to knowledge workers rest on an outdated understanding of the global economy, as the proportion of wealth creation accruing to the workforce rather than shareholders has declined. Global sourcing can be used to play off different groups of knowledge professionals scattered around the globe whether within the same or different organizations.

Stephen Roach, chief economist at Morgan Stanley, reported that the win-win scenario for globalization was in serious trouble well before the credit crunch. While he believed that some workers in the developing world were benefiting from global trade agreements, this was not the case for many workers in the rich developed world, as most of the benefits had accrued to owners of capital at the expense of labor. He observed a powerful asymmetry in the impact of globalization on the world's major industrial economies that led to record highs in the returns accruing to capital and record lows in the rewards going to labor. "Global labor arbitrage has put unrelenting pressure on employment and real wages in the high-cost developed world."[21]

These findings offer little support to those who subscribe to the "flat world" view of globalization and see the world becoming a level playing field on which people compete on creative knowledge applied to global markets. While most of the world's population stand outside the global economy described in this book, more people on the planet are gaining access to high skills, and within a context of shareholder capitalism, the inevitable consequence is price competition.

This would not be so calamitous for affluent economies if new jobs that offered interesting and rewarding careers were being created. We have shown how Thomas Friedman put his faith in a theory of comparative advantage. Although China and India are competing in knowledge-intensive fields, he believed that this would lead Americans to create new jobs, yet unimagined, because "there may be a limit to the number of good factory jobs in the world, but there is no limit to the number of idea-generating jobs in the world."[22] But there are limits to the ever increasing supply of knowledge-intensive, well-paid jobs not only because more of this work can be done in low-cost locations but also because of the growing realities of digital Taylorism.

Indeed, the collapse in corporate profits in America and Britain could accelerate corporate plans to offshore as a strategic imperative. Western companies may blame job cuts, hiring freezes, and reduced salaries on economic recession rather than corporate maneuvers within the global auction, as many of the spatial limitations of "where to think" have been overcome. But following the bailout of Wall Street by American taxpayers, offshoring jobs from financial services and the auto industry has become more politically sensitive.

In an interview with economic advisors in Washington during the Bush administration, we asked about the interests of American corporations in investing in the country's workforce. We were asked to turn off our recording equipment and in hushed voices, the two officials described their growing misgivings about the impact of free trade agreements working against the interests of American workers but to the benefit of American corporations. The consequences of this shift in economic power also led Robert Scott to conclude, "This shift has increased the global 'race to the bottom' in wages and environmental quality and closed thousands of U.S. factories, decimating employment in a wide range of communities, states, and entire regions of the United States. U.S. national interests have suffered while U.S. multinationals have enjoyed record profits on their foreign direct investments."[23]

The financial crash highlighted the economic catastrophe resulting from the failure of federal authorities to regulate financial markets, and the global auction highlights the social catastrophe of failing to regulate the relationship among education, jobs, and rewards. In putting its faith in the free market, the American government gave up the state's capacity to act as a strategic economic actor at a time when American workers and their families were being encouraged to pursue a better future. This chapter shows how far American corporations are removed from the interests of ordinary workers. In the next chapter, we turn our attention to the broken promise on incomes and examine the rise of a high-skill, low-wage workforce.

CHAPTER EIGHT

❧

High Skills, Low Wages

Income inequalities between countries will narrow, but wage inequalities
will increase amongst employees.

—*Global Head of HR, European Telecoms Company*

THE GLOBAL AUCTION for jobs is not based on a division between head and body nations despite the rhetoric of American technological superiority. Trump cards held by workers in the competition for high-value work have been reshuffled as they have been throughout the history of capitalism. Governments have a political duty to privilege their citizens, but capitalism has no such loyalty. Where it is given room to breathe, it tirelessly accumulates capital in whatever ways it can with scant regard for existing arrangements. Joseph Schumpeter highlighted a relentless capitalism, which "is by nature a form or method of economic change."[1] If alive today, even Schumpeter may have been surprised by the scale of "perpetual commotion" in the economy in recent decades. He would also have been reminded of Karl Marx and Friedrich Engels's words that under capitalism "all that is solid melts into air, all that is holy is profane, and man is at last compelled to face with sober senses, his real conditions of life, and his relations with his kind."[2]

The real condition confronting many well-qualified Americans is an economy of knowledge caught in two minds. For many, access to college credentials has not delivered on the promise because the auction for skills has shifted into reverse gear. As Thomas Friedman suggests, "Those who are waiting for this recession to end so someone can again hand them work could have a long wait."[3] At the same time, for those at the top of the pile, which Friedman calls the "new untouchables," with the skills, knowledge, and enterprise that will continue to be highly valued in the global economy, the opportunity bargain will remain alive. But for most, what was once taken as the normal life course for middle-class Americans can no longer be taken for granted.

The Next Normal

The full impact of the global auction will take time to work through into official figures, but there is a real danger that declining returns to human capital will be blamed on the aftermath of the economic crash rather than on a secular shift in the global balance of economic power. The repercussions of the financial crash are already part of the economic landscape that will make it more important for companies to return to profitability through cutting costs and doing more for less. Unemployment has risen and wages have fallen around the world. Today, many people will be earning less, alongside reduced benefits such as health care and pensions. The unprecedented collapse in consumer demand has led companies to restructure their global operations to reduce costs. Reflecting on a 10 percent cut in staff at Chanel, Karl Lagerfeld, the company's creative director, described the cut as a "horrible but healthy thing." Costs had mushroomed during the good times so while "it may be a difficult moment for a lot of people," he concluded that "in the end it was needed."[4]

The need for a fundamental shift in employee expectations was also voiced by Pat House, who is currently the CEO of the software company C3 and a stalwart of Silicon Valley. She believes that a "psychic change" is underway that will result in a new model of venture capital and entrepreneurship, bringing to an end what she called the "entitlement generation." Venture capital firms no longer hand over millions of dollars to start-ups, employing recent university graduates with "a fantastic salary and flying first class, and having an expense account, and not needing to be accountable for revenue while they build fantastically cool, not necessarily cash generating businesses." Those days are over.

The new model is driven by young entrepreneurs from India, China, and other Asian countries, who are coming to the valley with the same technical depth and with the creative talent to produce the same cool products but with a completely different sense of entitlement.

> Their intent is to come over and have seven people live in a two bed-room apartment, and work night and day out of the apartment…and they are asking for 10,000 dollars in funding from individuals rather than 10 million from venture firms. They are building the same out-rageously cool, highly innovative, extraordinarily world changing technologies and products…as the same colleagues of theirs who his-torically thought that they need to drive a BMW to work, work on the 18th floor of an all glass office, and have hot and cold running cafeteria at their disposal 24 hours a day. It's a mentality change. [5]

This psychic change is not restricted to private sector jobs, as huge budget deficits in both America and Britain have resulted in deep cuts in public services along with cuts to the pay, retirement plans, and health coverage for public sector workers at all levels of public organi-zations. This is reflected in investor interest in outsourcing companies such as Serco, as they lay claim to take over more public services due to their low-cost models. "Outsourcers of Serco's ilk stand to be among the few winners from the slash and burn in the public sector over the next five years." [6]

Winners *and* Losers

If the capitalist system has no loyalty to American workers, much the same can be said of American corporate elites. They have not simply played a game of winner takes all; they have created one. Before entering high office in the Obama administration, Lawrence Summers observed that the "growth in the global economy encourages the development of stateless elites whose allegiance is to global economic success and their own prosperity rather than the interests of the nation where they are headquartered." As a prominent chief executive at the 2008 annual meeting of business and government leaders in Davos, Switzerland, told Summers, "We will be fine however America does." [7]

This confidence is based on economic facts; many CEOs are so wealthy that they and their families are immune from the threat of economic destitution. And the companies they control are not tied to the United States; they will go wherever they can to make the highest profits. Top-earning Americans hadn't had it so good since before the first Wall Street crash in 1929. Based on market income, including wages, bonuses, dividends, and pensions, Berkeley economist Emmanuel Saez calculated the changing fortunes of America's top earners since 1917. He shows that the top 10 percent received almost half (49.7%) of national individual income in 2006, surpassing 1928, the peak of the stock market bubble in the Roaring '20s.[8] If the top 10 percent have done well over the last 25 years, it is those at the very top who struck gold. Saez's evidence shows that the top 1 percent captured about half of the overall economic growth in America over the period 1993 to 2006. These were the working rich, including the CEOs of major corporations. In 1965, American CEOs earned 24 times more than the typical worker; the ratio grew to over 100 by in the early 1990s and stood at 1:275 in 2007. For every $10,000 earned by the average employee, CEOs were earning $2.75 million. Put another way, a small to medium-sized company with 275 employees on average wages could be set up for the price of a single CEO, who averaged a staggering annual income of $12.3 million in 2007.[9] The rest of the workforce was not so fortunate.

Learning Isn't Earning

The major losers have been at the other end of the jobs pyramid. The 70 percent of the American workforce that does not have a college degree saw their entry-level wage drop from $13 to $11 per hour between 1973 and 2005, which is extraordinary. In Britain, average wages for the unskilled increased marginally but only through the state supplementing the wages of low-income workers. In both countries, around 25 percent of workers are paid poverty wages.[10] Given our focus on the promise of a college education, we need to consider the economic returns to education, even though it ignores the wider benefits of education because this is the evidence used to support the claim that education pays. Most of the superrich have a bachelor's degree or higher, usually from a highly ranked university, but they represent a fraction of employees with college degrees.[11]

Any review of the returns to human capital is hampered by the fact that many economists have been asking the wrong questions. Studies are usually based on comparing the average incomes of those who go to college and those who don't. This way, they can roughly calculate the lifetime premium associated with going to college. This is the evidence governments like to hear because it supports the claim that learning is earning, as average college-educated employees earned 75 percent more than noncollege workers in 2005, an increase from a figure of 68 percent in 1997. But it cannot be taken to indicate the rising value of a college education because it may reflect the declining incomes of those who did not go to college.

There is also a problem using averages to represent the fates of those with a college education, because, as the well-known joke goes, when Bill Gates walks into a bar, on average, everyone becomes a millionaire, even as Gates gives away most of his fortune to charitable causes. However, while the average shoots up when Gates enters the bar, the median doesn't change. That is, if you were to line up all the people in the bar in an income parade with Bill Gates at one end down to the lowest earners as the other, the median is the middle earner. Using an income parade allows comparisons between higher earners (standing at the 90th percentile) and low earners (standing at the 10th percentile). This type of evidence offers a much better way of understanding exactly who has or has not been earning through learning.

The headline story figure 8.1 presents is not one Americans have been accustomed to hearing. Only males and females in the higher earner category (90th percentile) enjoyed any significant growth in real income since 1973, as they accelerated away from the rest since 1989. Many of these top earners studied at elite universities, given the way employers target recruitment in search of top talent. For most, however, a college education has failed to deliver any additional premium on investments in human capital compared to those in the job market in the 1970s. Incomes have flat lined for men, and there has been a modest increase for median-earning women over this period.

This figure also shows that females with a college education continue to earn less in each of the earning categories than males, although the overall gap has narrowed. But the most striking difference is the way female and male top earners have raced away from the rest. They now earn around four times as much as lower earners of the same sex.[12] This underlines the need to avoid talking about the average college graduate because, when it comes to income returns from individual investments in education, some are far more equal than others.[13]

There are also huge variations in incomes when gender is linked to race. White men with a bachelor's degree on average earn around $12,000 a year more than black or Hispanic men with the same qualifications. The difference between white men and Hispanic females widens to more than $20,000 a year.[14] The fallout from the economic recession

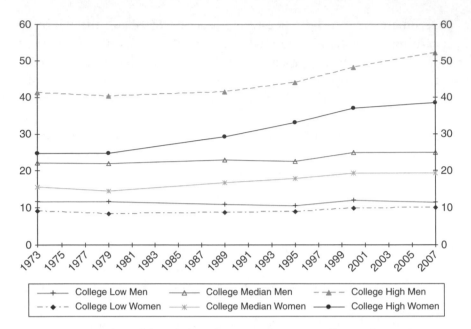

FIGURE 8.1 Male and female hourly wages for U.S. college-educated, 1973–2007 (deciles, 2007 dollars). *Note*: Low, median and high earners refer to, respectively the 10th, 50th, and 90th percentile wage. *Source*: Based on data from Lawrence Mishel, Jared Bernstein, and Heidi Shierholz, *The State of Working America 2008/2009* (Ithaca, N.Y.: Cornell University Press, 2009), p.174.

also shows unemployment rate for blacks with a college education rising more rapidly than for whites, Hispanics, and Asians. Figure 8.2 shows that unemployment for blacks jumped from under 3 percent to over 7 percent in just 2 years, almost twice the rate for whites.

In the United Kingdom, economists found a growing divergence in the incomes of male and female university graduates over the period 1994 to 2006. The benefits of a bachelor's degree at the top end of the wage distribution increased, but at the bottom end, they have sharply decreased.[15] They also found growing evidence of overqualification, forcing students into lower paying jobs for which a college education was not a requirement. This in part explains why a third of university students in England who had taken out government loans to pay for their studies since the introduction of tuition fees in 1998 have failed to repay anything. Their earnings were too low to reach the modest income threshold at which repayment is triggered.[16]

The divided fortunes of those in middle-class occupations is also shown in figure 8.3, which compares the hourly incomes of those in

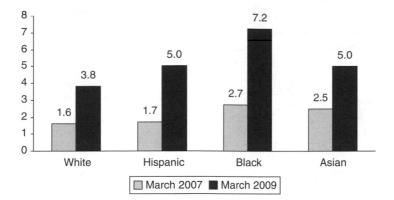

FIGURE 8.2 Unemployment rates for the college-educated, by race.
Source: Nonseasonally adjusted Bureau of Labor statistics data, http://www.
epi.org/economic_snapshots/entry/snapshots_20090422/

different occupations, including computer system analysts, lawyers, designers, and financial managers. Changes in the way occupations are classified make it difficult to compare over a longer time period, but figure 8.3 shows that those close to the top of the income parade earn two to three times more than those toward the lower end despite having the same occupation. In line with other evidence, it also shows how top earners pulled away from the rest as median earners in these occupations struggled to make much, if any, headway, whereas those paid less in each occupation saw their earnings flat line or decline.

There is a similar picture across all white-collar jobs, where only top earners increased their real incomes, and this was when financial markets were booming. There is little doubt that since 2005 there has been growing pressure on earnings that reveal a picture of static if not declining incomes for middle as well as low earners. There is also more pressure on top earners as they are being subjected to critical scrutiny.

Although it is difficult to assess the direct impact of the global auction on compensation,[17] evidence does show that the global auction is more than a bidding war between high- and low-cost workers—no matter how skilled—in different parts of the world. The auction has a different impact on Americans in the same occupation because the price competition tends to work as a forward auction for those at the top and as a reverse auction for those near the bottom of occupational groups. Take the example of university professors, where to date there is little evidence of competition involving cut-priced lecturers from

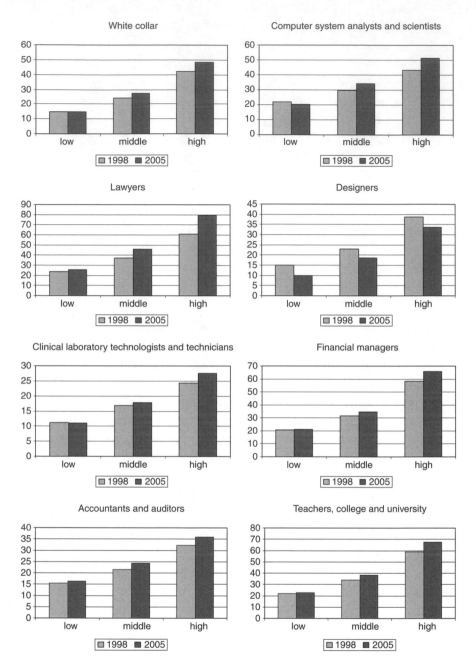

FIGURE 8.3 Hourly income for U.S. low, middle, and high earners within selected occupations, 1998–2005 (all workers, 2005 U.S. dollar). *Note*: Low refers to the 10th decile, middle to the 50th decile, high to the 90th decile. *Source*: Authors' own analysis of national compensation survey data, 1998 and 2005, Bureau of Labour Statistics. http://www.bls.gov/eci/

other countries. Yet global rankings of leading universities enhance the market position of elite academics in their field vis-à-vis other academic staff because they are seen to contribute to the reputational capital of the university for which they expect special privileges, including higher salaries. This does not obviously lead to pay cuts for the rest, but it weakens their bargaining position, especially when stringent budgetary constraints are imposed. This shows how the global auction operates in forward and reverse gears at the same time, shaping the relative fortunes of those in the same occupations in different ways.

More Than a Paycheck

Until now, we have focused on earnings which are only part of the overall rewards that accrue to workers, as health insurance and a decent retirement income also defined a middle-class occupation. But these are being slashed; in fact, for workers lower down the jobs pyramid, such benefits have been in decline for decades. In the 1970s, more than 60 percent of Americans had a company pension, but by 2006, fewer than 13 percent could rely on a company pension as their primary retirement plan.[18] This erosion of retirement income and health-care benefits has also become a characteristic of a growing proportion of those in middle-class occupations. Around 57 percent of college graduates had some form of private sector, employer provided pension in 2006, a decline from 61 percent in 1979.[19] These figures take no account of a major shift from defined benefit pensions to vastly inferior defined contribution 401(K) plans. A U.S. report on defined benefit pensions based on salary and years of service found that 51 percent of plans had been closed to new entrants and about half of the companies surveyed had one or more frozen plan.[20] Even before the stock market crash, the average person with a 401(K) plan was on track to retire with only 20–40 percent of what they need to maintain their standard of living, according to Ross Eisenbrey at the launch of Retirement USA.[21] The global downturn has accelerated the shift away from employer commitment to employee pensions, as many companies, including Forbes, J. P. Morgan, Chase, and Xerox, froze matched payments to employees on benefits plans, including 401(K)s, in response to the global recession.[22]

This story is repeated in respect to employer-provided health insurance. Remembering that about 45.7 million Americans had no private or public health insurance of any kind in 2007, the reduction in company-sponsored programs is putting increasing pressure on public funds when local, state, and federal budgets are in serious deficit.[23] Employer-provided health insurance fell from 51 percent in 2000 to 49 percent in 2006, with employees expected to pay over twice as much in annual premium contributions since 1999.[24] In the same period, executive, administrative, and managerial staff experienced a decline in coverage from 66 percent to 61 percent. Such evidence led Jared Bernstein and Heidi Shierholz from the Washington-based Economic Policy Institute to conclude that these losses in coverage in high-quality jobs are a reminder that occupational upgrading—the shift to jobs higher up the occupational ladder—does not ensure higher rates of health insurance coverage. "No one is immune to the slow unraveling of the employer-based system."[25]

Britain also has a pension crisis from which those in middle-class occupations are not immune, although a high quality National Health Service reduces the need for company-provided health insurance. In 1995, 5 million people remained in final-salary programs with a guaranteed proportion of their final salary in retirement, similar to the defined benefit pensions in the United States. But that number is now less than a million and likely to fall further as both public and private sector employers look to reduce costs. Three of four final-salary programs have already closed their doors to new members, and one in four of those that remain intended to follow suit.[26] This is to say nothing of longer working hours and the rise of the dual-earner family required to make middle-class ends meet in America and beyond.

Keeping the Promise of Human Capital Alive

To what extent are income inequalities in the earnings of those with a college education explained by the outstanding performance of a few in a global auction for skills? Gary Becker, awarded a Nobel Prize for his work on human capital, has highlighted what he sees as the "upside of income inequality," arguing that the earning gap has widened "because the demand for educated and other skilled persons is growing."[27] These inequalities, he argues, reflect the new realities of a global economy that offer exceptional rewards to those with scarce skills, knowledge, and talent at the same time as penalizing those with poor marketable skills or mediocre records of performance.

In *The Winner-Takes-All Society*, Frank and Cook are less sanguine about widening income inequalities in America, as they believe them to be unjust and a cause of economic inefficiency. They explain these inequalities in terms of winner-takes-all markets because they make "the most productive individuals more valuable, and at the same time have led to more open bidding for their services."[28] In line with Becker, they take for granted that the market value of the most talented is worth more due of their contribution to productivity.

The problem with this approach is that it continues to peddle the view that those who receive huge salaries deserve them, and the only thing stopping other people from doing the same thing is their failure to invest in their employability or to up their game. Here the analysis of the problem of wage inequalities is closely related to its remedy: if workers are in jobs that don't match their level of education or pay expectations, it is because they lack marketable skills. The solution is to give people incentives and opportunities to become more employable through education and training initiatives.

The growing number of high-skilled, low-wage workers is also considered to be a temporary phenomenon. As Americans start to read the market signals and retrain to enter new exciting areas of the economy, they will regain a competitive advantage over Chinese or Indian workers. We heard this view from Thomas Friedman in our earlier discussion, given a belief that there are no limits to the number of idea-generating jobs that could be created to compensate for those lost to Asia, even if there are limits to the expansion of manufacturing employment. But where are these new jobs?

They depend on an article of faith rather than hard evidence. It was difficult to find much support for a significant, let alone exponential, increase in demand for high-skill workers in new innovative fields even when the American economy was booming. Although the Bureau of Labor Statistics' estimate that most of the jobs with the fastest growth rate will require a bachelor's degree, most people will continue to work in occupations that require low levels of education and training. The bureau also shows that the proportion of the workforce requiring a bachelor's degree or higher is expected to remain almost unchanged between 2006 and 2016, rising from 20.6 percent to 21.7 percent.[29] This amounts to around a fifth of all jobs, whereas over a third of the workforce will be employed in low-skill jobs requiring little, if any, training.

The shift to a low-carbon economy is unlikely to change this picture despite predictions of up to 4 million new manufacturing jobs. Many of these jobs will be routine, although electronics engineers will be required to develop cost-competitive batteries for the next generation of electric cars, and mechanical engineers are needed to create new production facilities. But entry-level jobs in the green economy start at $12 an hour, "much less than the now extinct $28 an hour job that had allowed high school educated workers in the auto sector to achieve middle class status."[30]

Income inequalities in America cannot be explained by a global auction for skills as the pundits of human capital assert. Although skills are important, it is jobs that are auctioned for which the market price can rapidly change irrespective of educational level. Equally, what people are capable of doing as opposed to what they actually do and how much they get paid for doing it are not the same thing, as there is a growing void between brainpower and market power. We therefore need to focus on how occupational opportunities are being transformed in the global division of labor rather than simply focus on the supply of marketable skills.

What really counts is how American workers stand relative to others in the competition for jobs and rewards, where wages not only reflect productive contribution but also the outcome of a power play over how jobs are defined and rewarded. We have explained how corporate executives have extended their powers over the global organization of production, enabling them to retain a larger share of profits for corporate shareholders rather than employees.[31] The effect has been to break the promise of the opportunity bargain.

A Global Auction for Jobs

The trends outlined in this book reveal a complex interplay between the global and local. The importance of national context in shaping the global auction for American workers is shown in cross-national studies of income inequalities. If wage inequalities are a reflection of the returns to human capital in the global market, we would expect to find a similar pattern in all high-cost countries. But countries including Sweden, Japan, and France have maintained much lower levels of income inequalities at the same time that America and Britain experienced a headlong rush to inequality. Of course, it is possible that these differences reflect a time lag, and other countries will witness a similar increase in wage inequalities in the future. Germany offers initial support for this view, given a significant increase in income inequalities since the turn of the century.[32]

Nonetheless, national differences remain in the way labor markets are organized and incomes distributed. This is true even for global elites as revealed in a comparison of top earners in Japan and the United States. In 1970, the top 1 percent accounted for roughly 5 percent of earned income in each country. This proportion hardly changed in Japan, but the top 1 percent in the United States doubled their share of waged income to almost 12 percent.[33] So much for the claim from American and British bankers that the extortionate incomes they command reflect their international market value rather than a rigged system for assessing corporate compensation.

The runaway salaries of those at the apex of America's job pyramid have not only been justified by the stories that elites tell themselves and propagate to others about how necessary they are to the leadership of American corporations. It has also depended on free market reforms initiated by Ronald Reagan and Margaret Thatcher. It is not only the greed of executives that is at issue; they are also the beneficiaries of a free market system that distorts income distribution in favor of a few. Free market policies shifted the balance of power in favor of shareholders and corporate bosses as much as the deregulation of global financial markets. By removing the potential for collective bargaining with the decline of union representation, market power became even more concentrated on the upper floors of corporate headquarters. Much like a game of Monopoly, unregulated markets have their own internal logic, as most of the money goes to those who own the houses and hotels on the prized streets of Manhattan. At the same time, these policies removed the social shock absorbers that gave protection to workers in other countries such as Sweden, France, and Germany.

In concluding his historical analysis of income inequalities, Emmanuel Saez identifies a number of factors to explain rising inequalities that not only include "underlying technological changes but also the retreat of institutions developed during the New Deal and World War II—such as progressive tax policies, powerful unions, corporate provision of health and retirement benefits, and changing social norms regarding pay inequality." This led him to suggest that "we need to decide as a society whether this increase in income inequality is efficient and acceptable and, if not, what mix of institutional reforms should be developed to counter it."[34] Indeed, the rolling back of social entitlements such as retirement pensions and redundancy payments achieved by American and British workers after World War II has exposed the underlying reality of the global auction based on a cash nexus. Although this process began with the renaissance of neoliberalism under Reagan and Thatcher, it has accelerated under the austerity measures introduced after the 2008 financial crisis. This is an issue to which we will return in the final chapter, but there is another argument popular with American economists embracing the view that income inequalities are a result of changes in technologies.

Is There a Hi-Tech Elephant in the Room?

The idea that income inequalities are explained by the introduction of new technologies rather than global trade is intuitively attractive. It asserts that as new technologies are introduced into the workplace, some jobs are automated while more skilled workers are required to exploit the productive potential of new technologies. Widening income inequalities reflect the growing disparity in productivity achieved by high- as opposed to low-skill employees. "It seems undeniable," suggests Paul Krugman, a Nobel Prize winner, "that the increase in the skill premium in the advanced world is primarily the result of skill-biased technological change."[35] Other luminaries like Lawrence Summers reaffirmed this view, claiming that "most of the observed increases in income inequality in the American economy are due to new technology rather than increased trade," although he does recognize the threat of the global auction.[36]

The idea that new technologies usually demand higher levels of skill has led economists to present education and technology as a race in which the supply of educated workers needs to keep up with technology-led demand; otherwise, a shortage of skilled workers will lead to a polarization of incomes.[37] A major study by Claudia Goldin and Lawrence Katz documents how the supply of educated workers kept pace with demand for much of the twentieth century, which they called the century of human capital. But around 1980, they chart a slowdown in the supply of educated workers while the introduction of new information technologies increased demand for hi-tech workers. This mismatch between supply and demand is used to explain the polarization of incomes between higher- and lower-skill workers, as employers were forced to raise the salaries of qualified employees. As Katz suggests, information technologies are "complementary to workers at the top, a substitute for workers in the middle," and of little relevance to those at the bottom of the income ladder.[38] In line with human capital theory, their remedy is more high-quality education for American workers to close the gap between the supply and demand for skilled labor not simply because it would increase the wages of a large proportion of the workforce but also reduce the cost of skilled labor already in the job market.

Goldin and Katz's remedy rests on differences in earnings between college graduates and nongraduates, but this is only part of the story because as we've seen it ignores big differences in earnings among college graduates within the same occupations. It is little comfort to college graduates to be earning more than nongraduates if their incomes have either flat lined or declined.

One of the fundamental problems with a skill-biased explanation for income polarization is that it fails to consider the wider employment, organization, and political context that determine the way technology is used and rewarded in the workplace. The early days of mechanical Taylorism are worth revisiting to highlight the limitations of the skill-bias approach. We've already shown how the moving assembly line was developed to eliminate the need for skilled workers in the introduction of mass production. Although new technologies utilized low skills, it was the development of office work within corporate bureaucracies that led to a rise in the demand for more skilled workers, not the technology per se.[39] Without the creation of mass consumer markets, large corporate bureaucracies would not have emerged. In turn, corporate profits depended on paying high wages to low-skill workers to give them the money to buy consumer goods rolling off the production line. Where there were disputes between employers and labor unions, the state bought industrial peace through extending its welfare provisions. As the white-collar sector grew, so did the demand for educated labor, but the demand for skilled workers was largely a secondary effect of mass production and also dependent on a range of other social, political, and economic factors, including the expansion of public sector employment. The hypothesis, then, that there is a direct connection between income, technology, and the supply of skilled labor does not stand up to scrutiny.

It also falls foul of the growing evidence on the impact of new technologies in the global auction for jobs. Although Goldin and Katz offer an impressive account, they see the issue of new technology and education in national rather than global terms, perhaps because America was an early mover in the IT revolution and they consider that it will remain dominant. But we've shown how that advantage is rapidly eroding. The story of progress they want to tell can only be preserved at the cost of ignoring the role of new technologies in the creation of the global auction, especially a high-skill, low-wage workforce. There is little account of how low-cost locations have implemented hi-tech, low-cost solutions, reducing the market price of technical know-how in America.

It also ignores the employment implications of digital Taylorism, which could help explain why the fruits of technological innovation may not lead to high-skill, high-wage employment for college graduates. Digital Taylorism is not simply creating a polarization between high- and low-skill workers but also the fragmentation of middle-class occupations, where the benefits of productive growth are concentrated in the hands of executives and senior personnel, especially when combined with a shareholder model of corporate governance. The irony is that without the introduction of new information technologies, the global auction for high-skill, low-wage work would have been impossible.

A Global Middle Class

The idea of a high-skill, low-wage workforce is to look at the world through American eyes. What is regarded as a low wage for a college-educated employee in Chicago or Detroit is likely to be viewed as living the dream in Nanjing or Kolkata. The paradox of the global auction is that at the very time it threatens the livelihoods of America's middle classes, it creates the potential for new middle classes to emerge, as Asian workers use their price advantage in the competition for tradable goods and services. As their domestic economies expand, higher-skill workers are also required to meet the demand of local consumers for better goods and services, including accommodations, food, and education.

The people we met in China and India did not, at least openly, see themselves as winning at the expense of American workers despite considerable personal and national pride in what had already been achieved. A Chinese manager for a U.S. telecoms company in Beijing, told us that the economic rise of China and India was not a bad story for U.S. and European workers because when the Chinese take more professional jobs, Americans will move up their own value chain. "They will do something much more value added. It doesn't mean that they will lose their jobs. They may get another opportunity to upgrade themselves. Globalization means you serve me and I serve you. It doesn't mean I take your land, you lose your land. No, you have your own land. And you may have a better life; we may all have a better life."

We heard similar views expressed wherever we traveled, but in Bangalore, the chief information officer for a shared services company for U.S. clients recognized that American workers along with many Indians were not in a win-win global auction. "The way the world is structured, the rich always exploit the poor; it is a fact we can't deny it. Myself, I will look at the people who are lower than me in society, and I will take services and I will try to pay them lower. This is a fact; this is the way the whole world runs." He thought that the offshoring of information technology jobs to India had benefited well-educated Indians with better salaries, but most of the profits were going back to the Americans who fund the company. "That's the way it runs," but he also observed that "it's not going back to American workers. American workers are feeling more insecure; they're scared because they're losing their jobs."

He was also aware of a vast chasm in opportunities remaining in terms of education, jobs, or career prospects in his own country, as the economic boats which harbored the fortunes of individuals and families crisscross continents no longer restricted to national waters. They, too, face a global competition for jobs. In both India and China, employees with a college education working in managerial and professional jobs for international companies may have to work long hours and constantly feel the pressure of tough financial targets, but they are among the winners in the global auction.

In India, 76 percent of the population was living on less than $2 a day in 2005 despite having more billionaires than China. Before the global recession, Mumbai had the largest sales of Mercedes for any city in the world as well as large slums graphically depicted in the film *Slum Dog Millionaire*. Although there was a significant decline in the proportion of people living on less than $2 a day in China, from 85 percent in 1990 to 36 percent in 2005, a visitor to Beijing only has to walk through the marble malls to know that they have been built to serve a fraction of domestic customers who are wealthy beyond the imagination of many.[40] Winners and losers live side by side, creating first and third world conditions in both first and third world countries. Indeed, an overall decline in global economic inequalities is the flip side of widening social inequalities in affluent economies.[41]

Nevertheless, various attempts have been made to assess the growth of a global middle class, which depends on how the middle is defined, such as by income level preferred by economists or occupation preferred by sociologists. Invariably, studies attempting to assess the growth of the global middle class treat the world as a single country and use income data ranging somewhere between the rich and poor.

These definitions are also based on purchasing power parity (PPP) that offers a better indication of what you can buy with your dollars in different countries; a far lower level of income is required in China to achieve purchasing parity with people living in the United States.

Given wildly different definitions of middle-class income, it is unsurprising there is little agreement about the size of the global class.[42] Maurizio Bussolo and colleagues at the World Bank define the global middle class as those living between the per capita incomes of Brazil and Italy.[43] Using this definition, they calculate that it will expand from 7.6 percent in 2000 to 16.1 percent in 2030, which includes over a billion people in emerging economies able to buy cars, enjoy international tourism, and demand world-class products and quality higher education.[44] Figure 8.4 reveals the dominant role of the Chinese economy in explaining the rise of this new class. In 2000, China accounted for 13 percent of the global middle class, whereas by 2030, it is expected to account for 38 percent, with India accounting for a further 6 percent. Although the Indian proportion is much lower that China, it is expected to rapidly increase over the coming decades.

A study conducted by scholars at Nanjing University estimated that between 12–19 percent of the Chinese population were middle class based on having at least a bachelor's degree and earning 5,000 yuan

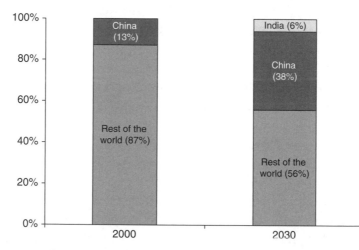

FIGURE 8.4 Chinese and Indians in the global middle class (percentage). *Source*: Maurizio Bussolo, Rafael E. De Hoyos, Denis Medvedev, and Dominique van der Mensbrugghe, *Global Growth and Distribution: Are China and India Reshaping the World?* The World Bank Development Economics Prospects Group Policy Research Working Paper 4392 (November 2007), 21.

($617) a month in a professional, technical, or managerial occupation.[45] In India, Rajesh Shukla, at the National Council of Applied Economic Research in New Delhi, reported that the middle class would rise from 5 percent in 2005 to around 20 percent in 2015.[46] But the problem with virtually all this evidence is that it bears little relationship to the way class has been historically understood. Being middle class is not only to stand somewhere between the rich and poor but is also defined by occupation linked to a lifestyle package, including a decent salary, career prospects, and a comfortable standard of living. There is little sense of a relationship between people in different social classes or between those in the same class living in different countries. It is far removed for Karl Marx's idea of a "class in itself" let alone a "class for itself" sharing worldviews with political significance. To date, in most of the studies of the global middle class, it means little more than a growing class of consumers who offer new market opportunities to Western companies.

The connection between the middle classes in developed and emerging economies hardly figures in their accounts because the American middle class is part of the global rich. Indeed, there is little expectation of a rapid convergence between incomes in rich and poor countries, as we've noted. The average resident in emerging economies receives about 16 percent of the average in high-income countries when measured in PPP terms: $4,800 versus $29,700. Average incomes in developing countries are projected to rise to 23 percent in 25 years time, as it is assumed that per capita incomes will continue to rise in high-income countries. Yet, as Bussolo and his colleagues acknowledge, "As the previous 25 years have shown, there is plenty of scope for surprises."[47]

Conclusion

This chapter reflects the reconfiguration of success, power, and progress shaping the future of America's middle classes. Global free trade was intended to deliver a high-skill, high-wage workforce, but it created something very different beyond even the imagination of the most Machiavellian of business leaders.[48] Corporate executives were the big financial winners, but in so doing, they not only unleashed an economic storm in Asia but also deep anxiety and disappointment eating away at the very foundations of American society. It has brought into question the rewards of a college education, and created an opportunity trap that is forcing people to go into self-denial in an attempt to win an advantage in the competition for a livelihood.

CHAPTER NINE

❦

The Trap

I think we are going to go through some very rough times here in the United States . . . even if they are very privileged, unless they are really focused they won't have a family supporting job.

—Leading Industrial Think Tank, Washington D.C.

We're not back there in '68 . . . our revolt is not to get more. It's to keep what we have.

—Nadjet Boubakeur (French Student Leader)[1]

T HE TRENDS PRESENTED in this book point to a chasm between the rhetoric of the opportunity bargain and the realities of the global auction because affluent societies find it difficult to provide middle-class jobs for their willing and educated workers. This has led social commentators to focus on the gap in life chances that results from inequalities in family wealth, racial discrimination, or gender rather than from the outcome of open competition based on individual abilities and efforts.

This focus on widening inequalities between winners and losers in the distribution of education, jobs, and rewards is to be welcomed, but at the same time, we should not lose sight of a deeper crisis at the heart of the American Dream. Explaining this crisis will show why extending opportunities based on human capital investment will not deliver individual freedom or prosperity but rather contribute to an opportunity trap. Far from being free to fulfill their aspirations, Americans are spending more time, effort, and money attempting to realize their opportunities, which inadvertently contributes to the social congestion they are seeking to avoid because we "are never really caught in a traffic jam, you are the traffic jam."[2] This suggests that at the same time that inequalities in the competition for a livelihood (gap) need to be addressed, we also need to consider the nature and consequences of the opportunity trap because it explains why a new opportunity bargain outlined in the final chapter requires a radically different approach to the typical policy prescriptions being offered today.

The Opportunity Gap

The opportunity gap remains a major political issue requiring urgent policy action. Although there have been significant improvements in the educational performance of female students and some evidence of a reduction in racial inequalities in academic performance, class divisions have widened at both ends of the social spectrum.

Commitment to the meritocratic ideal of a level playing field has been sacrificed in the battle for positional advantage. It has brought merit and the market into a head-to-head conflict. In the age-old battle between meritocratic competition and market choice that favors children from wealthier families, described by Michael Young in his classic account of *The Rise of the Meritocracy*, the commitment to meritocracy has been defeated by new forms of privilege, where millions are being excluded from any chance of receiving an education that would allow them an equal chance of competing with the sons and daughters of the wealthy.[3]

Evidence that inequalities are eating away at the capacity to rebuild the American Dream include James Heckman's influential research showing growth in both those gaining a college education and those entering the job market with no more that a high school education. The share of America's youth graduating with a college degree grew from 17 percent in 1980 to 36 percent by 2000 and is expected to rise to 43 percent by 2020. At the same time, young Americans entering the job market with only a high school education are also on the increase, from 31.5 percent of the age cohort in 1980 to 38 percent in 2000, and it is projected to reach 41.6 percent by 2020. Heckman argues that this polarization in educational achievement reflects income inequalities, as families living on poverty wages have lower educational aspirations and levels of achievement due to poor living conditions and a sense of hopelessness. Equally worrying is that more American children are being born into disadvantage than 50 years ago, contributing to a two-tier system of educational achievement.[4] Such evidence has led to a focus on early education, which is obviously to be welcomed. Yet the Scandinavian experience suggests that providing early childhood education on its own is not enough because the parents of poor children also need access to decent job prospects.

There is an equally urgent need to close the gap at the top end, as the elite universities from which the major corporations recruit are full of students from privileged backgrounds. In America, approximately 85 percent of those from the top income quartile go to a university, but just under 40 percent of those from the bottom quartile attend. However, among elite universities in America, those in the bottom quartile comprise only 11 percent. In Britain, those from the upper end of the social class structure dominate elite universities. The university with the highest percentage of students from professional and managerial backgrounds was Oxford with 90 percent followed by Cambridge with 89 percent.

Underlying these figures are inequalities in wealth and social capital. In America, the wealth amassed by a small elite, combined with changes to inheritance laws, has made it easier to transfer a larger share of assets to their children. This leads to a new form of privilege where the risks associated with the competition for a livelihood are removed. In a context of increasing positional competition, they seek to reproduce their advantage through wealth and ownership rather than credential competition. This is not to say that they will not buy access to elite kindergartens, schools, colleges, and universities, as this is an important source of social status and networking, but economic security has been bought in advance. This is likely to be seen as illegitimate even by the middle classes anxious to join them. Positional conflict has, therefore, not only cast the rich against poor but created a middle class at war with itself.[5]

If the American Dream is to be reclaimed, politicians cannot turn a blind eye to this elite self-recruitment. Even the right-wing Noble Prize winner James Buchanan has argued that when the wealthy die, their money should be returned to the community so as to preserve a meritocracy. It can't be right that selection to America's top universities amount to what Daniel Golden calls "affirmative action for rich white people" in his book on how America's elites buy their way into top universities. He argues that the children of wealthy or influential parents enjoy the "preferences of privilege." This means regular students applying to Ivy League universities may find themselves vying for only 40 percent of places because the rest are reserved for preferential candidates.[6]

Reforms to close the opportunity gap are therefore required at both ends of the social spectrum to create a fairer competition for a livelihood. We need to address the social exclusion of both the rich and poor. If we believe that the capabilities of all are worth cultivating as part of our common humanity, narrowing inequalities and attempting to create a level playing field in terms of family circumstances, neighborhood environment, and quality of schooling are not a recipe for a dull conformity. Rather, they are a way of ensuring that the cultural diversity of character, personality, and capabilities existing throughout the population may come to fruition.[7] The alternative is the development of resentment and despair for an increasingly disaffected middle and working class.

The Opportunity Trap

The trap points to increasing social congestion in the competition for decent jobs as people scramble for highly rated schools, colleges, and jobs. Indeed, increasing efforts to get ahead are contributing to the very social congestion that individuals and families are trying to avoid. If only a few adopt the same tactics to get ahead, such as intensifying efforts to get into a top university, do volunteer work to add value to one's résumé, or work late to impress the boss, it stands a chance of success. But if everyone adopts similar tactics, then no one gets ahead; it simply raises the entry bar or increases the number of hurdles. "If everyone stands on tiptoe, nobody gets a better view."[8] But if you don't stand on tiptoe, there is no chance of seeing.

In short, many aspiring Americans are compelled to take up the opportunity to enter this competition because it's the only game in town. This is why the opportunity bargain has turned into an opportunity trap. There are simply too many people wanting to make the same life journeys that depend on educational and occupational success highlighting the social limits to individual freedom.

Increasing social congestion is partly a consequence of greater personal freedom. Over the last century, there were more opportunities for people to break free of traditional roles within the family, employment, and wider community.[9] But the freedom to create one's own life project makes people more rather than less dependent on success in education and the job market. Today, opportunity comes with a responsibility to make something of oneself. To be judged by our own efforts is sacrosanct. The bottom line is that everyone is expected to work hard to build a livelihood and be self-sufficient rather than rely on welfare handouts. Although this has often given rise to a greater sense of personal freedom, individuals are not in control of their own destinies for the simple reason that the outcome of our efforts and abilities depends on the achievements of others.

Credentials, jobs, and income are all positional goods; what counts is how individuals are positioned relative to others, given a limited supply of places at highly ranked universities and with leading employers. When university rankings are taken to reflect differences in the caliber of students, where students are positioned within the academic status hierarchy is likely to have a significant impact on success in the job market. Likewise, at times of labor shortages, the long-term unemployed become employable, whereas when jobs are in short supply, they become unemployable if qualified job seekers are willing to accept poverty wages.

The role of positional goods is not readily understood in societies that are highly individualistic because people are encouraged to think of themselves as the agents of their own fate. This is obviously true in various aspects of our lives, such as the choice of a partner or whether to take illegal drugs, but we are all leading a *double life*. Fred Hirsch, who introduced the idea of positional goods, explains how our concept of the double life works in the context of education. He suggests that educational quality can be improved by having more receptive students, well-trained teachers, improved facilities, and so on, "but there is also a relative dimension, in which quality consists of the differential over the educational level attained by others." Therefore, if a key role of education is to judge students based on differences in academic performance, the possibility of general advancement is an illusion, even if there is an overall increase in educational standards.[10]

Unsurprisingly, the more stratified the society, the more position matters because social scarcity is a fact of life even in prosperous societies where most material needs could be met. Some will always be in better paid and higher status jobs than others, which is why there has been so much interest in whether these jobs are fairly allocated. Meritocracy is, after all, intended to give everyone an equal chance to be unequal, not to create social equality. This is also why it is misleading to focus on individual tales of personal triumph or failure. While we can all be encouraged to do our best, we cannot all be the best. We can't all go to the best universities or be a corporate executive (even if we wanted to) because such positions are relatively scarce. This means that what the American economy can offer to the winners cannot be offered to the population as a whole, no matter how well trained they are.

This reveals why the liberating consequences of a power shift from employers to knowledge workers has been greatly exaggerated and why it poses a major problem for the middle classes and aspiring working-class families who have little choice other than to trade on their human capital. The middle classes are only able to capitalize on their knowledge within employment. They are paid for doing a job, not for being well qualified. Consequently, power remains decisively with the employers. As German sociologist Georg Simmel observed a century ago, the freedom of workers is invariably matched by the freedom of employers in a money economy because workers may be free to change jobs, but they are not free from the need to make a living wage.

Far from being liberated from the jobs tournament, most people are more dependent on it than ever. In a buoyant job market, the balance of power between employees and employers is disguised by a healthy supply of job opportunities. But when the labor market slackens and unemployment rises, and as the reverse auction moves farther up the jobs pyramid, the realities of the opportunity bargain are thrown into sharp relief.

A High-Stakes Tournament

The opportunity trap is not a temporary problem resulting from economic recession but a capacity problem that afflicts many economies, including China and India. It is more acutely felt in America because it already has a large middle class in a high-stakes competition involving an increasing number of serious contestants.

Differences in the lifestyles of winners and losers in the jobs tournament have always existed, but increasing income inequalities since the 1980s have led to a dramatic increase in the stakes. These stakes have risen not only between those with high and low skills but also within jobs defined as managers, professionals, and executives. We have shown how the incomes of those within aspirational jobs have been stretched, making some far more equal than others, as pay and prospects for leadership talent pulled away from the rest.

The global auction for professional middle-class jobs also increased the stakes as areas of work previously thought to be immune from standardization or foreign competition now look vulnerable. The middle classes have little option other than to give it their best shot as they attempt to translate their financial and cultural assets into marketable knowledge, certificates, networks, and work experience. For most American families, there is little option other than to capitalize on these assets via education: there is no safety net for them, only the threat of downward social mobility with all that it entails. The daughters and sons from middle-class backgrounds may inherit material wealth, but usually, this extends to paying college tuition fees, contributing to a first mortgage, or purchasing a new automobile. However, it's inadequate to support a middle-class lifestyle.

America is also prone to the consequences of an opportunity trap for the simple reason that it already has a significant number of middle-class families that make further growth more difficult. Middle-class families now have to run faster and longer just to stand still. It is difficult for them to reach a higher social status than their parents simply because it is high in the first place.[11]

The expanding American middle classes since the 1950s increased the number of students that not only aspired to a university education but also expected to receive one. In some respects, this reflects a degree of success in opening educational opportunities to women, racial minorities, and those from less privileged backgrounds. Women, especially from more prosperous backgrounds, have become serious contenders for professional and managerial employment as they outperform male students in many areas of American education, although differences in subject choices and career prospects remain.

Widening educational opportunities have also helped working-class, mature, and ethnic minority students gain college credentials. While traditional patterns of working-class employment placed less emphasis on formal credentials, the opportunity to work up the organization from the factory floor has all but vanished. Cultural assumptions about manual work as proper work and the idea of a job well done no longer hold, leaving working-class males with few options other than to enter the competition for credentials or confront a life in dead-end, low-wage work. The decline of bureaucratic careers has made access to credentials an essential requirement, as there is less scope for occupational mobility within lean organizations without the appropriate certification. Consequently, aspiring working-class families have been forced into the scramble for paper qualifications even though they are at a distinct disadvantage compared to those from more affluent backgrounds.[12]

Credential Inflation and the Currency of Opportunity

A symptom of social congestion is credential inflation. The increasing numbers of college graduates entering the job market have forced employers to lift their entry requirements in an attempt to reduce the flood of applicants. The idea of credential inflation is similar to that of monetary inflation. If the increase in money supply and credit is greater than the supply of goods and services, it leads to rising prices. In other words, the dollar or euro in your pocket buys less. Equally, if more people gain the qualifications previously required for professional or managerial jobs and if the numbers of these jobs does not expand to meet the supply of qualified people, it leads to inflation and reduces the value of credentials in the job market.[13] As a result, the eminent sociologist Randall Collins observed that students who want to get ahead are forced to go back to college for longer periods to get more advanced qualifications. "One can predict that the process will continue to repeat itself at the more advanced level too. If in the future everyone had a Ph.D., law degree, M.B.A., or the like, then these advanced degrees would be worth no more than a job in a fast food restaurant, and the competition would move on to still higher degrees."[14]

Extended academic competition also adds to the rising cost of staying in the paper chase. The academic competition now extends well into students' 20s, and entrance fees at prep schools, colleges, and universities have risen steeply. The median cost for private high schools in America jumped by 79 percent over 20 years, with elite schools such as Milton Academy, Middlesex School, and Hotchkiss School all charging more than $33,000 a year for day students in 2009. To board costs another $10,000.[15] The cost of a bachelor's degree at private 4-year colleges also became more expensive. The annual cost of attending a private 4-year college doubled since the late 1970s from $15,000 to more than $32,000.[16] Although bursaries, scholarships, and endowment funds help those from less affluent backgrounds to meet the costs of higher education, 60 percent of new college graduates were averaging a debt of almost $23,000 in 2007. The debt for doctors, dentists, veterinarians, lawyers, and pharmacists averaged $100,000 with wide variations in future earnings.[17]

In England, private school fees rose by an average of 40 percent, double the rate of inflation over a 5-year period. As a result, the average worker in only 18 occupations in 2008 could reasonably afford to send his or her child to private school compared to 30 occupations in

2003. This made it more difficult for even scientists, engineers, veterinarians, and journalists to afford school fees, although at the time of writing university tuition fees are capped for home students.[18]

Credential inflation also has implications for employers' hiring practices. When employers are confronted with a large pool of applicants armed with the same credentials, they are forced into changing their hiring criteria. Simply lifting entry requirements as a way of reducing the numbers of applicants may prove to be counterproductive. It may lead to unrealistic expectations and job dissatisfaction. A number of companies told us that they carefully limited the number of M.B.A.s they hired because they were demanding and often had an inflated view of their own worth.[19]

Rather than constantly lift entry requirements, we have shown how employers pay more attention to the university's brand value as an indicator of quality: Does it carry the imprimatur of an elite or a second-chance institution? But as more paper qualifications enter circulation, employers have also turned to other ways of distinguishing between candidates. As one employer explained, "paper qualifications are the first tick in the box and then we move onto the real selection."[20] This suggests a change in the way company's view credentials because they are thought to reveal little about what they need to know when making hiring decisions. The credential represented discipline, perseverance, and rule-following behavior, highly valued in the bureaucratic organizations of the past.

Today, the selection criteria have been extended to include a range of behavioral competencies, including personal drive, self-reliance, and interpersonal skills. For aspirational jobs, individuals not only need the required credentials, but they must sell themselves to the employer by demonstrating, through interviews, psychometric tests, and assessment centers, that they are more employable than other candidates. Success in the labor market has come to depend on "personal capital": the (re)packaging of the self to capitalize on the personal qualities valued by employers.[21] This includes *hard* currencies, such as academic credentials, sporting achievements, or music prizes, and *soft* currencies, including social confidence, good communication skills, and social fit with colleagues and customers.

The focus on soft currencies gives the middle classes an additional advantage over those from less prosperous backgrounds due to their cultural capital, but it also threatens the value of their trade in credentials. At times, when employers freeze or slash their hiring plans, the problem of distinction through both hard and soft currencies becomes even more important as hundreds, if not thousands, of well-qualified candidates vie for scarce job openings with leading employers.

People may therefore be doing everything that is expected of them in terms of acquiring marketable skills, investing in further learning, or going that extra mile to meet unrealistic sales targets, but it may not deliver the expected returns in terms of jobs, salary, or career progression. The problem many confront today is that doing one's best may not be good enough. Even extraordinary efforts to improve performance will count for little if everyone else does the same thing. But whatever the outcome, the constant striving for distinction also comes at a personal price.[22]

The Price of Distinction

The personal costs of the trap continue to mount as individuals and families are forced to redouble their efforts to secure an advantage. Rather than opportunities extending individual freedom and fulfilling our dreams, they are making people increasingly self-centered, stressed, and unfulfilled as more and more effort, money, and time is spent doing what is necessary rather than for any intrinsic purpose. These unintended consequences of securing success reflect a lack of freedom for people to express their social worth or contribution to society other than through the job market. While those from disadvantaged social backgrounds confront the added obstacle of an opportunity gap, given a lack of material resources and often inferior schooling, they can at least point to these inequalities as evidence of a rigged competition that may preserve a degree of self-respect. But the middle classes have no one else to blame but themselves as they are assumed to have all the opportunities anyone could reasonably ask for, and even at times of economic recession, people continue to be judged by their own efforts to find employment.

In short, the pursuit of success harbors the danger of turning the self into a commodity.[23] We are being economically enslaved by our opportunities. Even the winners in the job market now live under permanent threat as their livelihood is not guaranteed for life. This was graphically illustrated by images of employees from Lehman Brothers being ushered out of a glass-plated corporate cathedral carrying their future employment prospects in cardboard boxes. Today, economic security involves a lifelong campaign to stay fit in a job—if currently in one—and to remain fit in the wider job market in the event of joining the ranks of surplus employees.

This democratization of job insecurity extends to all levels of the organization as companies constantly look to reduce labor costs. Robert Jackall observed in his study of corporate managers in the late 1980s that the real task for the ambitious manager became one of "how to shape and keep shaping others' perceptions of oneself...so that one becomes seen as 'promotable.'"[24] The same applies today, but this impression management is necessary to stay in a job. This relates to Richard Sennett's account of the new model worker, where people have to negotiate short-term relationships because there are no longer jobs for life. In the absence of permanent employment, people are forced to exploit their opportunities for permanent employability.[25] They also have to reinvest and reinvent themselves with new talents and skills because past performance is no guarantee of future employment, even discounting the achievements and talents they once had. The price of success becomes self-denial, the suppression of feelings, interests, and activities that do not conform to the perceived requirements of an occupational career.[26]

This adds to the importance of personal capital over human capital. Personal capital does not refer to the size of one's bank balance but to the extent the self can be packaged to capitalize on personal qualities valued by employers. It reflects the importance of the self as a key economic resource in the market for managerial and professional work.[27] The threads of identity, experience, knowledge, and social circumstances now need to be explicitly drawn together in the calculus of employer judgments of individual economic worth. Even those from more privileged backgrounds can no longer capitalize on their cultural backgrounds, extracurricular activities, and social networks, unless packaged in ways that organizations benchmark as indicative of managerial or professional talent.

Work and educational experience has to be packaged in a *narrative* of employability which involves constructing life stories of productive achievements and future promise that must be constantly sold to employers throughout a career. And while these are important now, more is required suggesting a significant extension of economic rationality. Even for the wealthy, the economy of experience is no longer a passive consequence of living a privileged life or coming from a privileged background. It has to be worked at as a life project where the things we do and how they are understood are packaged as personal capital rather than in terms of intrinsic human experience.[28] Sports, hobbies, voluntary work, and evening classes are all things that were done for fun, self-fulfillment, or through a sense of social responsibility.

But for those chasing their occupational dreams, they have become of strategic importance in adding value to their résumé.

Player Behavior

The battle for distinction has also resulted in increasing cultural confusion within the middle classes as the rules of meritocratic competition—that legitimated their social standing in the past—have crumbled under the competitive strain without any widely accepted alternative. The opportunity trap has led to increasing use of player tactics in the competition for a livelihood. In *The Mismanagement of Talent*, Phillip Brown and Anthony Hesketh draw a contrast between *purists'* and *players'* tactics in the competition for the tough entry jobs in the United Kingdom. The purists viewed employability as winning a competitive advantage in a meritocratic race, where differences in individual achievement reflected innate ability, effort, and ambition. Work was viewed as an expression of the self. Securing the right job involved developing good self-presentation skills so that employers could see the genuine article. Hence, individual employability amounted to a technical puzzle of finding employment that offered the right fit with their knowledge, skills, and aspirations. This was consistent with the middle-class ethos of meritocratic achievement; hence, the idea of the purists is synonymous with those who seek to preserve the established rules of the game.

But when the going gets tough, more college graduates are resorting to players' tactics. They reject the meritocratic ideal of matching the right person to the right job based on abilities, achievements, and the authentic self. Players seek a positional advantage by modeling and marketing themselves in ways that conform to the behavioral competencies required by employers. They use social contacts to decode the winning formula, attend workshops that simulate group exercises at assessment centers, read books on how to answer difficult interview questions, and practice psychometric tests. They understood the task as learning to be competent at being competent.[29]

The proliferation in player behavior extends to parents as they mobilize whatever material or cultural assets they can bring to bear on the outcome of the competition for the best schools, colleges, and universities. Some parents suddenly discover religion to get their child into a local faith school with a good reputation. The use of private education, tutors, counselors, and career specialists has become de rigueur. In a political system based on the sovereignty of the market, it is an expression of doing the best for one's child rather than cheating on society. In *The Cheating Culture*, David Callahan describes how Americans are breaking the rules to get ahead. "When profits and performance are the only measure of success, old-fashioned ideas about fairness go out the window."

Along with many other examples, he cites the case of Dr. Dana Luck, a psychiatrist in Westchester County, who had a sudden increase in the number of local teenagers she was asked to evaluate for even the slightest evidence of learning disability. The cause was a College Board ruling giving students with disabilities extra time on Standard Attainment Tests (SATs). This led to diagnosis shopping as wealthy parents attempted to gain official recognition of disability to allow their children a better chance of doing well in the SATs. Dr. Luck expressed little doubt that parents could find what they wanted at the right price, but students from poorer families with genuine learning disabilities may go without diagnosis because they can't afford the cost. As Callahan concludes, "Although it is well known that academic cheating by students has reached an all-time high, it's also true that parents and tutors and other adults are increasingly helping students do whatever it takes to get an edge in their high-stakes educational career."[30]

Players' tactics are not restricted to America, as cheating in examinations is on the increase almost everywhere. The global recession in China led to a 20 percent increase in the numbers taking the screening test to enter China's civil service, with 775,000 people competing for just 13,500 jobs. This produced a boom in dishonesty, as about 1,000 candidates were caught cheating during national entrance examinations, including the use of hi-tech listening devices so accomplices outside could whisper answers to the person taking the test. According to a newspaper report, one would-be cheater got into trouble with the authorities after paying a con artist 12,000 yuan ($1,756) for a copy of the entrance test paper. On realizing that the paper was a fake, as none of the questions appeared on the genuine paper, he complained to the police.[31]

This climate of players' behavior has a significant impact on the experience of childhood. The priority is to treat and train children in ways that are demanded for success in this new rat race rather than in ways that benefit the child as an intelligent and well-rounded individual. Many young people are "growing up absurd" in a grade-obsessed society.[32] In the United Kingdom, high school parent evenings to discuss student progress involve little discussion of the student's social development or what has been taught. Each student is represented by a set of benchmark grades: "Your child is working at a level five in geography," presumed to be good. "Your child is working at a level three in math," presumed to be bad. "To sum up your child, she is just above average"!

But anything less than top grades has become tantamount to failure. This leaves little room for experimentation, creativity, or mistakes. *Inquisitive* learning that is driven by an interest in knowledge and learning for its own sake is squeezed out by consumer-driven demand for *acquisitive* learning. It involves learning what is necessary to pass examinations or motivated by a need to impress employers with one's range of extracurricular activities and achievements. It is based on a model of individual rational calculation where the wider purpose of learning has been lost. This leaves many American students with a knowledge of how to get ahead but little understanding of why they do what they are doing.

This is not a problem restricted to America or Britain; children around the world now confront batteries of tests from the time they leave their baby carriages. It is a lengthening obstacle course that extends into their late 20s, and intense supervision gives children little room for individual expression. Given China's highly competitive education system, *Harvard Girl Yiting Liu* was on the bestseller booklist for over 16 months and sold more than 3 million copies within 2 years of publication. The book represents a do-it-yourself guide to getting your child into an elite foreign university such as Harvard or Oxford. It tells of how Yiting Liu's parents adopted a scientific method of child rearing based on the teachings of a little known eighteenth-century German priest named Carl Weter. The priest had applied his innovative approach to child rearing to his son who learned six languages by the age of 9 and obtained two doctorates by the age of 16. In a *Time Magazine* article "Eyes on the Prize," Yiting's parents explain that a lot of Chinese parents "just let their kids play until they're six," but Yiting's education started at 15 days old when she started to receive massages to stimulate her senses. Relatives were drafted to talk non-stop during the infant's every waking hour, a verbal barrage "crucial to developing IQ," according to Yiting's mother. "If we wanted Liu Yiting to grow up to be an exceptional person...she would have to be able to withstand great psychological pressures and physical trials," included long-distance swimming and holding ice cubes until her hand turned purple.[33]

This may sound extreme, but a world survey conducted by the journal *Nature* found that when asked what they would do if others in their child's class were using Ritalin—the widely used treatment for attention-deficit hyperactivity disorder (ADHD)—to improve their grades, more than a third felt they would feel under pressure to give it to their children.[34] Many middle-class parents have already taken the plunge as the numbers of children in America taking Ritalin or the like doubled in the 1990s. The U.S. National Institute on Drug Abuse reported that Ritalin was being used by 2.4 percent of 8th graders, 3.4 percent of 10th graders, and 4.4 percent of 12th graders, which amounts to millions of American schoolchildren in 2005. Such trends led Mary Eberstadt to ask why "millions of middle- and upper-middle class children are being legally drugged with a substance so similar to cocaine that, as one journalist accurately summarized the science, 'it takes a chemist to tell the difference?'"[35]

Conclusion

In the second half of the twentieth century, many appeared to benefit from widening opportunities linked to the expansion of white-collar work. This led the German-born sociologist Ralph Dahrendorf to conclude that "wherever possible, people will try to make headway by their own efforts. In the United States, this has long been the dominant mode of conflict. Today the same is true in most countries. Individual mobility takes the place of the class struggle."[36] Today, opportunity, rather than being the glue that bonds the individual to society, has become the focus for intense social conflict. The blind faith in the market to deliver decent jobs to American workers has contributed to social congestion and a waste of social resources and human effort, as many compete for prizes that only a few can achieve.[37]

The opportunity trap reflects this rupturing of the meritocratic link among education, jobs, and rewards that cannot be solved by further investments in human capital because the job market can no longer bear the weight of social aspiration, especially when there is an international bidding war for middle-class jobs. Any attempt to reconnect prosperity and justice will therefore require nothing less than a new opportunity.

CHAPTER TEN

A New Opportunity

This is our time—to put our people back to work and open doors of opportunity for our kids; to restore prosperity and promote the cause of peace; to reclaim the American Dream and reaffirm that fundamental truth—that out of many, we are one; that while we breathe, we hope, and where we are met with cynicism and doubt, and those who tell us that we can't, we will respond with that timeless creed that sums up the spirit of a people: yes, we can.

—President Barack Obama[1]

THIS BOOK EXPLAINS why the American Dream needs to be reclaimed as people struggle to live the promise of education, jobs, and rising incomes. Occupational change over the last century has been remarkable. However, the idea that a global job market would accelerate the demand for highly paid knowledge workers and that Americans would monopolize the best jobs and leave emerging economies to become the new workshops of the world has proved false.[2] We now confront the prospect of a high-skill, low-wage workforce that poses a challenge to all affluent economies.

The vast chasm between middle-class aspirations and the realities of the global auction reflects an explosion in education and know-how and the growing capacity for hi-tech work in low-cost locations. The rise of digital Taylorism involves the translation of various forms of knowledge work into working knowledge that can be digitally distributed worldwide. The war for talent, which focuses on the outstanding performance of a global elite of employees, leads to steeper income differentials between the best and the rest. For many, including well-qualified Americans, these trends have conspired to undermine the value of their human capital that promised individual prosperity and social justice.[3] Indeed, the need to bailout Wall Street was not only symptomatic of human avarice in the banking industry but also symptomatic of a faltering economy struggling to create jobs offering incomes needed to support middle-class lifestyles, even in many families where both partners were in waged work. Easy credit and the rising cost of real estate became substitutes for employment-driven prosperity.

The consequences of the global auction for American workers have been our main focus, but it is important to remember that this is only a part of the story, albeit an important one. A wider human story involves the astonishing development of China and India, which have made the global auction for knowledge and skills a reality. What took Western economies centuries of technological, educational, and economic change to achieve has been matched in emerging economies in decades.

But what we have called an inside-out model of economic development has given rise to social arrangements far removed from the "flat world" depicted by Thomas Friedman. The world has become more uneven, fragmented, and uncertain. It is common for those living in the same neighborhoods to inhabit different economic worlds in many emerging economies, but these inequalities and widening economic divisions are also evident in the developed economies as the connections between education, jobs, and incomes have broken down.

There is therefore nothing inherent in twenty-first-century economies that require them to become fairer or more egalitarian. Having said that, there are now signs that social inequalities are moving up the political agenda. On a return visit to assess the impact of global recession on government strategies in China and India in late 2009, the need to tackle rising inequalities because of their potential for social unrest has become a pressing policy issue. A senior business advisor in New Delhi had no doubts that a large young population locked outside the Indian Dream was "explosive material" that had to be defused by spreading the benefits of globalization more widely.[4]

The global auction offers further evidence, if any were now needed, that for this to be achieved, the market can't be left to its own devices. In America, it requires nothing short of a new opportunity bargain based on an alternative political economy of hope. Part of this hope results from the fact that recent economic change around the world shows that America is not locked into a neoliberal future from which there is no escape. This is because markets are socially constructed. They are shaped by political choices that will decide whether prosperity and social justice can be reconciled.[5]

The arguments presented in this book will no doubt generate contrasting reactions. In America, there will be those who will try to use it to support greater protectionism, whereas others will argue that we've exaggerated the nature and consequences of the global auction. Some will continue to assert that a neoliberal approach based on free markets (including international trade) remains the best way to deliver prosperity and social justice. We will briefly respond to these positions before arguing that they miss a window of opportunity to do things differently that would be of far greater benefit to present and future generations both in America and beyond.

A New Protectionism or Thinking beyond Borders

Even before the financial meltdown, people were losing faith in the neoliberal bargain. A survey on the future prospects for American families and workers found that 90 percent agreed with the statement, "25 years ago, if you worked hard and played by the rules, you would be able to have a solid middle-class life." When asked if this still applied, those who agreed plummeted to 49 percent. This 2006 survey also asked about returns on investments in education which found over half of those sampled believed that "even with a college degree, it is difficult to find good jobs and financial security in today's economy."[6]

Despite this growing skepticism, we thought that middle-class Americans would try to deal with the fallout from the global auction as a private trouble that would lead them to double their efforts to find a decent job. But following the global recession, the broken promises of education, jobs, and incomes have become more visible and painful. As good jobs remain hard to find, a sense of frustration, if not betrayal, may lead to a concerted backlash against the global auction, blamed for the declining fortunes of American workers. There are regular calls for American workers and companies to be protected from unfair foreign competition as their trade in knowledge and skills are undercut by low-cost competitors. International bodies such as the Organisation for Economic Co-operation and Development, United Nations, and World Bank have all expressed concerns about a rising wave of protectionism leading to new barriers to international trade.

Although these calls for protection against foreign competition are understandable, they ignore the fact that the neoliberal obsession with market forces left Americans exposed to the full impact of the global auction. It also ignores new global realities that mean America can no longer call all the shots. America's political elites took it for granted that they would win the knowledge wars, given the nation's technological and financial clout. This neocolonialist view of the world, shared by many in Western Europe, continues to color the way many Americans judge other countries. They map national divisions, including developed and developing, head and body, successful and failed, superior and inferior, or advanced and primitive, which in turn are never far removed from a world divided between us or them, eyeing up the threat that other nations pose to our jobs, our prosperity, and our future. Inequalities and a sense of social justice are equally bound to a sense of nationhood. The focus on inequalities within nations is obviously important, but it tends to draw an invisible border around the sphere of social concern and responsibility, fueling calls for protectionism. Perhaps this made more sense in an era of walled economies, where much of what was produced was for domestic consumption, but not today.

Our social, religious, and economic relations sprawl across the globe; we can no longer talk of comparative advantage without also talking about comparative responsibilities. The reality is that our economic interdependence doesn't stop at national borders. It is well known that paper, printing, gunpowder, and the compass were all invented in ancient China and later developed around the world with profound implications for modern civilization. Today, while we sleep, people in far-off countries are issuing us tickets for flights, building our cars, manufacturing components for our television sets, undertaking diagnostic tests for our medical conditions, as well as supplying doctors, nurses, and scientists, along with babysitters, cleaners, and janitors. If you look around the room or check the labels on the clothes you are wearing, it's a material United Nations. While it's true that most of these products are from a small number of emerging economies dominated by China, we can no longer pretend that the Chinese Dream, Indian Dream, or Vietnamese Dream has nothing to do with the American Dream. They are now intimately connected. Our opportunities shape the opportunity of others, often thousands of miles from home, and vice versa.[7]

In response, the temptation will be to protect American workers from foreign competition. The deeper the job cuts in the private sector—along with a cull of government-funded jobs to reduce the colossal national debt—the louder the calls for protectionism. Yet what exactly is being protected is not clear cut in an increasingly interconnected world, where the movement of data and information becomes as important as the exchange of goods, making it difficult to police border infringements. Returning to the economic nationalism of the 1950s would also harm the livelihoods of millions of families living in emerging economies, with as much right to aspire to a better standard of living as those living in affluent Western societies. It is worth remembering that it was not only Americans who lost their jobs when $4.32 trillion was wiped off the value of global markets.[8] There were also massive job losses in Guangzhou, individual destitution in Reykjavik, and corporate suicides in Mumbai.

Most important of all, the global economy cannot be shut down without disturbing consequences. China and India are on the move, and greater protectionism in the West holds the prospect of knowledge wars descending into real wars, given the ensuing scramble for the dwindling supply of natural resources, including oil, gas, and water. The huge federal bailout of America's financial sector has also made America more dependent on large inflows of foreign capital from China and the oil-rich Middle East, as they bought up debt on either side of the Atlantic. James Fallows, writing in *The Atlantic Magazine* shortly before the financial meltdown, observed how China's trade surplus was used to prop up the credit-driven lifestyles of American consumers. "In effect," he suggests, "every person in the (rich) United States has over the past 10 years or so borrowed about $4,000 from someone in the (poor) People's Republic of China."[9]

There would also be more than a whiff of hypocrisy as America and Britain championed global free trade and attempted to impose its model of free market capitalism as the only viable model for everyone else to follow. Some of the countries that rejected this ideology are now shaping the future of the global economy. After 30 years of preaching to the developing world about the virtues of deregulated markets and imposing them on Asian economies in response to the financial crisis of 1997, it would be hugely damaging for America to initiate a new era of protectionism.

There needs to be an alternative to both protectionist barriers to international competition and free trade of the neoliberal variety, which leaves workers exposed to the full force of the global auction, with little hope of competing against high-skill, low-wage workers across Asia, South America, and Eastern Europe. The neoliberal opportunity bargain has contributed to rising inequalities and market congestion that will not be resolved through greater protectionism. But whichever way we look at it, Americans can no longer be asked to depend on investing in human capital at the same time that welfare has been degraded and the trading position of the middle classes severely weakened.

Business as Usual

The neoliberal opportunity bargain has been so fundamental to the way prosperity and social justice have been understood that there is likely to be a strong reaction to our explanation of the global auction and the broken promises that it entails. There are those who will argue that we've exaggerated the threat of offshoring to middle-class jobs. Instead, they will argue that the global auction poses little more than a short-term blip as Americans respond to changing economic conditions on the way to a new win-win where all can still gain from the existing bargain.

We have acknowledged that it is difficult to assess the extent of offshoring or its future consequences. Yet this does not mean that we should ignore research, including Alan Blinder's calculation that between 22 percent and 29 percent of all U.S. service sector jobs could be offshored with little or no degradation in quality. Although some have argued that this exaggerates the problem, others have argued that it's an underestimation.[10] Time will tell. But an exclusive focus on the numbers of existing jobs being offshored from America to low-cost competitors ignores the question of where new jobs are going to be created.

This is why we need to consider the wider context of economic change that has witnessed the rising economic power of China along with the other BRIC economies. If we see the question of offshoring purely in terms of neoclassical theories of free trade, we miss the much larger point about how economic power in terms of capital, knowledge, innovation, and investment is being transformed.

Instead of the win-win scenario painted by free trade evangelists, some Americans are losing out. Leading American economists such as Paul Samuelson, Ralph Gomory, and William Baumol have shown that, even within neoclassical trade theory, it is possible to see that there are conditions under which some countries lose while others gain. Their argument is not that all trade is harmful to a country's interests but that under certain conditions, "the improvement of one country's productive capabilities is attainable only at the expense of another country's general welfare." The difficulty with this account is that it tends to ignore the fact that winners and losers live in the same country, as international trade has further enriched the wealthy and powerful in America at the expense of an increasing proportion of middle-class families.

Despite these disparities in economic fortunes, it remains widely assumed that a new win-win is just around the corner for those who invest in their human capital. This new win-win rests on the idea that China and India will provide exciting new opportunities for college-educated workers in the West as consumers in emerging markets begin to demand better-quality products and services. But we cannot return to business as usual for a number of reasons.

The first problem stems from the idea that the latest "gale of creative destruction" will release capital from dying sectors to new industries, enabling well-educated workers to capitalize on the new opportunities both at home and overseas.[11] This hope fails to understand that the next generation of innovative companies may not be American, and even if they are, they are likely to be less dependent on the talents of American workers.

The second reason that leads us to reject the idea of a new global win-win concerns the view that emerging countries have limited capacity to undertake high-level innovative research compared to America and other Western nations. This argument relies on an outdated view that has yet to acknowledge the globalization of research and development because there is less need for U.S. companies to concentrate their research activities at home. It also ignores the changing role of America's leading universities. When universities are free to play the global market, they are less constrained by national loyalties in the pursuit of knowledge (and profits). As we've documented, collaborative arrangements between universities mean that research breakthroughs in California can be capitalized on in Beijing, and vice versa. We have also expressed concern about the hollowing out of American and British science and technology, as graduate programs in these fields are dominated by Asian students. Overseas graduates once stayed to establish businesses in, for example, Silicon Valley and Route 128. Now they are returning to Asia to take advantage of expanding domestic markets.

A further contention is that while the elite institutions in China and India may produce graduates to rival the West, they have, as someone suggested to us, "no bench." They do not have the capacity to roll out the numbers of college graduates necessary to service the global demand for high skills. This is an optimistic view of a rapidly changing situation. Both China and India have policies and resources in place to raise the standards of their universities and hence the supply of good college graduates. And when the supply of graduates from all the developing countries is taken into account, it is not at all clear why Americans and others living in high-cost Western countries will be preferred. Having said that, some Americans with niche skills may make a decent living from the expansion of China and other emerging economies, but their numbers may be far fewer than hoped. In short, we have entered an era where business as usual is no longer an option.

A New Opportunity Bargain

The question is how to rebuild an opportunity bargain that can respond to the global auction and keep alive the prospect of a fairer and sustainable world. This will require a democratic conversation about new priorities that link economic activity to the quality of life that cannot be captured by the size of a person's paycheck or national per capita income. As the relationship between prosperity and justice has unraveled, a new bargain can no longer be limited to widening opportunities because it requires nothing short of a social revolution in the way we think about fairness both in access to education and jobs but in the way economic prosperity is shared. The moral bankruptcy of the financial markets and the scale of public debt that has engulfed America and Europe make the need for such a conversation all the more urgent. If this were not enough, there are also environmental limits to further economic growth that will also require a great deal of genuine knowledge work in the search for a progressive way forward.

To build a society that is both economically and socially sustainable will continue to depend on finding new sources of economic competitiveness along with government action to build a more inclusive society. This action will be required at both ends of the social spectrum, incorporating those who are currently marginalized by extremes of poverty and wealth. As American philosopher John Dewey observed, "Every expansive era in the history of mankind has coincided with the operation of factors which have tended to eliminate distance between peoples and classes previously hemmed off from one another."[12]

Prosperity

One of the most effective ways to respond to the global auction is by doing things differently from other national governments. Economic competitiveness is most likely to come from social innovations rather than intensifying efforts to do what has been done in the past. Again, education will be at the heart of a new bargain. Every effort needs to be made to equip American workers with the skills and support they need to succeed in the global auction. Reforming education to help people up their game to achieve world-class standards—especially in science and engineering—remains integral to America's competitiveness. It will require a social mobilization, the likes of which have not been seen since the former Soviet Union launched Sputnik, the world's first satellite in 1957, despite America's track record of invention, innovation, and entrepreneurial activities. Expertise in science and technology is crucial in a knowledge-driven economy, and unless there is a step change in education combined with quality job opportunities that enable students to utilize their technical knowledge, more of the jobs in knowledge-intensive fields will migrate to Asia regardless of cost differences.

The evidence presented in this book rejects the idea that the American economy will adapt to the aspirations of the population, given an almost limitless demand for creative and professional employment. It cannot be assumed that the labor market is going to offer exciting jobs for Americans who get a decent education. If the trend toward digital Taylorism proves to be accurate, it will play a major role in the economy, at the same time threatening to create new forms of workplace alienation among better-educated employees that expect more from their labors than a decent paycheck.[13]

In a nascent form, we may be witnessing a new correspondence between an education where students confront a modularized, pressurized, and metrics-driven system and a growing demand for work-ready demonstrators and drones outlined in our earlier discussion.[14] Hence, there seems little doubt that the current view of education for creativity and personal fulfilment bears little relationship to the future employment of many university graduates.

If the demand for creativity is limited, it raises fresh concerns about the role and content of mass higher education. But in the new opportunity bargain, the realities of digital Taylorism strengthen rather than weaken the case for an alternative approach to education by rejecting the narrow-minded (human capital) view of education as an economic investment.[15] By transforming the idea of education as an economic investment to an education system dedicated to enhancing the quality of life, we again move closer to John Dewey's idea of education as a freeing of individual capacity linked to social aims not limited to economic advantage.

Indeed, Dewey warned against treating education as solely an investment in human capital, which reduced learning to "trade" education rather than a tool for individual empowerment and social change. In his view, a democratic education "signifies a society in which every person shall be occupied in something which makes the lives of others better worth living, and which accordingly makes the ties which bind persons together more perceptible—which breaks down the barriers of distance between them."[16] This approach to education encourages people to think beyond narrow self-interest and to celebrate their mutual dependence as part of what it means to live in human society.

This widening of educational purpose is relevant to the economy. We've already argued that simply investing in skills upgrading is no longer a source of competitive advantage. It will be the creativity, knowledge, and collaborative skills of people to dream up better solutions both inside and outside the box that will define a key role for education in the future, even if creative work is in limited demand. It is the quality of educational experience that will determine the most inventive societies of the future, especially those that contribute to a low-carbon economy and create good jobs that add real value to people's lives.[17]

Social inventiveness depends on extending personal freedoms and giving people permission to think and to act upon them. This could contribute to a better society as well as economic prosperity, provided that this growth in innovative ideas could be supported through appropriate funding. After all, most creative ideas do not stem from a desire to make money; they arise out of a genuine interest in a subject. America's social capacity for creative thinking would also be difficult to replicate, as it derives from the hidden economic benefits of an open democratic society.[18]

But extending this invitation to think will be rejected by students and their families unless they are freed from the high-stakes competition for education and jobs that is robbing them of real choices and leads them to play it safe. Tackling inequalities in income and wealth would help reduce these stakes, as would reforms aimed at reducing the insecurities within the American job market. When locked into a high-stakes competition or gripped by the fear of job insecurity, people are not free.

Within Europe, there is an emerging interest in the idea of "flexicurity" rather than simply flexible labor markets. For people to pursue educational and occupational opportunities, it is correctly believed that people need access to learning opportunities, decent jobs, and income security when moving between jobs or retraining in periods of rapid economic change. It is "a policy approach geared less towards the protection of jobs, and more towards the protection of people."[19] Such an approach would require a radical shift in how the American economy is governed. In short, the state must assume a new active role in the development of a societal project, where a new opportunity bargain takes center stage.[20]

Smarter Government

Relying on market forces is no way to run an economy. The state must extend its role to become a strategic economic partner if America is to stand any chance of tackling the reverse auction and improving the quality of life for American workers and their families. America and Britain have been outsmarted by other nations that understand markets cannot be left to their own devices. East Asian economies have taken active measures to govern markets in the national interest. China, in particular, has mobilized huge resources investing in roads, airports, research facilities, and energy supplies. They insisted on joint ventures between foreign and domestic companies as a way of transferring technologies and know-how in exchange for access to its huge domestic market.

They also targeted major R&D investments in fields offering potential for employment growth, including green technologies. Although these attempts will not always succeed, they highlight an active role for the state, aimed at exploiting the global market to rapidly upgrade the Chinese economy. New forms of state capitalism also emerged, including the growth of sovereign wealth funds used by countries including China, Singapore, and the Gulf states to buy into Western companies or to launch national champions, akin to General Motors in the 1950s.

They recognized varieties of capitalism that do not correspond to the Anglo-Saxon hands-free variant. In many ways, there is nothing new about the way China has exploited the global economy to achieve rapid modernization, as Japan, Taiwan, South Korea, and Singapore all attempted to govern the market in pursuit of rapid economic growth.[21] We have also shown that it was Western corporations seeking to take advantage of new markets that gave emerging economies the opportunity for high-end growth, as it is difficult to stop knowledge from being passed on to competitors. Chinese and Indian companies also make it their business to capture and assimilate knowledge in the same way that the French tried to steal industrial secrets from the British in the nineteenth century or American and British companies poach key staff from competitors to acquire their trading secrets.

What is surprising is how little the American policy makers learned from these strategies, explained by their myopic belief in the superiority of a free market approach. The declining faith in neoliberalism is an opportunity to rebuild the state's capacity to take an active role in the economy, to share the nation's wealth for the benefit of all rather than a few, and to extend democratic freedom wherever possible.

The role of government can no longer be limited to filling gaps where the market doesn't work, given an assumption that corporate bosses and the financial markets should be left to run the economy with little interference from government. The collapse of corporate America, including banks and insurance companies along with the icons of America's auto industry, demonstrates how misguided such a view has been. It contrasts with the view expressed in an interview with a senior policy advisor in Singapore, who told us that the secret of a successful economy depended on building a government team "smarter than the smartest captains of industry." This is because national and business interests have been transformed as companies learn how to exploit the global auction. Their interests may overlap, but it is a relationship based on an uneasy truce, as governments seek to increase the prosperity of their citizens by raising the value of human capital, while companies seek to reduce it because it directly impacts on their profit margins.

The blind faith in the free market resulted in a trained incapacity to deliver the economic changes now required, as both American and British governments have lost much of the art of industrial policy making needed to shape the global auction in the interests of their workers.[22] Most Americans continue to rely on the quality of the countries education system to compete in the global auction at the same time that companies have more global options in terms of where to establish high-tech operations. This is going to require a more active industrial strategy to ensure that jobs remain in America, while establishing new niche markets for well-qualified workers.

Saying that the state has a key role to play in the economy is not to suggest that the state should try to monopolize knowledge of new technologies, innovations, or market opportunities. Rather it is based on an understanding that markets can be organized in different ways and with different consequences for the supply of, and demand for, trained workers. Globalization and advances in information technologies have exponentially increased the amount of market knowledge and intelligence that governments would need to govern. But it is precisely because of this growing complexity that coordination needs to become more systematic. It now, for instance, includes identifying key areas of innovation-led economic development through indigenous investment and inward investment, where efforts can be made to create new employment and increase the skill content of jobs, such as in high-performance manufacturing and exportable service clusters, including telecommunications, biotechnology, precision engineering, nanotechnology, international business services, health, education, and the creative industries.

It also involves a smarter approach to skills utilization because having large numbers of highly educated workers is no longer enough. The key question is how they are individually and collectively engaged in innovative and enterprising activities that cannot be easily performed elsewhere. It is the societal, state, or local capacity to exploit the collective intelligence of workers, sometimes in collaboration with those living in other countries, in the production of goods and services that people want. This is what counts rather than merely increasing the supply of college graduates.[23]

However, rebuilding a productive economy that contributes to the quality of people's lives is difficult to envisage within a model of shareholder capitalism that rewards senior executives for short-term profit maximization based on driving down labor costs both at home and overseas. It has been too easy for the short-term interests of corporate managers and shareholders to be put before those of American workers and the longer-term interests of the nation's economy. Companies need to operate within a regulatory framework where they are encouraged to balance immediate competitive pressures to reduce costs and increase profits with an eye on the medium term and the interests of employees and local communities. Stock options for senior management should, for example, be restricted and rewarded only on the medium- to long-term performance of the company. This would reduce the risks managers take and enable them to focus more on the development of productive assets rather than inflating share prices or company profits for personal gain.

Governments around the world, including the U.S. administration, also need to change the rules of the global auction. This would include new rules for the conduct of corporations and their executives designed to limit the race to the bottom that the reverse auction implies for many college-educated as well as less qualified workers. International labor standards would have to be reformed, allowing workers to counterbalance the power of global corporations by strengthening their rights to act collectively across national borders.

Equally, at the same time that low-cost competition is a legitimate facet of the global auction, the exploitation of cheap labor (including child labor) is not legitimate and will require the introduction of a minimum wage for all countries based on national per capita income. It would also include a more active role for international agencies, including the International Labor Office (ILO) and support for their campaign for decent work and a stronger role for the International Federation of Unions. These initiatives are intended to create a better system of checks and balances that recognizes the legitimate claims of all stakeholders—employees, managers, consumer, shareholders, and local communities—that must tackle the way companies excessively profit from the global auction at the expense of working families.

There are other possibilities such as that proposed by Barry Lynn, where antitrust laws could be used so that no corporation controls more than a quarter of the American market. The sourcing of goods in the global supply chain could also be limited to only a quarter of products from any one country, which could lead to greater openness in the global economy with workers in many countries being able to gain from it.[24]

Justice: Beyond Human Capital

A new bargain is also more than a matter of equalizing opportunities to join occupational elites even if, as we've argued, moving toward a level playing field in the competition for a livelihood is a key policy goal. Social justice is also about giving people a sense of dignity and recognition for their contribution to society regardless of whether they are an out-and-out winner in the global auction. This part of a new bargain challenges the winner-takes-all society based on neoliberal assumptions about talent, contribution, and rewards. It challenges an economic world of empty suits that knows nothing other than bottom-line numbers and return on investment (ROI) and thrives on the global auction through cutting the incomes of middle-class Americans. It also questions the perverse social priorities that lead talented professionals to dedicate themselves to finding novel ways of making bigger profits or personal bonuses even if it threatens the viability of the financial system if not the whole economy.

Today, the winners in society are encouraged to see themselves as self-made and to feel little sense of obligation to the losers because the competition is judged to be fair and based on individual performance. We are told that we get what we deserve, and those with the most marketable skills are assumed to be the most productive and consequently deserve much larger incomes than other workers. In his description of *The Revolt of the Elites*, Christopher Lasch argues that although hereditary advantages play an important role in the attainment of professional and managerial status, the new elite have "to maintain the fiction that its power rests on intelligence alone. Hence it has little sense of ancestral gratitude or of an obligation to live up to responsibilities inherited from the past. It thinks of itself as a self-made elite owing its privileges exclusively to its own efforts."[25]

When encouraged to see our education as an economic investment, our jobs solely as a source of income, and the size of our wallets as the measure of our social contribution, it obscures the fact that how people develop (or otherwise) depends on many factors, including the century one is born in, the place one lives, the wealth of one's parents, the quality of schooling, and job prospects, as these all shape opportunities, ambition, and a willingness to learn.[26] In presenting themselves as self-made, those Americans who are the winners in the global auction ignore the fact that their achievements, including their university degrees, are not only "'badges of ability" prized as a symbol of innate talent but also a social gift.[27]

Indeed, there has been a silent revolution around the globe that calls into question the idea that raw talent is in limited supply. The rise of mass college education suggests that the pool of ability is not as limited as many elites would like us to believe. They assert an "aristocracy of talent" and that mass higher education reflects the "dumbing down" of educational and cultural standards,[28] but we are led to a different conclusion. Without denying evidence of credential inflation, the overheated competition for credentials and jobs reflects the fact that the capabilities of a few Americans have been greatly exaggerated, and those of the majority have been greatly underestimated. Much the same is true of Western ideas about the capabilities of workers in emerging countries.

This book exposes the dim view of intelligence for what it is, a social fiction.[29] It is the social rather than the human limits to opportunity that represent the main problem in developed and emerging economies. This was clearly recognized by the senior manager working in India's IT industry that we referred to earlier when he told us that "the average IQ of people all over the world has been the same." He suggested that in India they did not have the right processes or right type of environment needed to tap the potential of their population. But he concluded that "luckily now, thanks to the Internet and thanks to the changing world order, I think we have more opportunities to give our population the chance to come up to a global level."

This offers a source of optimism, as it suggests that many classes of human species are not as stupid as Western elites have historically encouraged us to believe, but it poses a fundamental challenge to the legitimacy of social inequalities based on innate talent and acquired expertise. Although companies talk of a war for talent, the crucial issue to be tackled is what to do with the wealth of talent being created in America and beyond.

First, we can stop undervaluing the productive contributions of the many rather than overvaluing those of a few. There is clearly something wrong with an existing reward structure that has become dangerously skewed toward occupational elites. The global auction has conspired to increase inequalities between the best and the rest, but what is being rewarded is not differences in innate talent. In many respects, it is not the unique talents of the few that make them so valuable but the privileges of their education and job-market opportunities. In part, they are being rewarded for success in the paper chase—in gaining access to the most prestigious universities for reasons of breeding as much as brains. It also reflects their success in making it to the top in the positional division of labor that confers privileged access to share options and other corporate incentives restricted to corporate executives in an attempt to align their interests to those of shareholders. And as we have seen, their wealth often bears little relationship to their actual productive contribution in comparison to other employees.

Rather that being held to ransom by those at the top who threaten to be on the next flight out of the country if they are burdened with higher taxation or more government red tape interfering with the way they run their affairs, we could begin to redefine established views on talent and the distribution of rewards, including a reassessment of human capital.

Economists have thought of capital as investments in land, machines, or individuals leading to flows of income. But the idea that human societies are the source of capital accumulation has largely been forgotten. In the mid-nineteenth century, Auguste Comte, the founder of modern sociology and the man said to have inspired the motto on the Brazilian flag—*Ordem e Progresso* (Order and Progress)—defined capital as every permanent advance in material products, which included advances in knowledge and services as well as material goods. The development of capital was initially spurred by the struggle for human survival followed by attempts to enhance economic prosperity. This led Comte to see capital as combining the "labor of generations."

Capital represents a facet of human culture lost in the way economists define capital as the private property of individuals, shareholders, or business owners.[30] Human capital is an example of this social amnesia, as it involves individuals learning what are defined as the most important ideas society has to offer. These are then translated into credentials and sold privately to employers in exchange for the highest price possible.[31]

When all can benefit from these cultural riches by finding decent well-paid employment, there is less of a problem, but this is far removed from the realities of today's job market. Indeed, the benefits of increasing productivity have been concentrated in the hands of senior executives and major shareholders rather than the bulk of the workforce despite the fact that they are not only cashing in the labor of past and present generations but also publicly funded research. Most radical shifts in technology over the last century were the direct result of public funding. In the case of the electronics industry, it was publicly funded military spending that enabled Silicon Valley to take off and brought Bill Gates and others their fortunes. Equally, while companies label their goods such as mobile phones under their corporate brands, it should not be forgotten that today's cell phones are a pocket-sized chunk of technical civilization that is being exploited for private profit.

Jeremy Rifkin poses the question of whether every member of society has a right to participate in and benefit from increases in productivity brought on by the information and communication technology revolution. "If the answer is yes," he believes, as we do, "some form of compensation will have to be made to the increasing number of unemployed whose labor will no longer be needed in the new hi-tech automated world of the twenty-first century."[32] But it is not only the unemployed. More than a quarter of working families in America exist on poverty wages alongside a better-off category of workers in high-skill but low-wage jobs.[33]

In short, in any new bargain, the distribution of rewards needs to reflect the real contribution to productivity made by those both directly and indirectly involved in the production of goods and services, such as those involved in child care, community improvement, and the welfare of the elderly.[34] If the development of human talents is the foundation for a new bargain, then the work of those who are not employed in the formal economy will also need to be given greater recognition. A reduction of social inequalities will involve rewarding those who further the growth potential of others, whether in the home, community, school, or workplace. This is not intended to undermine individual ambition but to serve as an ethical correction that ties rewards more closely to social contribution rather than exclusively driven by market competition and private gain.

Conclusion

In the opening chapter, we began with de Tocqueville's depiction of America as a land of opportunity. He saw it as a bold social experiment that has come to define American society. We have shown that the American Dream has faltered as the neoliberal opportunity bargain exposed individuals and families to relentless market competition both at home and overseas that has broken the promise of education, jobs, and incomes. The question is whether American democracy will give rise to another bold experiment needed to bring together prosperity and justice in new ways based on a fundamentally different set of social priorities, including a shared prosperity that exists beyond job markets or national borders. Today, there seems little prospect of political leaders taking up the challenge of converting the private troubles felt by middle-class Americans, as well as the enduring suffering of less affluent families, into public issues of policy reform. However, a major lesson that we have learned in writing this book is always to remain open to surprises. So we will continue in the hope that Americans, along with other developed and emerging nations, will ultimately rise to the national as well as global challenges that will shape the quality of life for the next generation.

Notes

Chapter One

1. Alexis de Tocqueville, *Democracy in America*, vol. 2 (New York: Harper and Row, 1966 [1835]).
2. See Richard Rosecrance, *The Rise of the Virtual State: Wealth and Power in the Coming Century* (New York; Basic Books, 1999), xi.
3. Joseph Schumpeter, *Capitalism, Socialism and Democracy* (New York: Harper, 1947), chap. 7.
4. Ed Michaels, Helen Handfield-Jones, and Beth Axelrod, *The War for Talent* (Boston, Mass.: Harvard Business School Press, 2001).
5. Here "low wages" is a relative concept relating to the expectations of the rewards and career prospects associated with professional and managerial occupations. This relative idea of low wages is discussed in chap. 8.
6. See "Struck Down by Strikes," *Hindustan Times*, October 21, 2009; Peter Wonacott "Deadly Labor Wars at Factories in India Hinder Country's Rise," *Wall Street Journal* (Asia), November 24, 2009.
7. Robert H. Frank and Philip J. Cook, *The Winner-Takes-All Society* (New York: Penguin, 1996). The idea of a winner-takes-all job market may exaggerate these trends. As Frank and Cook admit, "it would be more accurate to call them 'those-near-the-top-get-a-disproportionate-share market'" (p. 3). But this is a mouthful and hence our simpler, if somewhat less descriptive, label.
8. Gary Becker, "The Age of Human Capital," in Hugh Lauder et. al. (eds.), *Education, Globalization and Social Change* (Oxford: Oxford University Press, 2006).

Chapter Two

1. Robert Reich, *The Work of Nations* (New York: Vintage, 1991), 247.
2. W. Norton Grubb and Marvin Lazerson, *The Education Gospel: The Economic Power of Schooling* (Cambridge, Mass.: Harvard University Press, 2004).

3. See Adam Smith, *An Inquiry into the Nature and Causes of the Wealth of Nations*, Edwin Cannan (ed.) (Chicago: University of Chicago Press, 1976 [1776]), 8. By the dawn of the twentieth century, the fate of the workforce was looking more promising, at least according to another famous economist, Alfred Marshall. In a essay on "The Future of the Working-Classes" presented to the Reform Club in Cambridge, England, in 1873, he spoke of new technologies accelerating the demand for a skilled workforce ending the distinction between blue- and white-collar workers. Although this would not lead to equality, Marshall told his audience, it could lead to a significant narrowing in income inequalities as the value of human skills increased. However see Harry Braverman's classic account *Labor and Monopoly Capital: The Degradation of Work in the Twentieth Century* (New York: Monthly Review Press, 1974).

4. Emma Rothschild, *Paradise Lost: The Decline of the Auto-Industrial Age* (New York, Vintage Books, 1973), 34. See also Huw Beynon, *Working for Ford* (Harmondsworth: Penguin, 1973).

5. Gary Becker, *Human Capital* (Chicago: University of Chicago Press, 1964); Theodore W. Schultz, *Investment in Human Capital: The Role of Education and Research* (New York: Free Press, 1971).

6. Theodore W. Schultz, "Investment in Human Capital," in Jerome Karabel and A. H. Halsey (eds.), *Power and Ideology in Education* (Oxford: Oxford University Press, 1978), 314.

7. George Psacharopoulos (ed.), *Economics of Education: Research and Studies* (Oxford: Pergamon, 1987); Organisation for Economic Co-operation and Development, *Human Capital Investment: An International Comparison* (Paris: OECD, 1998).

8. Schultz, "Investment in Human Capital," 314. This is assumed to create more inequalities between workers as some contributed, through differences in ability and application, more than others. Moreover, it is not difficult to see how by sleight of hand "learning is earning" eliminated the inconvenient fact that you need to be in a job to earn (unless self-employed) and that some appear to be overpaid for their talents whereas many more are undervalued.

9. Daniel Bell, *The Coming of Post-Industrial Society* (New York: Penguin, 1973), 409.

10. Peter Drucker, *Post-Capitalist Society* (New York: HarperCollins, 1993), 22.

11. Sumantra Ghoshal and Christopher A. Bartlett, *The Individualized Corporation: A Fundamentally New Approach to Management* (London: Random House, 2000), 8.

12. Michael B. Arthur and Denise M. Rousseau (eds.), *The Boundaryless Career: A New Employment Principle for a New Organizational Era* (New York: Oxford University Press, 1996).

13. Ibid., 4 and 6.

14. Maureen S. Bogdanowicz and Elaine K. Bailey, "The Value of Knowledge and the Values of the New Worker: Generation X and the New Economy." *Journal of European Industrial Training*, 26 (2002): 127.

15. Peter Sheahan, *Generation Y: Thriving and Surviving with Generation Y at Work*. Hardie Grant Books. http://www.managementbooks.com.au/bookweb/details.cgi?ITEMNO=9781740663175

16. Richard Rosecrance, *The Rise of the Virtual State: Wealth and Power in the Coming Century* (New York: Basic Books, 1999), xi.

17. R. Reich, *The Next American Frontier* (New York: Penguin, 1983), 127, taken from D. Coates, *Models of Capitalism, Growth and Stagnation in the Modern Era* Cambridge: Polity Press, 2000).

18. Phillip Brown and Hugh Lauder, *Capitalism and Social Progress: The Future of Society in a Global Economy* (New York: Palgrave, 2001).

19. Richard Florida, *The Flight of the Creative Class* (New York: Harper Business, 2005); Phillip Brown and Stuart Tannock, "Education, Meritocracy and the Global War for Talent," *Journal of Education Policy*, 24, no. 4 (2009): 377–392.

20. AnnaLee Saxenian, *The New Argonauts: Regional Advantage in a Global Economy* (Cambridge, Mass.: Harvard University Press, 2006).

21. Thomas Friedman, *The World Is Flat* (New York: Penguin, 2005), 230.

22. Gordon Brown, "We'll Use Our Schools to Break Down Class Barriers," *The Observer*, February 10, 2008.

23. President Barack Obama, "Explaining the Promise of Education in America," White House Briefings, March 10, 2009. http://www.whitehouse.gov/the_press_office/Fact-Sheet-Expanding-the-Promise-of-Education-in-America/

24. See Daniel Yergin and Joseph Stanislaw, *The Commanding Heights: The Battle between Government and the Marketplace That Is Remaking the Modern World* (New York: Simon and Schuster, 1998); James Buchanan and Richard E. Wagner, *Democracy in Deficit* (New York: Academic Press, 1977).

25. Ronald Reagan quoted in Stephen Weatherford and Lorraine M. McDonnell, "Ideology and Economic Policy,: in Larry Berman (ed.), *Looking Back at the Reagan Presidency* (Baltimore: Johns Hopkins University Press, 1990), 125.

26. Hugh Lauder and David Hughes, *Trading in Futures: Why Markets in Education Won't Work* (Buckingham, U.K.: Open University Press, 1999).

27. President Barack Obama's Address to Joint Session of Congress, February 24, 2009. http://www.whitehouse.gov/the_press_office/remarks-of-president-barack-obama-address-to-joint-session-of-congress/

28. National Commission on Excellence in Education, *A Nation at Risk* (Washington, D.C.: National Commission on Excellence in Education, 1983), 5. For a more recent discussion in education, skills, and the workforce, see National Center on Education and the Economy, *Tough Choices or Tough Times: The Report of the National Commission on the Skills of the American Workforce* (Hoboken, N.J.: Jossey-Bass, 2006); Robert Birgeneau has also warned in *Time Magazine* that we have a different kind of war from the war on terror, which is an economic war, but "the importance of investing in long-term research for winning that war hasn't been understood." Quoted in Michael D. Lemonick, "Are We Losing Our Edge?" *Time Magazine*, February 13, 2006.

Chapter Three

1. Ministry of Education, People's Republic of China and Guangzhou International. Ministry of Education of the People's Republic of China. www.moe.edu.cn/english/

2. The club of rich nations is usually defined as leading members within the OECD, which includes 30 member countries, Australia, Austria, Belgium, Canada, Czech Republic, Denmark, Finland, France, Germany, Greece, Hungary, Iceland, Ireland, Italy, Japan, South Korea, Luxembourg, Mexico, Netherlands, New Zealand, Norway, Poland, Portugal, Slovak Republic, Spain, Sweden, Switzerland, Turkey, United Kingdom, and United States.

3. It is important to remember that being highly qualified does not necessarily mean being highly skilled, especially as employers put greater store on social skills, alongside any technical requirements for the job in question. But here we want to highlight the global transformation in the capacity of some emerging economies to compete for high-skilled work.

4. There was significant expansion in all of the major developed economies with the exception of Germany because of the way a college education is defined excludes German students in high-quality technical apprenticeships. See Phillip Brown, David Ashton, Hugh Lauder, and Gerbrand Tholen, *Towards a High-Skilled, Low-Waged Workforce? A Review of Global Trends in Education, Employment and the Labour Market*, Monograph No. 10, Centre on Skills, Knowledge and Organisational Performance, Cardiff and Oxford Universities (2008). http://www.skope.ox.ac.uk/publications/towards-high-skilled-low-waged-workforce

5. See "Enrollment in Educational Institutions, by Level and Control of Institution: Selected Years, 1869–70 through Fall 2016," *Digest of Educational Statistics: 2007*. http://nces.ed.gov/programs/digest/d07/tables/dt07_003.asp?referrer=report

6. President Barack Obama's Address to Joint Session of Congress, February 24, 2009. http://www.whitehouse.gov/the_press_office/remarks-of-president-barack-obama-address-to-joint-session-of-congress/

7. Japan's formal membership to the OECD was on April 28, 1964.

8. See The World Bank, *The East Asian Miracle: Economic Growth and Public Policy* (Oxford: Oxford University Press, 1993). For an alternative account, see David Ashton, Francis Green, Donna James, and Johnny Sung, *Education and Training for Development in East Asia* (New York: Routledge, 1999); Phillip Brown, Andy Green, and Hugh Lauder, *High Skills: Globalization, Competitiveness and Skill Formation* (Oxford: Oxford University Press, 2001).

9. This represented a 41 percent increase in the number of full-time teachers in secondary education since 1988. See China Education and Research Network (CERNET). http://www.edu.cn/english_1369/index.shtml

10. Brown, Ashton, Lauder, and Tholen, *Towards a High-Skilled, Low-Waged Workforce?*

11. Government White Paper, China's Employment Situation and Policies, *Section VI. Employment Prospects for the Early Part of the 21st Century*. (People's Republic of China, Beijing, April 2004). See http://www.china.org.cn/e-white/20040426/6.htm

12. China's Ministry of Education, www.moe.edu.cn/english/; see China Education and Research Network (CERNET) (2009). http://www.edu.cn/english_1369/index.shtml

13. *Eleventh Plan to Focus on Education: PM*, December 28, 2007. http://www.domainb.com/economy/general/20071228_eleventh_plan.html

14. *Eleventh Plan to Focus on Education*, Syed Amin Jafri, January 3, 2008. http://in.rediff.com/money/2008/jan/03education.htm

15. *Eleventh Plan Will Be the Education Plan: PM*, January 11, 2008. http://www.siliconindia.com/shownews/38448

16. Richard Freeman. *The Great Doubling: The Challenge of the New Global Labor Market* (2006). http://emlab.berkeley.edu/users/webfac/eichengreen/e183_sp07/great_doub.pdf

17. Diana Farrell, Martha A. Laboissière, and Jaeson Rosenfeld, "Sizing the Emerging Global Labor Market," *The McKinsey Quarterly* (August 2005). http://www.mckinseyquarterly.com/Sizing_the_emerging_global_labor_market_1635

18. See Phillip Brown and Stuart Tannock, "Education, Meritocracy and the Global War for Talent," *Journal of Education Policy*, 24, no. 4 (2009): 377–392.

19. See *Tapping America's Potential: The Education for Innovation Initiative* (2005). http://www.uschamber.com/publications/reports/050727_tap.htm

20. These figures are based on the *Digest of Education Statistics* provided by the National Center for Educational Statistics. http://nces.ed.gov/

21. See the Higher Education Statistic Agency's Web site in the U.K. http://www.hesa.ac.uk/

22. *Research Insight (2008) A Study on the IT Labour Market in the UK*, Report Commissioned by The Council of Professors and Heads of Computing (CPHC). http://www.cphc.ac.uk/publications.php

23. Harold Salzman, *Globalization of R&D and Innovation: Implications for U.S. STEM Workforce and Policy*. Statement Submitted to the Committee on Science and Technology, U.S. House of Representatives (2007): 2.

24. One of the unintended consequences of a deep economic recession is that people may reevaluate what constitutes a good job and also reevaluate what is of real social, ethical, and economic value.

25. National Science Foundation, *Science and Engineering Indicators* (2008). http://www.nsf.gov/statistics/seind08/c2/c2s5.htm#c2s53

26. Ibid.

27. See Vivek Wadhwa, AnnaLee Saxenian, Ben Rissing, and Gary Gereffi, *America's New Immigrant Entrepreneurs: Part I*. Duke Science Technology & Innovation Paper No. 23 (2007); Huma Khan, "Trend of Foreign Workers Leaving Likely to Accelerate as Economy Struggles," *ABC News*, November 7, 2008. http://abcnews.go.com/Business/Economy/Story?id=6200335&page=2

28. Khan, "Trend of Foreign Workers Leaving"; Vivek Wadhwa, a leading researcher in this field, predicts that between 2008 and 2015 around 100,000 Indian and Chinese workers and students will move back. Also see Michael G. Finn, *Stay Rates of Foreign Doctorate Recipients from U.S. Universities* (Oak Ridge Institute for Science and Education, 2007).

29. Kent H. Hughes, Testimony before the U.S.-China Economic and Security Review Commission, July 16, 2008. http://www.uscc.gov/hearings/2008hearings/

30. See Tamar Lewin, "Global Classrooms: U.S. Universities Rush to Set Up Outposts Abroad," *New York Times*, February 10, 2008. http://www.nytimes.com/2008/02/10/education/10global.html?_r=1&pagewanted=print

31. Madelyn C. Ross, *China's Universities Look Outward* (Institute of International Education, Fall 2004). http://www.iienetwork.org/?p=Ross

32. Xiong Yan, *SOEs, Private Firms Set Acquisition Targets Overseas*, November 25, 2008. www.chinastakes.com

33. Ming Zeng and Peter Williamson, *The Dragons at Your Door: How Chinese Cost Innovation Is Disrupting Global Competition* (Boston, Mass.: Harvard Business School Press, 2007).

34. See Cong Cao, "China's Innovation Challenge," in Mark Mohr (ed.), *China's Galloping Economy: Prospects, Problems and Implications for the U.S.*, Asia Program Special Report (Washington, D.C.: Woodrow Wilson International Center for Scholars, 2008).

35. Ibid., 27.

36. See http://www.nanotechproject.org/inventories/consumer/analysis_draft/

37. James Ellenbogen, "Toward Molecular-Scale Computers, Computation as a Property of Matter, and Matter as Software, The Future of Computing," *The Edge*, 6, no. 1 (January 2002). http://www.mitre.org/news/the_edge/january_02/ellenbogen.html

38. Ernest H. Preeg, Testimony before the U.S.-China Economic and Security Review Commission, Technological Advances in Key Industries in China, July 16, 2008. http://www.uscc.gov/hearings/2008hearings/written_testimonies/08_07_16_wrts/08_07_16_preeg_statement.php

39. Eve Zhou and Bob Stembridge, "World IP Today," *Thomson Reuters* (December 10, 2008). http://scientific.thomsonreuters.com/press/2008/8494659/

40. World Bank, *Global Economic Prospects: Managing the Next Wave of Globalization* (Washington D.C.: World Bank), 109.

41. Farrell, Laboissière, and Rosenfeld, "Sizing the Emerging Global Labor Market."

42. Figures quoted from John Daniel, Asha Kanwar, and Stamenka Uvalić-Trumbić, "Mass Tertiary Education and the Developing World: Distant Prospect or Distinct Possibility?" *Europa World of Learning* (2007). www.col.org/resources/speeches/2007presentations/Pages/2007-*massTertiary*Ed.aspx

43. Cited in *The Observer*, January 25, 2009, p. 36.

44. Again, it is important not to assume that the highly qualified are necessarily highly skilled, given the frequent gap between the products of the education system and the skill needs of employers.

Chapter Four

1. Quoted in the *Financial Times*, May 12, 2006.

2. J. Bradford Jensen and Lori G. Kletzer, *Tradable Services: Understanding the Scope and Impact of Services Outsourcing* (Washington, D.C.: Peterson Institute

for International Economics, 2006). http://www.iie.com/publications/papers/print.cfm?doc=pub&ResearchID=638. There is also little agreement about what services could become tradable as this will have a major impact on the potential for offshoring. This is a key issue, and we will consider some of the evidence in the next chapter.

3. Rafiq Dossani and Martin Kenney, "Went for Cost, Stayed for Quality? Moving the Back Office to India," Asia-Pacific Research Center, Stanford University, Working Paper (2003), 29. http://APARC.stanford.edu. See also Stephen Cohen, Bradford De Long, and John Zysman, "Tools for Thought: What Is New and Important about the E-economy?" Berkeley Roundtable on the International Economy, BRIE Working Paper 138 (January 1, 2000); Martin Kenney and Richard Florida (eds.), *Locating Global Advantage* (Stanford, Cal.: Stanford University Press, 2003).

4. The WTO superseded the General Agreement on Tariffs and Trade (GATTS) established following World War II.

5. See United Nations Conference on Trade and Development (UNCTAD), *World Investment Report 2005: Transnational Corporations and the Internationalization of R&D*, 88–89. www.unctad.org/wir

6. Organisation for Economic Co-operation and Development, *Information Technology Outlook* (Paris: OECD, 2006), 8.

7. See "Motorola Eyes Research China 3G Market." http://www.cn-c114.net/577/a318213.html; see also http://www.motorola.com.cn/cn/about/inchina/default.asp

8. See United Nations Conference on Trade and Development, *World Investment Report 2006: FDI from Developing and Transition Economies: Implications for Development* (Geneva, UNCTAD, 2006), 56.

9. http://www.unctad.org/Templates/Webflyer.asp?docID=6337&intItemID=2068&lang=1

10. *The Washington Times*, November 24, 2008; see also, "U.S. Automakers Say Labor Costs Must Shrink to Compete," June 20, 2007. www.workforce.com/section/00/article/24/96/64.html

11. See Steve Hargreaves, "The New 'Good' Job: 12 Bucks an Hour," *CNNMoney.com* (2009). www.money.cnn.com/2009/06/04/news/economy/green_jobs/

12. *Financial Times*, July 9, 2007.

13. Amy Lee, "Dr Reddy's Charts New Path for Indian Drugmakers," *Financial Times*, December 19, 2006.

14. See http://money.cnn.com/magazines/fortune/global500/2009/

15. Ming Zeng and Peter J. Williamson, (2007) *Dragons at Your Door: How Chinese Cost Innovation Is Disrupting Global Competition* (Boston, Mass.: Harvard Business School Press, 2007), 2.

16. Ibid., 89.

17. Ibid., 14.

18. See Manjeet Kripalani and Josey Pullyenthuruthel, "India: Good Help Is Hard to Find," *Business Week*, February 14, 2005.

19. World Bank, *Global Economic Prospects. Managing the Next Wave of Globalization* (Washington, D.C.: World Bank, 2007), 41. These figures are based on a measure of purchasing power parity (PPP).

20. UNCTAD, *World Investment Report, 2006*, 92.

21. This is based on figures for 2002; see Dieter Ernst, *Why Is Chip Design Moving to Asia?* http://www.eastwestcenter.org/research/research-projects/?class_call=view&resproj_ID=182

22. Accenture, "The Kindest Cuts: The Vital Role of Cost Optimization in High Performance Financial Services," *The Point*, 9, no. 2 (2009): 3.

23. *China Today*, "Chinese Cities and Provinces"; based on 2005 data from the Ministry of Construction. http://www.chinatoday.com/city/a.htm

24. See Walt Whitman Rostow, *The Stages of Economic Growth: A Non-Communist Manifesto* (Cambridge: Cambridge University Press, 1960) and Daniel Bell, *The Coming of Post-Industrial Society* (New York: Penguin, 1973).

25. Alexander Gerschenkron, *Economic Backwardness in Historical Perspective: A Book of Essays* (Cambridge, Mass.: Harvard University Press, 1962). See also Albert Fishlow's review of Gerschenkron's book published through Economic History Services (2003). www.eh.net/bookreviews/library/fishlow.shtml

26. See Oswaldo De Rivero, *The Myth of Development: The Non-Viable Economies of the 21st Century* (London: Zed Books, 2001).

27. An example is Alfred Marshall's nineteenth-century essay on "The Future of the Working Class," delivered at the Reform Club in Cambridge, England. Arthur C. Pigou (ed.), *Memorials of Alfred Marshall* (London: Macmillan, 1925).

28. Pierre Garrouste and Stavros Ioannides (eds.), *Evolution and Path Dependence in Economic Ideas: Past and Present* (Cheltenham, U.K.: Edward Elgar, 2000); Peter A. Hall and David Soskice (eds.), *Varieties of Capitalism* (New York: Oxford University Press, 2001).

29. Hugh Lauder, Phillip Brown, and David Ashton, "Globalisation, Skill Formation and the Varieties of Capitalism Approach," *New Political Economy, 13*, no. 1 (2008): 19–35.

Chapter Five

1. Jay Tate, "National Varieties of Standardization," in Peter A. Hall and David Soskice (eds.), *Varieties of Capitalism: The Institutional Foundations of Comparative Advantage* (New York: Oxford University Press, 2001), 442.

2. See Peter F. Drucker, *Post-Capitalist Society* (New York: HarperCollins, 1993). Taylor's ideas will be discussed later in the chapter.

3. As Peter F. Drucker observed, "the only thing that increasingly will matter in national as well as in international economics is management's performance in making knowledge productive." *Post-Capitalist Society*, 176.

4. Ibid., 40.

5. Thomas Friedman, *The World Is Flat* (New York: Penguin, 2005), 200.

6. It is not innovation or standardization but innovation as standardization.

7. We credit the idea of "permission to think" to Ian Jones, who was a doctoral student of Phillip Brown.

8. David Landes, *The Wealth and Poverty of Nations* (London: Abacus, 1998), 187.

9. Ibid., chapter 13. It is this rationalization of economic activity that has been an enduring issue within the social sciences. Max Weber observed what he called the "routinization of charisma" and the prospects of an "iron cage" of bureaucracy, and Steven Brint has argued that the rhetoric of the knowledge economy is ahistorical: "Many years in the future, we shall see the same standardization in the computer software industry that a previous generation witnessed in the insurance and automobile industries." Steven Brint, "Professionals and the 'Knowledge Economy': Rethinking the Theory of Post Industrial Society," *Current Sociology, 49,* no. 4 (2001): 116.

10. See Werner Holzl and Andreas Reinstaller, *The Babbage Principle after Evolutionary Economics*, MERIT-Infonomics Research Memorandum Series, Maastricht, the Netherlands. http://edocs.ub.unimaas.nl/loader/file.asp?id=812

11. Barbro I. Anell and Timothy L. Wilson, "Prescripts: Creating Competitive Advantage in the Knowledge Economy," *Competitiveness Review, 12,* no. 1: 26–37.

12. Holzl and Reinstaller, *The Babbage Principle*, 14.

13. Frederick W. Taylor, *Principles of Scientific Management* (New York: Harper and Brothers, 1911), chap. 2, p. 6. http://www.archive.org/details/principlesofscie00taylrich. Peter Drucker argues, "Few figures in intellectual history have had greater impact than Taylor. And few have been so willfully misunderstood and so assiduously misquoted." Drucker, *Post-Capitalist Society*, 31.

14. See Robert Kanigel, *The One Best Way: Frederick Winslow Taylor and the Enigma of Efficiency* (London: Abacus 1997), 9.

15. Frederick W. Taylor quoted in Robert Kanigel, *The One Best Way*, 473.

16. Frederick W. Taylor, *The Principles of Scientific Management*, chap. 2, p. 4. http://www.archive.org/details/principlesofscie00taylrich

17. Ibid., 2. http://www.archive.org/details/principlesofscie00taylrich

18. See Kanigel, *The One Best Way*, 460.

19. Taylor, *The Principles of Scientific Management*, chapter 2, p. 4. http://www.archive.org/dctails/principlesofscie00taylrich

20. Kanigel, *The One Best Way*, 282.

21. Henry Ford, *My Life and Work* (New York: Garden City Publishing, 1922), 85.

22. See Emma Rothschild, *Paradise Lost: The Decline of the Auto-Industrial Age* (New York: Random House, 1973), 34.

23. See Phillip Brown and Hugh Lauder, *Capitalism and Social Progress: The Future of Society in a Global Economy* (Basingstoke: Palgrave Press, 2001).

24. Quoted in Kanigel, *The One Best Way*, 472–473.

25. See Judith Merkle, *Management and Ideology: The Legacy of the International Scientific Management Movement* (Berkeley: University of California Press, 1980).

26. John K. Galbraith, *The Liberal Hour* (New York: Penguin, 1960), 140–141.

27. In mechanical Taylorism, the application of knowledge to work focuses on the development of hardware, such as machines, production lines, and factory buildings; in digital Taylorism, the application of knowledge to work focuses on the development of software. Although mechanical Taylorism relates closely to manufacturing and its digital variety to service sector occupations, it should be noted that the mechanical and digital are being applied to both factories and offices. Mechatronics, for example, is indispensable to the production of automobiles, which combines mechanics, electronics, and computing not only in the use of industrial robots but also reflects the increasing importance to the value of an automobile.

28. Paul Romer, "Beyond the Knowledge Worker," *Worldlink* (January/February 1995), 56–60.

29. Simon Head, *The New Ruthless Economy: Work and Power in the Digital Age* (New York: Oxford University Press, 2003), 61.

30. Ibid., 69–70.

31. Ibid., 63.

32. Suresh Gupta, "Financial Services Factory," *Journal of Financial Transformation*, (The Capco Institute, 2006): 46.

33. Jon Ronson, "Cold Sweat," *The Guardian Weekend*, January 28, 2006. See also Adria Scharf, "'From 'Welcome to McDonalds' to 'Paper or Plastic?' Employers Control of Speech of Service Workers,' *Dollars and Sense, The Magazine of Economic Justice* (September/October 2003). www.dollarsandsense. org/archives/2003/0903scharf.html. After developing the distinction between mechanical and digital Taylorism, we came across this article by Parenti Christian that used the term *digital Taylorism*. The focus is mainly on technologies of surveillance, and although this is important, we want to emphasize that control is not being imposed for its own sake but to drive profits by lifting productivity and reducing costs. We have also sought to understand digital Taylorism within its wider context of the modular corporation. Parenti Christian, "Big Brother's Corporate Cousin," *Nation*, *273*, no. 5.

34. Accenture, *The Point: Automation for the People* (2007), 1. https://www. accenturehighperformingbusiness.com/Global/Services/By_Industry/Financial_ Services/The-Point/Archive/fsi_thepoint47.htm. This article suggests, "When manufacturing companies seek greater economies of scale across product lines while retaining each product's distinctive brand traits and characteristics, they 'industrialize' their operations: deconstructing the product and the manufacturing processes into smaller, more discrete components that can be efficiently combined in various combinations depending on what is being built. The automotive industry is a perfect example. With their 'platform' approach to building cars, companies such as Volkswagen and Toyota can combine different

parts in different ways to spread engineering and production costs across a greater number of vehicles while ensuring that, for example, a Volkswagen Passat remains different from an Audi A4—even though they share many components and are built on the same assembly line."

35. Nora Denzel, *Standardization: Reduce Cost, Simply Change*, HP Feature Story, (February 2004). http://h41131.www4.hp.com/hk/en/stories/standardization–reduce-cost–simplify-change.html; see also Suzanne Berger, *How We Compete* (New York: Currency Doubleday, 2005); Raghu Garud, Arun Kumaraswamy, and Richard N. Langlois (eds.), *Managing in the Modular Age* (Malden, Mass.: Blackwell, 2003); Andrew Holmes, *Commodification and the Strategic Response* (Aldershot: Gower, 2008).

36. See Richard Waters, "Big Blueprint for IBM Services," *Financial Times*, March 2, 2009.

37. Gupta, "Financial Services Factory," p. 43.

38. Craig Schneider, "The New Human-Capital Metrics," *CFO Magazine* (February 15, 2006), 1. www.cfo.com/printable/article.cfm/5491043. This is likely to change in the future as a survey by the Conference Board of Canada found that 84 percent of HR executives in the 104 medium to large organizations surveyed where planning to use human capital metrics. Ibid. See also *The Strategic Value of People: Human Resource Trends and Metrics* (Ottawa: The Conference Board of Canada: 2006). http://www.conferenceboard.ca/documents.asp?rnext=1707

39. During the 1950s and 1960s, the extent to which Taylor's approach was adopted varied considerably both within and across industrial sectors and countries. But it's well worth reading Harry Braverman, *Labor and Monopoly Capital: The Degradation of Work in the Twentieth Century* (New York: Monthly Review Press, 1974).

40. Harold Wilensky, "Work, Careers, and Social Integration," *International Social Science Journal, 12* (1960): 557.

41. Drucker, *Post-Capitalist Society*, 35.

Chapter Six

1. C. Wright Mills, *The Power Elite* (New York: Oxford University Press, 1956), 141.

2. "The Battle for Brainpower, A Survey of Talent," *The Economist*, October 7, 2006, p. 12.

3. Daniel Muzio and Stephen Ackroyd, "On the Consequences of Defensive Professionalism: Recent Changes in the Legal Labour Process," *Journal of Law and Society, 32*, no. 4: 640. Also see Eliot Freidson, *Professionalism: The Third Logic* (Chicago: University of Chicago Press, 2001).

4. Ed Michaels, Helen Handfield-Jones, and Beth Axelrod, *The War for Talent* (Boston, Mass.: Harvard Business School Press, 2001). See also Phillip Brown and Anthony Hesketh, *The Mismanagement of Talent* (Oxford: Oxford University Press, 2004).

5. Ibid., 3.

6. Ibid.

7. "The Battle for Brainpower," 12.

8. Michaels et al., *The War for Talent*, 4–5. Equally, Elisabeth Marx suggests, "This new class of global executive has common features: they have an MBA from a top business school; they have several years of international experience and are typically fluent in several languages...Executives are also expected to have far more cross-sector experience than before with a track record of making lateral moves during their careers" (Heidrick and Struggles, *Mapping Global Talent* [Chicago, IL: Heidrick and Struggles, 2007], 4; http://www.heidrick.com/PublicationsReports/PublicationsReports/MappingTalentGlobal.pdf). It would be interesting to know how many managers and professionals defined as key talents get anywhere near these criteria, especially in terms of language skills.

9. This segmentation of employees is related to the rise of digital Taylorism discussed earlier because if you emphasize the contribution of a few, the contribution of the rest of the workforce functions below the talent radar. The focus on top talent is not only reflected in job titles, salaries, or career opportunities but also shapes the way organizations and jobs are being reconfigured on a global scale.

10. Author's calculations based on United Nations Conference on Trade and Development (UNCTAD), *World Investment Reports* 2002–2009.http://www.unctad.org/

11. Richard Florida, *The Flight of the Creative Class* (New York: Harper Business, 2005), 3.

12. Britain's then Secretary of Trade Alistair Darling quoted in Alok Jha, "Minister Moves to Attract Foreign Scientists to UK," *The Guardian*, October 24, 2006, p. 15. See also Phillip Brown and Stuart Tannock, "Education, Meritocracy and the Global War for Talent," *Journal of Education Policy*, 24, no. 4 (2009): 377–392.

13. Brown and Tannock "Education, Meritocracy and the Global War for Talent."

14. Ibid.

15. Frederic Docquier and Abdeslam Marfouk, "International Migration by Education Attainment, 1990–2000," in Caglar Ozden and Maurice Schiff (eds.), *International Migration, Remittances and the Brain Drain* (Washington, D.C.: World Bank: 2005), 167–168.

16. Gurmeet Bambrah, *Canadian "Experiments" in Diversity*. CERIS Working Paper No. 41 (2005), 40.

17. Bob Pond and Barbara McPake, "The Health Migration Crisis: The Role of Four Organisation for Economic Cooperation and Development Countries," *Lancet* (March 26, 2006). All the above references are from Brown and Tannock, "Education, Meritocracy and the Global War for Talent."

18. House of Lords, *The Economic Impact of Migration*, vol. 1 (Select Committee on Economic Affairs, 2008), 5. http://www.publications.parliament.uk/pa/ld/ldeconaf.htm

19. AnnaLee Saxenian, *The New Argonauts: Regional Advantage in a Global Economy* (Cambridge, Mass.: Harvard University Press, 2006).

20. John Carvel, "Nursing Drive 'Like People Trafficking,'" *The Guardian*, May 12, 2004.

21. Joel D. Adriano, "Politics of Poverty in the Philippines," *Asia Times Online*, March 21, 2008. http://www.atimes.com/atimes/Southeast_Asia/JC21Ae01.html

22. David L. Llorito, "Brain Drain Saps the Philippines Economy," *Asia Times Online*, June 20, 2006.

23. Michaels, *The War for Talent*, xii.

24. Ibid.

25. Ibid. In *Winning the Talent Wars*, Bruce Tulgan sees little point in trying to define talent because, "You know very well that a single truly great person on your team is worth two, three, four, or five mediocre ones. The difference in value is hard to quantify, but the truth of the matter is clear: Nobody is more valuable than that person you can rely on without hesitation. That person almost always gets the job done right and ahead of schedule, takes exactly the right amount of initiative without over-stepping, makes the tough judgement calls as well as the easy ones, and makes it look routine" (2001), 32.

26. In these companies, hiring for diversity often involves recruiting elites from other countries. To qualify, individuals have to go to the best universities whatever country they live in. See Daniel Golden, *The Price of Admission* (New York: Random House, 2006). He shows how many top schools in the United States adopt various forms of restricted practices that make it doubly difficult for students from nonelite backgrounds to gain entry.

27. See Phillip Brown and Richard Scase, *Higher Education and Corporate Realities* (London: UCL Press, 1994).

28. Mats Alvesson, "Knowledge Work: Ambiguity, Image and Identity," *Human Relations*, 54, no. 7 (2001), 863–886.

29. Charles A. O'Reilly and Jeffrey Pfeffer, *Hidden Value: How Great Companies Achieve Extraordinary Results with Ordinary People* (Boston, Mass.: Harvard University Press, 2000), 2.

Chapter Seven

1. Nicholas Donofrio, "Global Strategy and Corporate Resource Needs." Keynote Speech, *The Evolving Global Talent Pool. Issues, Challenges and Strategic Implications* (The Levin Institute, State University of New York, June 16–17, 2005), 34 and 31.

2. See *The Challenge of Customization: Bringing Operations and Marketing Together.* http://www.strategy-business.com/sbkwarticle/sbkw040616?pg=all&tid=230

3. Michael Chanover, *Mass Customizi-Who?—What Dell, Nike and Others Have in Store for You.* http://www.core77.com/reactor/mass_customization.html

4. See Stephen Foley, "Boeing's Dream Finally Flies," *The Independent*, December 16, 2009.

5. Kenichi Ohmae, *The Invisible Continent: Four Strategic Imperatives of the New Economy* (London: Nicholas Brealey, 2000), 64.

6. See Albert O. Hirschman, *Exit, Voice and Loyalty: Responses to Decline in Firms, Organizations and States* (Boston, Mass.: Harvard University Press, 1970).

7. Robert Hayes and William Abernathy, "Managing Our Way to Economic Decline," *Harvard Business Review* (July/August 1980): 70. See also Robert Reich, *The Next American Frontier* (New York: Penguin, 1984); Bennett Harrison and Barry Bluestone, *The Great U-Turn* (New York: Basic Books, 1988); Lester Thurow, *Head-to-Head* (London: Nicholas Brealey, 1993); William Lazonick, "Industry Clusters versus Global Webs: Organizational Capabilities in the American Economy," *Industrial and Corporate Change, 2* (1993): 1–24.

8. Hayes and Abernathy, "Managing Our Way to Economic Decline," 68. In Fordist plants, although there had been a clear division between those who did the company's thinking and those who did the company's producing, the former often had experience of the industry in which they had based their careers.

9. Phillip Brown and Hugh Lauder, *Capitalism and Social Progress* (New York: Palgrave, 2001), 139–140.

10. Robert Reich referred to this as the "bastard child of scientific management" in *The Next American Frontier*.

11. See Lawrence Katz and Kevin M. Murphy, "Changes in Relative Wages, 1963–1987: Supply and Demand Factors," *Quarterly Journal of Economics, 107* (1992): 35–78: George Borjas, Richard Freeman, and Lawrence Katz, "How Much Do Trade and Immigration Affect Labour Market Outcomes?" *Brookings Papers on Economic Activity, 1* (1997): 1–90. However, a key dissenting voice was that of Adrian Wood, *North–South Trade: Employment and Inequality: Changing Fortunes in a Skill Driven World* (Oxford: Clarendon Press, 1994).

12. Robert E. Scott, *The China Trade Toll: Widespread Wage Suppression, 2 Million Jobs Lost in the U.S.*, Economic Policy Institute, Briefing Paper No. 219 (2008). www.epi.org

13. Ibid., 12.

14. *Zhi Wang's presentation at a conference*, China's Increasingly High Technology Trade, *Carnegie Endowment for International Peace (September 26, 2007)*.

15. Alan Blinder, *How Many U.S. Jobs Might Be Offshorable?* CEPS Working Paper No. 142 (March 2007). http://econpapers.repec.org/paper/pricepsud/60.htm

16. Ibid., 1.

17. Organisation for Economic Co-operation and Development, *Offshoring and Employment: Trends, and Impacts* (2007). http://www.oecd.org/document/22/0,33 43,en_2649_33927_38743126_1_1_1_1,00.html

18. A. T. Kearney Consultants. http://www.atkearney.com/main.taf?p=1,5,1,130

19. *Financial Times*, September 28, 2005.

20. Blinder, *How Many U.S. Jobs*, 1.

21. Stephen Roach, "From Globalization to Localization," in Morgan Stanley, *Perspectives*, (January 7, 2007). Back in 1993, Ravi Batra had warned that while the free trade associated with economic globalization might raise wealth in America, he also argued that it reduced the wages of ordinary workers. Now his heterodox views look like orthodoxy. See Ravi Batra, *The Pooring of America: Competition and the Myth of Free Trade* (New York: Collier Macmillan, 1993).

22. Thomas Friedman, *The World Is Flat* (New York: Penguin, 2005), 230.

23. Scott, *The China Trade Toll*, 4.

Chapter Eight

1. Joseph A. Schumpter, *Capitalism, Socialism and Democracy* (London: George Allen and Unwin, 1943), 82.

2. Karl Marx and Friedrich Engels, *The Communist Manifesto* (New York: Penguin, 1967), 83.

3. Thomas L. Friedman, "The New Untouchables," *New York Times*, October 21, 2009.

4. See Charlie Porter, "Blood on Catwalk as Cutbacks Bite," *The Observer*, January 4, 2009.

5. Pat House, interview on *BizDaily*, BBC World Service, December 30, 2008.

6. James Moore, "Outsourcing Mania Makes Serco a Buy," *The Independent*, December 16, 2009.

7. Lawrence Summers, "America Needs to Make a New Case for Trade," *Financial Times*, April 28, 2008.

8. Emmanuel Saez, "Striking It Richer: The Evolution of Top Incomes in the United States," *Pathways Magazine*, Stanford Center for the Study of Poverty and Inequality (Winter 2008): 6–7. http://elsa.berkeley.edu/~saez/saez-UStopincomes-2006prel.pdf

9. See Lawrence Mishel, Jared Bernstein, and Heidi Shierholz, *The State of Working America 2008/2009* (Ithaca, N.Y.: Cornell University Press, 2009), figure 3AE. Emmanuel Saez also shows that the bottom 90 percent of earners accounted for just 9.1 percent of the growth in American income from 1989–2006.

10. Francis Green, *Demanding Work: The Paradox of Job Quality in the Affluent Economy* (Princeton, N.J.: Princeton University Press, 2006), 124; see also Karen Gardiner and Jane Millar, "How Low-Paid Employees Avoid Poverty: An Analysis by Family Type and Household Structure," *Journal of Social Policy*, 35, no. 3 (2006): 351–369.

11. See David Rothkopf, *Superclass: The Global Power Elite and the World They Are Making* (New York: Farrar, Straus and Giroux, 2008), 290.

12. In 2007, the 90:10 ratio was 3.9 for women and 4.5 for men. The ratio for high-earning females as opposed to low-earning men was 3.3. Calculated from table 3.20 in Mishel, Bernstein, and Shierholz, *The State of Working America, 2008/2009*.

13. The within-group inequality in earnings for college graduates is not only far greater than that of the lower skilled, but it has also been growing more rapidly, whereas nongraduates experienced slow or no growth in within-group variance in earnings. See T. Lemieux, *Residual Wage Inequality: A Re-examination*. University of British Columbia, CLEER Working Paper 2 (2003). http://www.econ.ubc.ca/cleer/papers/cleer002.pdf

14. See U.S. Census Bureau, *Current Population Survey* (2005). http://www.census.gov/population/www/socdemo/education/cps2004.html

15. Francis Green and Yu Zhu, *Overqualification, Job Dissatisfaction and Increasing Dispersion in the Returns to Graduate Education*, London School of Economics and Political Science, Manpower Human Resources Lab, Centre for Economic Performance (2007), p. 3.

16. Polly Curtis, "1 in 3 Graduates Not Repaying Student Loans," *The Guardian*, October 6, 2008.

17. Further analysis is obviously required to compare occupations that are more tradable than others as in the work of Alan Blinder, *How Many U.S. Jobs Might Be Offshorable?* CEPS Working Paper No. 142 (March 2007). Some of the differences will reflect the age profile of an occupation where the younger employees on lower hourly rates are assumed to climb the hierarchy over time to become high earners. We suggested that for various reasons, including the segmentation of knowledge-based occupations, this cannot be taken for granted. Occupational differences are also likely to reflect gender and racial differences that require further analysis.

18. Maura Jane Farrelly, "'Fewer Employers Offer Pensions," *Voice of America*, January 26, 2006.

19. Lawrence Mishel, Jared Bernstein, and Heidi Shierholz, *The State of Working America, 2008/2009* (Ithaca, N.Y.: Cornell University Press, 2009), Table 3.13, p.150.

20. Government Accountability Office (GAO), *Defined Benefit Pensions: Plan Freezes Affect Millions of Participants and May Pose Retirement Income Challenges*, GAO-08–817 (2008).

21. Ross Eisenbrey, *Why We Need Retirement USA*, National Press Club, March 10, 2009. http://www.epi.org/publications/entry/why_we_need_retirement_usa/

22. The Pension Rights Center in Washington is monitoring the companies that have frozen pension contributions. http://www.pensionrights.org/

23. See Institute of Medicine, *America's Uninsured Crisis: Consequences for Health and Health Care* (2009). www.iom.edu/americasuninsuredcrisis

24. Ibid.

25. Jared Bernstein and Heidi Shierholz, *A Decade of Decline: The Erosion of Employer-Provided Health Care in the United States and California, 1995–2006*, EPI Briefing Paper No. 209 (2008), 6. In America, perhaps the clearest signal of a retreat from a commitment to nonwage compensation has come from Peter Peterson, founder of Blackstone, the leading private equity company, who established a billion-dollar foundation to spread the message that the social risks of working in a capitalist economy should be privatized because the American economy cannot afford the cost of pensions, health care, and social security. "Blackstone Founder Backs Apocalyptic Warning with $1 billion," *The Guardian*, February 18, 2008.

26. Ruth Sunderland, "After the Credit Crisis, the Pensions Crunch," *The Observer*, April 26, 2009.

27. Gary S. Becker and Kevin M. Murphy, "The Upside of Income Inequality," *The American*, May/June 2007, p. 3.

28. Robert H. Frank and Philip J. Cook, *The Winner-Takes-All Society* (New York: Penguin, 1995), 6.

29. See Arlene Dohm and Lynn Shniper, "Employment Outlook: 2006–16, Occupational Employment Projections to 2016," *Monthly Labor Review* (November 2007): 103. http://www.bls.gov/opub/mlr/2007/11/art5full.pdf

30. Steve Hargreaves, *The New "Good" Job: 12 Bucks an Hour,* CNNMoney.com, June 4, 2009. www.money.cnn.com/2009/06/04/news/economy/green_jobs/

31. These are EPI data on productivity and rewards. Moreover, the rich and the poor may feel worlds apart, but they are locked into a set of social and economic relations which bind them into alternative fates. See Lawrence Mishel, Jared Bernstein, and Heidi Shierholz, *The State of Working America 2008/2009* (Ithaca, N.Y.: Cornell University Press, 2009).

32. See Phillip Brown, David Ashton, Hugh Lauder, and Gerbrand Tholen, *Towards a High Skilled, Low Waged Workforce?* ESRC Centre for Skills, Knowledge and Organizational Performance (SKOPE), Monograph No. 10 (2008).

33. Emanuel Saez and Chiaki Moriguchi, "The Evolution of Income Concentration in Japan, 1886–2005: Evidence from Income Tax Statistics," *Review of Economics and Statistics, 90,* no. 4 (2008): 713–734. See also Frank Levy and Peter Temin, *Inequality and Institutions in 20th Century America,* MIT Department of Economics Working Paper No. 07–17 (2007).

34. Saez, "Striking It Richer," 4.

35. Paul Krugman, "Past and Prospective Causes of High Unemployment in Reducing Unemployment," *Federal Reserve Bank of Kansas City, Economic Review* (Fourth Quarter 1994), 37.

36. Lawrence Summers, "America Needs to Make a New Case for Trade," *Financial Times,* April, 28, 2008; see also "The Global Middle Cries Out for Reassurance," *Financial Times,* October 30, 2006.

37. Claudia Goldin and Lawrence Katz, *The Race between Education and Technology,* (Cambridge, Mass.: Harvard University Press, 2008).

38. See Krishna Guha, Edward Luce, and Andrew Ward, "Middle America Misses Out on Benefits of Growth," *Financial Times Online,* November 1, 2006.

39. Alfred Chandler, *Scale and Scope: The Dynamics of Industrial Capitalism* (Cambridge, Mass.: Harvard University Press, 1990).

40. See Martin Ravallion, *The Developing World's Bulging (but Vulnerable) "Middle Class,"* Policy Research Working Paper No. 4816 (Washington, D.C.: World Bank, 2009), table 1: Poor by the Standards of Developing Countries.

41. It is largely explained by the growth performance of BRIC economies, especially China, at the same time sub-Saharan Africa has fallen farther behind. But economic fortunes within the developing world have also become more polarized. Ibid., 18.

42. Some studies include people living on little more than $2 a day as part of a global middle class. See Ibid., 8; Abhijit Banerjee and Esther Duflo, "What Is Middle Class about the Middle Classes around the World?" *Journal of Economic Perspectives, 22,* no. 2 (2008): 3–28; Dominic Wilson and Raluca Dragusanu, *The*

Expanding Middle: The Exploding World Middle Class and Falling Global Inequality,
Goldman Sachs, Global Economic Paper No. 170 (2008).

43. This definition was developed by Branko Milanovic and Shlomo Yitzhaki. "Decomposing World Income Distribution: Does the World Have a Middle Class?" *Review of Income and Wealth, 48,* no. 2 (2002): 155–178. Italy's per capita is used as the upper limit because it has the lowest per capita income in the G7, and Brazil represents the lower threshold because its per capital income is close to the official poverty line in the United States and Germany (about $PPP 10 a day).

44. Maurizio Bussolo, Rafael E. De Hoyos, Denis Medvedev, and Dominique van der Mensbrugghe, *Global Growth and Distribution: Are China and India Reshaping the World?* World Bank, Policy Research Working Paper No. 4392 (2007), 19.

45. Zhou Xiaohong, *Social Changes in China and the Urban Middle Class Growth* Beijing: Academic Press, 2005).

46. See John Parker, "Burgeoning Bourgeoisie: The New Middle Classes in Emerging Markets," *The Economist,* February 12, 2009; Rajesh Shukla, *The Great Indian Middle Class* (New Delhi: National Council of Applied Economic Research, 2008).

47. Bussolo, De Hoyos, Medvedev, and van der Mensbrugghe, *Global Growth and Distribution,* 10.

48. Kevin T. Leicht and Scott T. Fitzgerald argue that today's American middle class bears a striking similarity to peasants in the system of debt peonage in agrarian societies. " 'In agrarian systems, peasants were indebted to specific landlords; in contemporary America, post-industrial peasants are indebted to an economic system. In both cases, workers are locked into arrangements that force them to struggle continuously to make a living with little hope of breaking free from their subordinate positions." *Postindustrial Peasants: The Illusion of Middle-Class Prosperity* (New York: Worth Publishers, 2007), 29.

Chapter Nine

1. A 26-year-old history major at a public university in Paris and a leader of the student movement UNEF. Reported by Elaine Sciolino, "History Repeats Itself in France," *The Times of India, New Delhi,* March 18, 2006.

2. *Times of India,* http://www.indiapoised.com/

3. See Michael Young, *The Rise of the Meritocracy* (Harmondsworth: Penguin, 1961). Moreover, Brown has argued that educational selection is based on the ideology of parentocracy, where the wealth and wishes of parents matter as much as the abilities and efforts of students. Here the equation "ability + effort = merit" is reformulated into "resources + preferences = choice." Phillip Brown, "Cultural Capital and Social Exclusion: Some Observations on Recent Trends in Education, Employment and the Labour Market," *Work, Employment and Society, 9,* (1995): 29–51.

4. James Heckman, *Schools, Skills and Synapses,* Discussion Paper No. 3515, The Institute for the Study of Labor (IZA), Bonn, Germany, 2008.

5. Phillip Brown, "The Globalization of Positional Competition," *Sociology, 34,* no. 4 (2000): 633–653; Stephen Ball, *Class Strategies and the Education Market: The Middle Classes and Social Advantage* (London: Routledge Falmer, 2003).

6. See Daniel Golden, *The Price of Admission* (New York: Crown, 2006), 6–7.

7. One of the most outstanding contributions to our understanding of these issues comes from the democratic socialist Richard Henry Tawney. See *Equality* (London: George Allen and Unwin, 1931), 55; John Dewey, *Democracy and Education* (New York: Macmillan, 1916); A. H. Halsey, *Democracy in Crisis* (London: Politico Books, 2007).

8. Fred Hirsch, *The Social Limits to Growth* (London: Routledge and Kegan Paul, 1977).

9. Ulrich Beck, *Risk Society: Towards a New Modernity* (London: Sage, 1992).

10. Hirsch, *The Social Limits to Growth*, 6; Phillip Brown, "The Opportunity Trap: Education and Employment in a Global Economy," *European Educational Research Journal*, 2, no. 1 (2003): 142–180; revised and abridged as "The Opportunity Trap," in H. Lauder et al. (eds.), *Education, Globalization and Social Change* (Oxford: Oxford University Press, 2006).

11. Raymond Boudon, *Education, Opportunity and Social Inequality* (New York: Wiley, 1973), 6.

12. David K. Shipler, *The Working Poor: Invisible in America* (New York: Vintage Books, 2005).

13. Ivar Berg, *Education and Jobs: The Great Training Robbery* (New York: Penguin, 1970).

14. Randall Collins, *Four Sociological Traditions* (New York: Oxford University Press, 1994), 146; *Credential Society: An Historical Sociology of Education and Stratification* (New York: Academic Press, 1979).

15. Tom Van Riper, *Most Expensive Private High Schools*, December 11, 2006. http://www.forbes.com

16. College Board, *Trends in College Pricing, 2007* (2007). http:/www.collegeboard.com/trends

17. Beth Lattin, "A Graduate Degree in Debt," *Forbes Magazine*, March 10, 2009. http://www.forbes.com

18. The current capped rate for full-time undergraduate students in England is £3,225, but this is under review and likely to rise. The definition of affordability is based on occupations where school fees represent 25 percent or less of gross average annual earnings for full-time employees. See Halifax Financial Services, *School Fees Rising at More Than Twice the Rate of Inflation* (2008). http://www.HBOSplc.com

19. Unlike money, credentials are not a currency of exchange but one of entitlement. If you have the appropriate qualifications, you are entitled to enter the competition for specific kinds of employment. It confers an entitlement to barter.

20. See Phillip Brown and Anthony Hesketh, *The Mismanagement of Talent* (Oxford: Oxford University Press, 2004).

21. Ibid., 34.

22. It may also count for less not because of increasing market congestion but because the rules of the game have changed. Although the opportunity bargain is based on preparing people with the skills to compete in the global job market, American workers find themselves in a bidding war where cost is a key factor.

23. Nikolas Rose, *Governing the Soul: The Shaping of the Private Self* (London: Free Associations Press, 1999).

24. Robert Jackall, *Moral Mazes: The World of Corporate Managers* (New York: Oxford University Press, 1988), 64; see also http://www.sunyit.edu/~harrell/billyjack/book_reviews.htm

25. Rosebeth M. Kanter, "Nice Work If You Can Get It," *American Prospect*, 6, no. 23 September 21, 1995); Martin Carnoy, *Sustaining the New Economy: Work, Family and Community in the Information Age* (Cambridge, Mass.: Harvard University Press, 2000).

26. Madeleine Bunting, *Willing Slaves: How the Overwork Culture Is Ruling Our Lives* (London: HarperCollins, 2004).

27. This is not to suggest that *social* qualifications were eliminated in recruitment to bureaucratic organizations. The selection of elites has traditionally been associated with a cultural code consistent with images of masculine managerial authority, expert knowledge, and the right school tie.

28. Obviously, these can and often do overlap.

29. Brown and Hesketh, *The Mismanagement of Talent*.

30. David Callahan, *The Cheating Culture: Why More Americans Are Doing Wrong to Get Ahead* (Orlando, Fla.: Harcourt, 2004), 9.

31. Tania Branigan, "Boom in Exam Cheats Battling for China's Top Jobs," *The Guardian*, January 21, 2009.

32. Paul Goodman, *Growing Up Absurd* (New York: Random House, 1956).

33. These quotations are from Andrew Marshall, "Eyes on the Prize," *Time*, February, 10, 2003. http://www.time.com/time/magazine/article/0,9171,421086,00.html; also see Eugenia V. Levenson, "Harvard Girl," *Harvard Magazine*. http://harvardmagazine.com/2002/07/p-harvard-girl.html

34. See James Randerson, "One in Five Admit Using Brain Drugs," *The Guardian*, April 10, 2008. Although an international study, most of the respondents were from the United States. http://www.guardian.co.uk/science/2008/apr/10/medicalresearch.health

35. Mary Eberstadt, "Why Ritalin Rules," *Policy Review*, Hoover Institute (April/May 1999). http://www.hoover.org/publications/policyreview/3552192.html

36. Ralf Dahrendorf, *The Modern Social Conflict* (Berkeley: University of California Press, 1990), 159.

37. Robert H. Frank and Philip J. Cook, *The Winner-Takes-All Society* (New York: Penguin, 1996).

Chapter Ten

1. Presidential speech, November 4, 2008.

2. This overexuberance in terms of what the global economy could deliver led to credentials, as the currency of opportunity, being treated in much the same way as financial derivatives. Easy access to consumer credit was used to keep the American and British economies in full swing while the underlying fundamentals were falling apart. Likewise, the increasing numbers of credentials

in circulation created a climate of widening access and opportunities while in reality many credentials were subprime, and students found themselves in debt as their investments in education failed to deliver.

3. Rather than offering a law of economic development, human capital, at least as understood in official policy circles, characterized by the slogan learning equals earning, looks to be more appropriate to American society in the 1950s and 1960s. This was when the expansion of education coincided with a rising demand for white-collar technicians, managers, and professionals.

4. The disconnection between prosperity and justice would come as no surprise to Karl Marx as they capture the Janus-headed nature of market capitalism. Although its innovative powers for dramatic economic change are clearly evident, it has also created chronic instability and inequality.

5. Economists call the way countries are locked into a predetermined future "path dependency" because it's difficult to break free of past ways of organizing various forms of economic activity. A classic example is the QWERTY keyboard, which once established makes it difficult to shift to another format. See Paul A. David, "Clio and the Economics of QWERTY," American Economic Review, 75, no. 2 (1985): 332–337.

6. David Kusnet, Lawrence Mishel, and Ruy Teixeira, *Talking Past Each Other: What Everyday Americans Really Think (and Elites Don't Get) about the Economy* (Washington, D.C.: Economic Policy Institute, 2006).

7. Doreen Massey, winner of Nobel Prize geography's, correctly talks about space as relational and the need to extend our understanding of responsibility beyond the local because we are all locals as well as global citizens.

8. See Gary Duncan, "Alistair Darling Calls for World's Financial Leaders to Take Decisive Action: £2.7 Trillion Wiped off the Global Value of Shares as Confidence Collapses," The Times, October 11, 2008. http://business. timesonline.co.uk/tol/business/economics/article4922053.ece

9. James Fallows, "The $1.4 Trillion Question," The Atlantic, January/February 2008. http://www.theatlantic.com/doc/200801/fallows-chinese-dollars

10. See Jagdish Bhagwati and Alan S, Blinder, *Offshoring of American Jobs* (Cambridge, Mass.: MIT Press, 2009).

11. Tom Nicholas, "Innovation Lessons from the 1930s," The McKinsey Quarterly, 84, no. 1 (2009). Nicholas argues that economic recessions result in the movement of high-quality, skilled workers toward stronger employers, so for "companies with cash and ideas, history shows that downturns can provide enormous strategic opportunities."

12. It is more likely to bring people from different walks of life into contact both in America and beyond, sparking new ideas, approaches, and rebuilding social trust, which is currently in short supply. See John Dewey, *Democracy and Education* (New York: Free Press, 1916).

13. It is paradoxical that in a knowledge-driven economy, job enrichment will become more important if the commitment of well-qualified workers is to be achieved.

14. See Samuel Bowles and Herbert Gintis, *Schooling in Capitalist America* (New York: Basic Books, 1975).

15. This takes us back to Adam Smith's view that education should seek to compensate for work in a complex division of labor.

16. Dewey, *Democracy and Education*, 369–370.

17. The need for fresh thinking is reinforced by the environmental limits to middle-class lifestyles based on material consumption. The politics of more has led to unimaginable wealth since the eighteenth century, but our understanding of the stakes also needs to be questioned as the Western model of economic growth that has been exported around the world brings 3 billion new consumers with profound environmental consequences. This poses a huge challenge to us all in working out how to create a sustainable world based on justice and improving the quality of life for the world's 6 billion plus population rather than the world's 950 billionaires. Currently, much of education remains organized on a mass production model corresponding to digital Taylorism. But this is precisely the kind of work that is subject to global price competition. It's little more than an intense factory education churning out credentials with often dubious value despite students working hard to get them.

18. We are grateful to Ian Jones, Head of Innovation and Engagement, School of Social Sciences, Cardiff University. His regular conversations with Phillip Brown have helped shape some of our thinking on sources of creativity and innovation.

19. *What Is Fexicurity*, European Employment Strategy. http://ec.europa.eu/social/main.jsp?catId=116&langId=en

20. The distinction between "society-as-it-is" and a "societal project" draws on Manuel Castells's work on the developmental state. See his book *The Rise of the Network Society* (Malden, Mass.: Blackwell, 2000), 198.

21. Robert Wade, *Governing the Market: Economic Theory and the Role of Government in East Asian Industrialization* (Princeton, N.J.: Princeton University Press, 1990).

22. It would also require immediate action to disband what James K. Galbraith sees as a new class that set out to influence the state not for ideological reasons but to profit both individually and as a group from the public purse. This kind of predator state, he argues, amounts to "the systematic abuse of public institutions for private profit" and "the systematic undermining of public protections for the benefit of private clients." James K. Galbraith, *The Predator State: How Conservatives Abandoned the Free Market and Why Liberals Should Too* (New York: Free Press, 2008). See also Benjamin M. Friedman, "A Challenge to the Free Market," *The New York Review of Books*, November 6, 2008, pp. 43–47.

23. These ideas are developed in P. Brown, A. Green, and H. Lauder, *High Skills: Globalization, Competitiveness and Skill Formation* (Oxford: Oxford University Press, 2001); D. Ashton, F. Green, D. James, and J. Sung, *Education and Training for Development: The Political Economy of Skill Formation in East Asian Newly Industrialised Economies* (London: Routledge, 1999).

24. See Barry Lynn, *End of the Line: The Rise and Coming Fall of the Global Corporation.* (New York: Doubleday, 2006).

25. Christopher Lasch, *The Revolt of the Elites and the Betrayal of Democracy* (New York: Norton, 1995), 39.

26. Capitalism is nothing if not inventive. In an advertizing campaign for Orange, a European telecom company, their strap line is "I am what I am because of everyone," which offers an excellent counterblast to market individualism. It is based on the simple insight that "I am everyone"; we are inextricably connected to everyone else in human societies. "I am my mate who never speaks and the one who won't shut up. I am my older sister and unfortunately my younger brother. I am all the girls I've kissed and all the ones I will not."

27. As individuals, we are born with the capacity for intelligence—an ability to acquire and interpret information, to solve problems, to think critically and systematically about the social and natural world, to communicate ideas to others, and to apply new skills and techniques. Developments in the social world stimulate the mind's potential for new forms of feeling, reasoning, and understanding.

28. Richard Herrnstein and Charles Murray, *The Bell Curve* (New York: Free Press, 1994).

29. Phillip Brown and Hugh Lauder, *Capitalism and Social Progress* (New York: Palgrave, 2001).

30. Yet in the nineteenth century, the emerging concepts of culture and capital were Siamese twins. Culture was capital in its public form (libraries, museums, civic buildings, public universities, etc.), and capital was culture privatized through private property. It is this private capture of culture that has dominated our understanding of who gets what. Alvin Gouldner, *The Future of Intellectuals and the Rise of the New Class* (New York: Macmillan, 1979).

31. What we are arguing for has occurred in reverse in the form of socialism for the rich. The financial crash of 2008 clearly demonstrated the scale of corruption to the principles of meritocratic achievement and social justice. Corporate executives and financiers rigged a "casino" economy. They "draw up the rules of the game, rig the odds in their favor and disown their losses" because when things got difficult they persuaded governments to socialize the private debt of individuals and companies while executives of failed companies walked away with private fortunes. If the same principles were applied to tackling poverty in America, it could be abolished tomorrow. See Simon Caulkin, "Stock Exchange: A Casino Where the Rich Can't Lose," *The Observer,* October 5, 2008; James K.Galbraith, *The Predator State* (New York: Free Press, 2008).

32. Jeremy Rifkin, *The End of Work* (New York: Tarcher/Putnam, 1996), 267.

33. The Working Poor Families Project, *Still Working Hard, Still Falling Short* (2006). http://www.workingpoorfamilies.org/still_working.html

34. See Brown and Lauder, *Capitalism and Social Progress.*

Index

Page numbers in bold indicate figures.

WITHDRAWN

182918